Christian Ethics

ISPCK Contextual Education Series No. 3

Christian Ethics
and
Indian Ethos

(Revised & Enlarged)

Somen Das
M.Th., Ph.D..
Principal, Bishop's College
Calcutta, W. Bengal

I.S.P.C.K., Delhi
1994

Published by the Indian Society for Promoting Christian Knowledge
(ISPCK), Post Box 1585, Kashmere Gate, Delhi-110006.

First Published 1989
Revised and Expanded Edition 1994

Price :   Rs. 50 CC $ 7
           Rs. 65 HC $ 10

ISBN - 81-7214-168-8

Lasertypeset at:
ISPCK
1654 Madarsa Road
Kashmere Gate
Delhi 110006.

Printed at:
Printsman
18A/11 Doriwalan
New Delhi.

Acknowledgements

I am immensely grateful to the General Secretary, Dr. James Massey and Associate General Secretary, Mr. Ashish Amos of the ISPCK for encouraging me to revise and expand my book which was published in 1989. As a result of their initiative and inspiration I am glad that it has been possible for me to complete the writing in the midst of my heavy academic and administrative work. I am thankful to the ISPCK for republishing it and seeing it through the press.

June, 1993   **Dr. Somen Das**
Bishop's College   *Principal*
224 A.J.C. Bose Road,
Calcutta 700 017

Contents

Introduction: Fundamental Presuppositions

I have been teaching in the area of Christian ethics and Indian ethos at the graduate and Post-graduate levels for last twenty four years. I am glad that I had the opportunity to publish in a book form the fruit of my teaching and research in 1989. In fact that was an attempt to put together many of my articles in this area which have been published in learned journals both in India and abroad. But I am happy that it is now possible to review, revise and expand those articles and establish a relationship for this second edition of the book.

In the following pages I have tried to relate self-consciously the discipline of Christian ethics to the present Indian ethos which has been formed and informed by its long unbroken history. I would like to reflect on the social, economic and ethical perspective. In the process we will discover the interaction and the inter-relationship of the personal, inter-personal as well as the societal or structural aspects of those areas of life. This is what constitutes the content of the ethos which I will be examining and evaluating. As I develop these topics I hope my theological-ethical perspective will emerge and become clear. I will now try to clarify the fundamental presuppositions of the book.

Firstly, to do Christian ethics in a context, it is important to understand critically the ethos. Etymologically, ethics and ethos are integrally related. Therefore the ethicists have the onerous task of unveiling or unmasking the real reality as against the apparent reality (maya) which so often deceives and distorts our judgement. In this encounter of ethics and ethos we will avoid giving easy answers to complex and very often ambiguous situations. It is not a straight-forward either or situation. Very often we are hovering around the "twilight zone" or the "borderline situations" to use the helpful term of Helmut Thielicke. Thus it has been rightly said, "Every choice however responsibly made carries the calculated risk of being wrong. And it is part of human responsibility in choosing to accept that risk. This means that *morality is not moralism* - not giving easy answers to difficult moral questions but to clarify the context of decision-making, to crystallise as far as possible the fundamental issues and problems and helping the people to ask the right questions. That is the beginning of ethical wisdom. Therefore morality is not didactic in character nor does not belong to the domain of homiletics. The 'is' and the 'ought' or the descriptive and the normative have to be related carefully and critically.

Secondly, this book assumes that morality cannot be reduced to sexuality. In the Indian context, even till today, an immoral or a characterless person refers primarily to some sexual actions or aberrations. We must realise that sexuality is only a part of ethical study and even that has to be conceived in the wider context of family and society.

Thirdly, this book presupposes that *morality is not to be identified with legality* - 'do's' and 'don'ts'. It is much larger in scope and character.

Fourthly, the assumption of the following pages is that ethics is not common sense or intuitively-derived. It has to be carefully thought out and organised. This means that it has to do not only with action but reflection, not only with involvement but with detachment. Thus Gustafson has asserted,

> Both as serious moral agents and as scholars, both as persons
> of deep moral passions and as intellectuals, the burden of the
> ethical for us lies in the dialectic between involvement and
> disinterestedness.[1]

As we venture to study the socio-economic-political reality of India we must maintain the attitudinal polarity between the cerebral and the visceral.

I may mention that Christian ethics has to do with thinking (cognitive), feeling (affective) and willing (volitional). It must promote and practise these three-dimensional reality. We have to think through an issue carefully but it is not enough to be intellectually aware of an ethical issue. We have to feel it passionately (anubhava). But again it is not

---

[1]   James Gustafson, *Theology and Christian Ethics* (Philadelphia: United Church Press, 1974), p. 35.

enough to think or just feel the sense of justice or injustice about a problem but be willing to *do* something about it. There must be a practical-pedagogical dimension to Christian ethics. Thus I had written,

> God's will has to be done on earth in accordance to his vision of the Kingdom. So in the ultimate sense we have to have a Kingdom perspective to discern God's will, otherwise there is the conflict of wills. We are called to fulfill God's will on the basis of God's Kingdom. There is no confusion or ambiguity about this both in the Old and the New Testaments.[2]

Fifthly, Christian ethics is a systematic and rational study of situations using norms and principles, values and visions. This means it is a scientific discipline but it does not exclude imagination and intuition as long as the latter is examined and corrected in the light of the former. I had stated in my earlier book.

> The Christian life is not a static possession which we passively enjoy but we are always becoming Christians by the kind of choices we make — those that will either preserve, protect and promote life in all its dimensions or those that would frustrate and obstruct the coming of his Kingdom... Therefore Christian life demands decisions but life does not merely demand decisions but life is decisions.[3]

Briefly I should also mention that as we think Christian ethics, it has to be theoretical-theological. We have to reflect on the tools of Christian ethics from the disciplines of sociology, anthropology, theology and others. By theology I mean the God-human-World matrix. Ultimately, what matters the most in Christian ethics is the nature of God. Is he/she socio-economic-politically perceived God? Or is he/she so spiritualised and privatised that ethics particularly, corporate-community ethics become peripheral to or optional for God? Fundamentally, we affirm an ethical (moral) God. Thus by now we have realised that law and grace, faith and work, seed and fruit, body and soul are not opposed or

---

[2] Somen Das, *Weakness of Power and Power of Weakness: Seeking Clarity, Credibility and Solidarity* (Delhi: ISPCK, 1990), p. 61.

[3] Somen Das, *Jesus' Coming is our Becoming* (Madras: Christian Literature Society, 1985), p. 50-51.

contradictory. They are integral and whole. Thus "Blumhardt said that a conversion to Christ must be followed by a conversion to the world."[4] Thus Christology is in fact transcendent anthropology. We need to develop an attitude of *Against the world for the world* or an "Undivided Vision" to do Christian ethics. John Cobb had said, "ontological dualism is profoundly unsatisfactory and cannot be used as a way of understanding God's relation to the physical world, except very *provisionally*"[5] We need to go beyond this tentativeness and affirm that God and the world cannot, must not be separated ontologically or functionally.

I hope this brief introduction will help us to get into the topics with a proper perspective and attitude.

4   H.J. Schultz, *Conversion to the World: Perspectives for the Church of Tomorrow* (London: SCM Press Ltd., 1967), p.62.
5   John B. Cobb, Jr. *God and the World* (Philadelphia: The Westminster Press, 1969), p.69.

I

Fundamental Modes of Moral Discourse

How do we determine the 'ought'? In this chapter I will seek to answer this question briefly so that the methodology in the following chapters will be clear. Basically, there are three discernible modes or approaches to moral reasoning which are not exclusive in character.

Firstly, there is the *deontological* mode of moral thinking. It has to do with duties to be observed and rules to be obeyed. This is an understanding of the right which is primarily oriented towards the past in the sense of what we have inherited. History and tradition have much to teach us. We have to learn from the mistakes and wisdom of the past. Therefore past has its legitimate place in the present in our determination of the 'ought'. It is important to know the kind of training and discipline that were sought to be inculcated — What rules governed and guided their thinking and doing?[1] All throughout history and among all civilizations, they stipulated stringent permissions, *vidhis* and prohibitions, *nisedhas*. In India from time immemorial, the pundits have been engaged in formulating such injunctions which are enshrined in the *dharmasāstras* and *dharmasūtras*. The *Manusmriti* (laws of Manu) or *Manudharmasāstra* is an example of a systematised scheme of codified conduct. It had its problems and serious limitations but it guided the behaviour of people in India for a long time. Similarly, in ancient Babylon they had the Code of Hammurabi; the Hebrew people had their *Torah* and the Muslims their

---

[1] I have looked at history and tradition briefly from the perspective of Spirituality in my earlier booklet, *Christian Spirituality and Indian Reality* (Bombay: BUILD, 1988)

Shariat. Many people even till today adhere to these codes very faithfully in spite of their historicity and time-conditionedness. Very often these rules and regulations contained in the sacred scriptures, came to be interpreted in a legalistic, rigid, offensive and absolute ways. This resulted in their distortions and consequent failure to respond to the living situations. In such a situation codes are considered valuable and valid independently of whether they promoted the good and welfare of all concerned. In this context ethics becomes pre-conceived and predetermined, automatic and mechanical. It is simplification of reality and restricts human freedom and creativity. We need rereading of these 'sacred' texts and make sense for ethics. Fidelity to God is replaced by a rigid faithfulness to rules. Because of some of these problems, some scholars have made the distinction between *rule-deontologists* and *act-deontologists*, indicating the kind of emphasis given by the two groups of people. The latter group maintain that the basic judgements of obligations are particular ones like, "In this situation I should do so and so." This code-morality has been designated by Richard Niebuhr as "Man-the-citizen" who only obeys and follows. He has said,

> We come to self-awareness if not to self-existence in the midst of *mores*, of commandments and rules. Thou shalts and thou shalt nots, or directions and permissions. We come into being under the rules of family, neighbourhood, and nation, subject to the regulation of our action by others. Against these rules we can and do rebel, yet find it necessary—morally necessary, that is—to consent to some laws and to give ourselves rules, or to administer our lives in accordance with some discipline.[2]

Paul Ramsey, another ethicist, conceives of deontology in terms of obedient-love. For him neighbour-love is not good but obligatory. It defines what is right or obligatory. So he affirms categorically, "Certainly Christian ethics is a deontological ethic, not an ethic of the good."[3] Obviously in the Bible there is no opposition between law and love or law and grace. On the contrary, Jesus gives a new command that his disciples love one another (John 13:34; 15:17).

[2]   H. Richard Niebuhr, *The Responsible Self: An Essay in Christian Moral Philosophy* (New York: Harper & Row, Publishers, 1963). p. 52-53.

[3]   Paul Ramsey, *Basic Christian ethics* (New York: Charles Scribner's Sons, 1952), p.116. See also his *Deeds and Rules in Christian Ethics* (New York: Charles Scribner's Sons, 1967), p. 107-108.

Therefore there is a definitive place for laws and the duty to obey those laws in Christian ethics. It gives us space or indicates the boundaries within which we can move. It is an occasion to learn from other people's freedom. Indeed it is an occasion to learn from other people's experience as it is not possible or necessary to make innumerable agonizing appraisals undertaken *de novo*. Such arbitrary and ad-hoc actions break up time, the moral life and the moral community. Voting Rights Bill and the Civil Rights Bill were necessary in the United States, which of course cannot abolish or eliminate racism but certainly they can regulate and control human behaviour. Similarly in India we are in the struggle to formulate a Uniform Civil Code which would transcend and integrate the various religious communities. It is in this spirit we can understand and use injunctions in the Old Testament like the *Decalogue* or the ones inscribed in the New Testament. In its richer versions, according to Max Stackhouse, deontological ethics attempts to articulate the warrants, procedures or the public criteria, to adjudicate the right against wrong. In this sense deonotology has a hidden indicative tone although its explicit language is imperative and prescriptive.

The second methodology has emerged in Christian ethics particularly as a response to the problems of authoritarianism and legalism in deontology. This is called *situation* or *contextual* ethic which asks the questions like, "What is happening?" or "Who is affected?" rather than asking, "What does the rule state?" The normative is derived from the active interaction of the human indicative in history and the divine imperatives as enshrined in the sacred scriptures. Ethics become sensitive to and having an analytical understanding of the historic and human context. It is an approximation to the Kantian proposition that theory without praxis is empty, while praxis without theory is blind. Situation ethic is very much person or people-oriented and thus it is inductive in character. It did a service to Christian ethics by exposing the complexity and the predicament of the human condition and concomitantly moral decisions and actions. It clarified that there cannot be a fixed or once-and-for-all solution to any human and historical problem. Therefore Paul Lehmann rightly wrote that the 'ought' factor cannot be ignored in ethical theory. The primary ethical reality is the human factor, the human indicative in every situation. Thus he went on to assert,

The complexity of the actual human situation, with which a *Koinonia* ethic tries seriously to deal, is always compounded of an intricate network or circumstances and human interrelationships bracketed by the dynamics of God's political activity on the one hand and God's forgiveness on the other.[4]

Therefore for Lehmann the fundamental criterion for contextual ethic is "What God is doing in the world to make and to keep human life human." The other exponent of this methodology is Joseph Fletcher who worked out systematically this position on the basis of certain presuppositions and propositions.[5] The basic criterion for him is love understood in terms of *agape*. Thus he indulged in love monism and made it the great simplifier of ethics. According to Bernard Haring, "The concept of love is structureless" in Fletcher. Because of this norm he calls this mode as "principled relativism." Even the well-known scholar, Bishop John A.T. Robinson advocated this approach in Christian ethics on the basis of love. He made a radical opposition between fixity and freedom, law and love, and authority and experience. Robinson and those scholars who belonged to this school of ethical thinking took isolated verses as it is and agreed to them. They took literally when Paul states that you are not under law but under grace (Romans 6:14; also I Cor. 9:21). They used Jesus' saying, "The Sabbath was made for man, not man for the Sabbath" (Mk.2:27). This interpretation made Robinson utter. "Love *alone*, because, as it were, it has a built-in moral compass, enabling it to 'home' intuitively upon the deepest need of the other, can allow itself to be directed completely by the situation."[6] Paul Tillich called this methodology as ethics of *Kairos* and affirmed, "Love *alone* can transform itself according to the concrete demands of every individual and social situation without losing its eternity, and dignity and unconditional validity."[7] Such reductionism underestimates the depth of the Discipline and simplifies

---

[4]   Paul Lehmann, *Ethics in a Christian Context* (New York: Harper & Row, Publishers, 1963), p. 141. The whole chapter V is relevant for the above discussion.

[5]   Joseph Fletcher, *Situation Ethics: The New Morality* (Philadelphia: The Westminster Press, 1966).

[6]   John A.T. Robinson, *Honest to God* (Philadelphia, The West-minister Press, 1963), p. 115.

[7]   Paul Tillich, *The Protestant Era* (London: Nisbet and Co., Ltd, 1951), p. 173. See the discussion on "Relativism" in Arthur C. Dyck, *On Human Care: An Introduction to Ethics* (Nashville: Abingdon Press, 1977), Ch. VI, pp. 114-134. Read the discussion on Relevance and Context in my article "A General survey of Asian Christian Theology", in *Bangalore Theological Forum*, December, 1988, pp. 17-22

and distorts the human reality. Such ethical thinking leads to confusion and anarchy in life. Christian ethics becomes individualistic, completely subjective and relativistic. Its estimation of the human is highly optimistic and thereby unrealistic. Thus Macquarrie has rightly stated, "Prohibitions can sometime be stifling but they can also be protective. They save us from our worst selves."[8] We have the onerous task of clarifying norms and establishing clear criteria in our ethical decision and action. The better version of this mode is found in Richard Niebuhr who espouses the ethics of

He calls it a fitting response or cathekontic ethics. The value of Niebuhr's thinking is that he clarifies the nature and content of the concept of responsibility in detail. But its limitation is that it focuses too sharply on the present. Therefore we have to take the warning of Thomas Oden seriously when he says,

> The proper *modus vivendi* between situation ethics and legal
> principle has not been achieved in our time. The persistent
> antinomian inclinations of current Protestantism toward an
> ethic of self-affirmation without self-denial, gospel without
> law, freedom without obedience, and grace without obliga-
> tion, constitutes the most urgent problem of protestant ethics.[9]

The third mode of moral discourse is *teleological* which is primarily end or goal-oriented. It looks towards the future, for the *summum bonum*, the highest or the ultimate good. It is concerned with clarification of values, visions, goals and ideals. This methodology first appeared in the philosophical ethics of the early Hellenistic thinking. One of the pioneers was Aristotle who formulated this method in his book, *Nicomachean Ethics* (it was either dedicated to or edited by Aristotle's son, Nicomachus). The book commences with the sentence, "Every craft and every inquiry and similarly every action and project, seems to aim at some good; hence the good has been well defined as that at which everything aims."[10]

8   John Macquarrie, *Three Issues in Ethics* (New York: Harper & Row, Publishers, 1970), p. 35.
9   Thomas C. Oden, *Radical Obedience: The Ethics of Rudolf Bultmann* (Philadelphia: Westminster Press, 1964), p. 133.
10   Aristotle, *Nicomachean Ethics* Trans. Martin Ostwald (New York: Bobbs-Merriil company, Inc., 1962). See also Alasdair MacIntyre, *A Short History of Ethics: A History of Moral philosophy from the Homeric Age to the Twentieth Century* (New York: The Macmillan Company, 1966), Ch.7, pp. 57-83.

Thus began Aristotle's exploration of the good as the aim and end of action sometime between 350 B.C. and 320 B.C. According to him the good of every action is relative because every action is individual and unique. He was the first philosopher to make the definitive distinction between the science of the Good and the science of the Truth and so he subordinates the life of acting (praxis) to the life of knowing. For him the *summum bonum* attainable by action is happiness. This is the first principle of the practical sciences. What constitutes this happiness (eudaemonia)? Is it wealth, or honour or reputation or health? Aristotle rejects these because they are means to some other end or good. For him it must be final and self-sufficient. So he defines happiness as, "the active exercise of the faculties of the soul, in conformity with excellence or virtue, if there are several virtues, in conformity with the best and most perfect among them, during a complete lifetime." Then Aristotle went on to elucidate and elaborate about the nature and content of good in terms of virtues.

At this juncture it may be useful to remember that in Hindu ethical thought, increasingly there has been a significant shift from the deontological mode to the teleological thinking. Therefore modern Hindu thinkers like Sri Aurobindo, Radhakrishnan, Rabindranath Tagore and Gandhi wrote about the future-oriented goals and values. They visualised such a future that would motivate and move people to ethical action in the present. Sri Aurobindo formulated his concept of the 'Superman' who would sum up in himself all that is true, good and beautiful. Radhakrishnan in his numerous writings beckon humanity to "Commonwealth of the Spirit", "Fellowship of faith", and "Partnership of religions." For this he called for a new *dharma* — a new *smrti*. He was looking for a new "world civilization." Tagore had the vision of the "Universal Man" (Common humanity) who would represent the integration of the East and West, Martha and Mary, the Brahmin and Sudra. Gandhi in his life - long work and writings looked forward to the *Ramarajya* which for him stood for the morally best. Such is the dream and vision of the modern Indian stalwarts. *Dharma* is related to *Karma* (action) which together gives us a vision (darsana) of the new world order.[11]

There is a great emphasis on teleological methodology in the Bible and consequently in Christian thinking. From the time of the Old

---

[11]   See my forthcoming book, *New Dharma: A Theological-Ethical Paradigm*. (Delhi, ISPCIC, 1993). I have elaborated this concept further in the book.

Testament, the patriarchs and prophets of the Hebrew people, envisioned the future in terms of the "Day of the Lord" - "Where there is no vision the people perish" (Prov. 29:18). Michael Keeling says "Vision is not an absence of discipline, but the basis of it."[12] There was the old covenant and the new covenant that promised a new day — "new heaven and new earth" or the "new Jerusalem". Jesus himself began his ministry by proclaiming, "The Kingdom (rule) of God is at hand, repent and believe in the gospel" (Mark 1:15). The coming Kingdom constitutes the gospel, the good news of Jesus. Indeed futurity is fundamental to Jesus' message. He taught his disciples to pray for it daily (Matt. 6.10a). Related to this is the *Parousia* referring to the Second Coming of Jesus. On the basis of this, eschatological teaching of the church developed. Thus we may safely conclude that the Bible from the beginning to the end is concerned with teleological-eschatological thinking. Followers of Jesus are expected to pattern their character and conduct on the basis of this decisive future of God in Jesus Christ. We will explore this area further in chapter fourteen.

In our movement from the 'is' to the 'ought' it is important to take cognizance of the right, fitting and the good - past, present, and the future as far as possible. This means that in our moral decision-making and action we cannot conceive of the above-mentioned methodologies in isolation — apart from each other. Each of these modes of moral discourse have their possibilities and limitations, advantages and weaknesses. Precisely for this reason it is necessary to achieve a certain measure of integration of these three modes to help us to achieve discernment and judgement. The basis of this integration or the integrative principle will be teleology-eschatology. On the one hand it gives us faith and hope and on the other a sense of universality, transcendence and objectivity so necessary for ethical decision-making. Keeping this in mind, I would like to proceed to examine and evaluate ethically some areas of social, economic and political structures of life.

---

[12] Michael Keeling. *The Foundations of Christian Ethics* (Edinburgh: T. & T Clark, 1990), p.232.

II

Sex, Marriage and Family

Introduction

We live in a world of sexplosion. T.V., Cinema, various advertisements, many magazines and such other mass media have aggravated and accelerated the exposure and explosion of sex in our time. It is very much publicised, commercialised, glamorised, or sensationalised and thus in the process it is being trivialised. As a consequence of this process a lots of people suppose that we live in a sex-saturated society but in fact people are sex-starved in an authentic sense. Their knowledge of sex is superficial and therefore their use of it is very often distorted or depraved. This kind of distortion is quite evident when the basic thrust of books like *Mahatma Gandhi and His Apostles* by Ved Mehta, or *Reminiscences of the Nehru Age* by M.O Mathai and the *Dairy* by Frances Stevenson is misconstrued and thereby the fundamental lessons are not learnt from such great biographical writings. None of the authors mentioned above wanted to exaggerate and magnify the sexual life of these famous people. They were eager to put them in a proper perspective and view them with "warts and all". They did not want to put them on a pedestal, deify them and then become oblivious of the magnanimity of their character and conduct and magnitude of their impact. The last book mentioned above is about David Lloyd George who was the Prime Minister of the United Kingdom between 1916 and 1922. It has been rightly said,

> Sexuality seems to be so precariously poised on the boundary between irrationality and rationality, anarchy and sobriety, as to nullify every attempt to bring the counsels of judgement and virtue to bear upon the guidance of sexual behaviour.[1]

[1] Paul Lehmann, *Ethics in a Christian Context*, p. 133.

It is imperative that people have a clear understanding of and a responsible participation in the life of sexuality because of such distortions and perversions.

Past attitude towards Sexuality

In the past and to a great extent even in the present, attitude towards sexuality is characterised by inhibitions from within and prohibitions from without, by do's and don'ts and by fear, anxiety and unhealthy guilt-complex. It is basically a negative position determined by authoritarianism and legalism. It was the mood and fundamental manner of the Victorian age which had been strongly influenced by the Puritans and the Pietists. Among the Roman Catholics for a long period of time there was the exaltation of the ascetic life. This was institutionalised in many of the traditional Orders in terms of chastity and celibacy. Such a negative attitude is very much embedded in the cultural and religious norms of India. This had delivered countless generations of adolescents over to the "destructive depersonalization of sexual emotions, caught between venereal fears and venereal frivolity." What is the reason for this kind of libidinal sexual repression? Basically, there are two reasons which are intrinsically related. Firstly, throughout human history people every where have lived with a false dualism or a radical dichotomy between the body and spirit. This way of thinking was very pronounced in the Graeco-Roman world and in certain aspects of classical Hindu thought. Such a thinking has exalted the spirit at the expense of or to the exclusion of the flesh. They considered the body as the tomb from which the immortal soul must be released. So the body with its organs was disparaged and repudiated. Asceticism and other-worldliness were held in high esteem. Mortification of the flesh and the suppression of the natural desires and instincts were thought to be worthy and virtuous. Holiness and spirituality were considered in the negative term. Although Christianity rejected Gnosticism and Manichaenism as heresies because they denied any genuine incarnation, the Christian church has persisted in thinking of the human as an exile or captive in an alien or demonic world with its sexual urges. Morality came to be equated with sexuality in this context. Therefore Bertrand Russell had noted, "To this day Christians think an adulterer more wicked than a politician who takes bribes, although the latter probably does a thousand times as much harm." It may be added that for a similar reason, it is possible to consider masturbation more serious than rape because the former wasted the seed while the latter preserved the biological structure of procreation.

The other extreme attitude towards sexuality was antinomianism, having no rules or laws about sexual conduct. There were the Libertines and Gnostics who held this view for different reasons. The Gnostics thought that they had a special knowledge and therefore needed neither principles nor rules to guide and govern their sexual behaviour. Morality with regard to sexuality was reduced to spontaneity, made ad hoc and casual. They assumed a biological-hedonistic or physiological-hedonistic posture, meaning that they conceived of sex only in physical terms and only in terms of pleasure. Because of the problems mentioned above, it is important to look at the nature and extent of human sexuality - its depth and dimension.

What is Human Sexuality?

We must realise that human sexuality is divinely-ordained nature. It is not to be considered as inherently evil, given by the devil. It embraces the whole range of feelings and actions dominated by the relations between persons. This means that sexuality cannot be reduced to genitality - dealing only with the sexual organs of the humans. That is to entertain a very narrow and perverted notion of human sexuality. That would be to conceive of sex only in terms of pleasure or recreation. This dimension cannot be negated in human life, particularly pertaining sexual life. It is important to have a naturalistic and realistic perspective about it. The great psychologist and psycho-analyst, Sigmund Freud, had highlighted this characteristic of the human. Repression of sexual urges drives them to the subconscious where they assume vicious forms and very often emerge in the conscious mind sometime or the other and express in dubious and devious ways. Therefore it is very necessary to realise that human beings are inescapably and irreducibly a sexual creatures. Sexuality is part of the distinctiveness of humanity. It is not just a blind impulse but an expression of the selfhood or the personhood. It is essential to humanity and basic to one's life. Thus it has been affirmed.

> ...that there can be no self without a body, for it is in virtue of the body that we are in the world. Only as embodied selves can we act in the world or be acted upon by the world. The body is not an appendage to the self, still less an encumbrance to the self, but an essential part of personal being.[2]

---

[2]   John Macquarrie, *Three Issues in Ethics*, p. 53. See also Frederick C. Wood Jr. *Sex and the New Morality* (New York: Association Press, 1968).

So it is necessary to accept our own body with its sexual needs and wants and deal with them positively - constructively. Similarly we have to have an affirmative relationship with other bodies knowing our possibilities and limitations.[3] This mutual recognition constitutes the essence of being human. Somebody has put it very simply, "We have to have a body to be somebody, otherwise we are nobody." This is the crux of the matter. This brings us to the religious basis for human sexuality.

Religious Basis for Human Sexuality

From a Biblical perspective, we believe that God has created the humans and consequently human sexuality is a divine gift. There is an essential goodness or an affirmative relation to the whole created order. According to the Genesis story, sexuality is basic to the human structure. Adam was incomplete without Eve. She was created to be "a helper fit for him."[4] This complementarity is not just physiological. According to Macquarrie it is a true being-with-another. Therefore the basic sexual attraction of woman to man is a gift of God and must be inherently good. Helmut Thielicke calls this "immanental bisexuality," and human beings exist in this differentiation. Thus woman and man are constitutive of each other. Long before Berdyaev and Buber, Feuerbach wrote,

> The distinction of sex is not superficial, or limited to certain parts of body; it is an essential one... Hence personality is nothing without distinction of sex; personality is essentially distinguished into masculine and feminine.[5]

The very life of God entered into the world and became flesh in Jesus Christ (John 1:14). The divine initiative in the incarnation does not negate or exclude the physical and the bodily manifestation. Our affirmation of the body with its senses is reinforced by the Christian belief in the resurrection of the body and not the immortality of the soul in isolation.

---

[3] D.H. Lawrence helps us to see this point through his novels. See Mark Spilka, *The Love Ethics of D.H. Lawrence* (Bloomington: Indiana University Press, 1955), pp. 205-231.

[4] Genesis 2:18

[5] Ludwig Feuerbach, *The Essence of Christianity*, George Elliot, introductory essay by Karl Barth and Foreword by H. Richard Niebuhr (New York: Harper & Row, publishers, 1957; Originally published in German in 1843), p. 92.

Christians cannot be ashamed of the body. There is sufficient grounding in the Bible to warrant proper use and enjoyment of sexual life with responsible freedom. Bible makes it clear that the body and its senses are not only organs of pleasure but also the means by which and in which our personality, our very self, comes to being and growth. Sex contains the capacity for personal affirmation and mutuality. It is not an object to be used but to be seen as a medium of human relationship. There is a healthy and wholesome attitude towards human sexuality in the Bible. Abuse of sexuality and its perversions are noted and categorically condemned whether perpetrated by the kings or the commoners. In the Bible, a person is a psychosomatic unity and thus the Hebrew people could not indulge in opposition of the physical and the spiritual. There was a wholistic understanding of the human and the best paradigm of it was the incarnation of Jesus. The Hebrew word for soul, *nephesh*, refers to the whole human being, including the body with its senses. In the light of this it is important to use the sexual gift to make us fully human. It needs to be humanised and personalised.

At this juncture it will be useful to take note of the Hindu religious tradition. The Hindu pundits had stipulated four *āshramas* (stages of life), namely, *brahmacharya* (celibate or period of training), *grhastha* (householder), *Vānaprastha* (forest-dweller or mendicant) and *sanyās* (ascetic life). Thus in the Hindu scheme of life, one is expected to marry and be responsible as a husband and father. Similarly they stipulated four *purusārthas* (goals or values) from very ancient time. They were *artha* (wealth), *kāma* (emotional, sensual or sexual life), *dharma* (righteousness) and *moksa* (release or salvation). Again we must note that sensual or sexual life is not repudiated. On the contrary, it is to be practised and promoted as it happened in the long history of India. Her art and architecture, her music and painting, her love poems and songs, her *kāmasūtra* and other related *śāstras* bear testimony to the healthy and robust attitude towards and participation in the sexual dimension of human life. Thus it is naive to categorise the Hindus under the typology of life and world negation as opposed to life and world affirmation as Albert Schweitzer and other scholars have done. *Dharmaśāstras* and *dharmasūtras* clearly formulated the requirements of the householder, *grhastha* and of sexual life but definitively guided and governed by *dharma* or righteousness. Of course over a period of time this scheme of life became stratified and consequently *sanyas-dharma* and *moksa* came to be divorced from the rest. In the process there was a glorification of asceticism at the cost of or to the detriment of life as a whole.

Understanding of Marriage

Differentiation of sex is in the very purpose of God and attraction to the opposite sex is a God-given nature of the human. The Lord specifically declares that it is not good for man to be alone (Gen. 2:18). They together were to mutually help and "be fruitful and multiply, and fill the earth" (Gen. 1:28). Therefore the final affirmation in the creation myth is, "Therefore a man leaves his father and his mother and cleaves to his wife, and they become **one flesh**" (Gen. 2:24). Later Jesus shared in this conviction that marriage was ordained by God and declared, "What therefore God has joined together, let no man put them asunder" (Matt. 19:6). It is believed that Paul was unmarried and suggested the celibate state to other people (I Cor. 7: 8-9, 32-35). But it must be remembered that this preference was mainly due to eschatological considerations, believing that Jesus would return soon. But if one cannot be a celibate it would be better for him to marry (I Cor. 7:25-28). It must be noted that although the Bible teaches that marriage is 'honourable' (Heb. 13:4), sexual asceticism became a norm in the Roman Catholic Church. This was primarily due to the impact of the Graeco-Roman and Oriental thinking. Marriage came to be subordinated to celibacy in the writings of the early Fathers of the Church like St. Jerome, Tertullian, St. Ambrose, and St. Augustine. For the last-named Father, sexual act is always accompanied by *concupiscence*, which is sinful but within marriage this involves only a venial sin. It has been stated,

> Roman Catholic ethics is able also to structure and limit sexual love through the sacramental character of marriage and the insistence upon procreation as the primary end of marriage. Ultimately the sovereignty of grace and the spirit over natural impulse is maintained by the adroit insistence that the exaltation of the ascetic life contributes gradually to the ennoblement of natural impulse.[6]

At the Council of Nicea in 325 A.D., an attempt was made to compel married bishops to abandon their wives but that did not succeed. Gregory VII (Hildebrand), the Pope from 1073 to 1085, insisted upon the disposition of all married priests. It was only after the demise of that Pope, the celibacy of both priests and deacons was enjoined by Canon Law. It

---

[6] Paul Lehmann, *Ethics in a Christian Context*, p. 134.

may be noted that Peter himself was married and Jesus did not ask him to leave his wife (Matt. 8:14; Luke 4:38; I Cor. 9:5).

Protestant sexual ethics has basically rejected the glorification of asceticism and upheld marriage as an ordinance of God. Although Martin Luther himself considered it as a 'medicine' and a "hospital for the sick", the Protestants have accepted it both theologically and practically. The marriage of woman and man is a "symbol of the eschatological marriage in which Christ is the bridegroom of humanity as such." In that context, "the sexual act is fundamental to and the most concrete and intimate condition of human fulfillment in marriage." Therefore it is rightly mentioned that it is not marriage which legitimizes or fulfils the sexual act but the sexual act which legimitimizes or fulills marriage. It is "the communion of the body" that results in a complete and transforming partnership. Essentially it is not meant only for procreation but for companionship and creativity. Love has to be the bounding and binding factor in marriage. There has to be a certain measure of stability and security in this relationship.

Dowry-deaths and *sati*-deaths in India raise fundamental issues about attitudes towards women and marriage. Obviously, marriages are not made in heaven - preordained. They have to be carefully thought out and entered into witn freedom and responsibility. We cannot be guided solely by absolutist, supernaturalist and deductive standards. It is not a fate nor does it happen by a fiat. Knowing fully well the miserable condition of many of our married women it is imperative to emphasise the mutual or reciprocal relationship in marriage. Marriage is not a "bed of roses" and even if it is, it has its share of thorns. It must take two people to make it successful and creative. This brings us finally to a brief discussion about the understanding of the family.

Understanding of Family

Family is the basic institution of humanity - of any society. It is the nursery of human nature. In India it is the basic unit which has functioned from time immemorial in the form of the joint family. It was not only the centre of social intercourse but generated economic power and began to have political leverage.[7]

In the Old Testament and the New Testament the relationship of God to the human is understood in terms of imageries drawn from the family.

---

[7]   See P.D. Devanandan and M.M. Thomas ed. *The Changing Pattern of Family in India* (Bangalore: C.I.S.R.S., 1966).

Jesus was born into a family and was nourished and nurtured by it (Luke 2:52). Bible mentions about the family of Jesus - his mother, Mary, his Father, Joseph and his brother, James (Mark 6:3; Jude 1:1; Gal. 1:19). It is significant that Jesus expanded the meaning and scope of the concep. of the family and thus becoming theological-ethical in nature. He said,

> And stretching out his hand toward his disciples, he (Jesus) said, "Here are my mother and my brothers. For *whoever does the will of my Father* in heaven is my brother, and sister, and mother". [8]

Consequently, Paul and Peter conceived of the church as the "household of faith" (Eph. 2:19; Gal. 6:10; I Tim. 3:15 and I Peter 4:17). It must be realised that from a Biblical perspective, fidelity to the Kingdom of God does not exclude but subordinates the loyalty to the immediate family. It is important to keep alive this element of transcendence in our relationships at the social level. The Biblical witness does not negate the life of the family but views it in the context of the Kingdom of God. The family is not conceived only in terms of the blood relation but viewed in terms of common values and meanings. Thus we can talk of the "human family". We should never think of it narrowly or exclusively.

Seen from this perspective it is imperative to practise and promote the life of the family through mutual respect and love. Each member of the family has to be treated as subject and not object, of love and concern. There has to be mutual accountability between the spouses, parents and the children. Thus this kind of relationship can be nurtured and encouraged through love, freedom and responsibility. As the family had been instituted for mutual comfort and common happiness, it is important to develop a responsible partnership and parenthood.[9] This will become a model and an example for the children who quickly and quietly learn from this part of the social life.

Conclusion

We are living in a technological age which is decisively affecting and changing the human attitude and action towards sex, marriage and family. But people are also beginning to learn that they cannot live by technique

---

[8] Matt. 12:50, See also Mark 3:35.
[9] William Johnson Everett, *Blessed be the Lord: Christian Perspectives on Marriage and Family* (Philadelphia: Fortress Press, 1985), Ch. 6.

and technology alone. They have to live by meanings, values and goals.[10]
For this reason, we cannot separate the life of sex, marriage and family,
from the values that constitute human existence. Unfortunately there is
a naive identification of quantity with the quality of life in this area. In
the final analysis, "It is the pursuit of meaning that makes sex a source of
renewal as persons who care for one another and find in their sexual
experience a symbol of their union and mutual concern." Precisely for
this reason sexual life has to be seen in the context of marriage and family.

It will be useful to remember the Upanishadic distinction between
preya and *sreya* - between gratification and satisfaction. It said,

> The better (sreya) is one thing, and the pleasanter (preya) quite
> another.
> Both these, of different aim, bind a person,
> Of these two, well is it for him who takes the better;
> He fails of his aim who chooses the pleasanter.
> Both the better and the pleasanter come to a man.
> Going all around the two, the wise man discriminates.
> The wise man chooses the better, indeed, rather than the
> pleasanter.[11]

For the pundits in ancient India, *preya* was indicative of that which is
pleasing to the feelings and emotion - ephemeral and subjective. *Sreya*
represented for them something of abiding value, enjoying a measure of
objectivity. As all human beings have to struggle with their sexual life,
it is normatively valuable to take cognizance of this subtle distinction
between *preya* and *sreya*. It is not easy to make this definitive distinction
but with responsible freedom people should be able to discern the good
as opposed to the bad in sexual, marriage and family life.

---

[10] Peter A. Bertoeci, *Sex, Love and the Person* (Kansas; Sheed and Ward, Inc.,
      1967), Ch. 2 and 3.
[11] *Katha Upanishad* 1:2. 1. Translation and revised edition of Robert Ernest
      Hume, *The Thirteen Principal Upanishads* (London: Oxford University
      Press, 1931).

III

The Liberation of Women

Introduction

In the previous chapter I have already indicated the negative attitude towards sexuality in general and woman in particular. In this chapter I would like to elaborate this issue and seek to understand their genuine search for liberation from an ethical-theological perspective. To do this it is necessary to grasp at the outset the traditional attitude towards woman both in India and abroad, in the oriental and the occidental world - in the so-called Christian countries as well as in the 'non-Christian' countries. As we begin our study of the traditional attitude towards woman, it will be useful to remember the general principle of tradition advocated by Romila Thapar, the well-known Indian historian. She has stated that what we consider to be 'traditional' has been deliberately selected by the modern people. She says, "Nothing comes to us in a completely pristine form through the centuries...so the way in which present day society picks up a tradition is determined by present day attitudes to women."

Traditional attitude towards Women in the West

Women have been discriminated both at the conceptual as well as at empirical level - at the theological as well as at the practical level. Consequently they have been deprived of power and privileges for centuries. Plethora of prohibitions and consequent inhibitions afflict women all over the world. The imposition from outside have been internalised by women and this has resulted in an inferiority-complex. This negative attitude has been inculcated through the thinking of the ancient church Fathers who displayed an attitude of the misogynists.

As we examine the attitude of the early church Fathers, it is necessary to take cognizance of their historical antecedents. I have mentioned in the previous chapter the prevalence of dualism in the Graeco-Roman world. The Pythagoreans sounded their hymn of *soma sema*, the body is a tomb and this kind of thinking influenced Plato. The dualism of Egypt, Mesopotamia and of India decisively affected the Hellenistic age and *ataraxia*, detachment, freedom from passion, became the goal. The Stoics and the Epicureans withdrew from the world of the flesh into the citadel of the soul. Salvation was understood as the immortality of the soul. It has been rightly noted that,

> Even Judaism, with its naturalistic heritage from patriarch and prophet, was not unaffected in the Persian and Greek periods of Israel's history. The mystery cults of Isis and Osiris, the Persian Mithras, the Syrian Baals proffered release from bondage to the mortal flesh and multitudes responded.[1]

This kind of thinking persisted in the life and work of the early church. Gnosticism denied that creation was the work of God; Marcion negated the place of the Old Testament in the Christian Scripture and Montanism went to extremes in its other-worldly asceticism. It is to the credit of the church that she declared these movements as heresies. But in spite of these rejections, Origen castrated himself in order to escape the temptations of lust; John Chrysostom declared that "virginity is greatly superior to marriage", and Tertullian regarded sex even within marriage as sinful. The apocalyptic-eschatological thinking of the church was supported and sustained by the dualistic thrust of the classical time. This in turn maintained and strengthened the alienation between woman and man.

This kind of dualism and consequent alienation became crystallised in the thought of St. Augustine in the fourth century. He describes the Fall or the Original Sin in sexual terms. After the Fall, Adam and Eve became conscious of a new impulse, independent of their minds and wills and Augustine designated this as *concupiscence*. The whole of humanity is driven in all aspects of life by concupiscence whose chief characteristic is insatiability. Therefore for him no sexual union takes place without the corrupting effect, without burning desire and compulsiveness of concupiscence. This is the result of sin and the punishment of sin according to him. After his own encounter and experiment with the opposite sex, he boldly advocated virginity and celibacy. Indirectly, he

William Graham Cole, *Sex in Christianity and Psychoanalysis* (New York: Oxford University Press, 1955), p.7.

rejected loving and pure marital intercourse and even wholesome and healthy relationship with the opposite sex was not looked with favour but a frown. Obviously this kind of thinking laid the foundation for the attitude of the succeeding generation of stalwarts of the Church towards women. St. Jerome does not hesitate to call woman a gate leading to hell, a path towards vice, useless creature, and the sting of the scorpion.

This way of thinking continued even with Thomas Aquinas who is considered the official theologian of the Roman Catholic Church. In the thirteenth century he continued with the thinking of Augustine and Jerome with regard to women in spite of his great erudition and depth. He believed that the natural person had the capacity to distinguish between good and evil which he called *synteresis*. But unfortunately he did not exercise this ability for discernment with regard to women. He thought of her as a rapidly growing weed, a being which is less perfect than man since nature devotes less attention to her. He had stated, "Woman was made to be a help to man. But she was not fitted to be a help to man except in generation, because another man could prove a more effective help in anything else." His masculine arrogance becomes explicit with regard to menstrual period of the women in marriage. She is expected to "render the marriage debt" even during that period to her husband lest he fall into sin through her refusal. Aquinas had written,

> If however, the husband ultimately persists in his request, she must yield to his demand. But it would not be safe for her to make known her dissatisfaction, lest this make her husband entertain a revulsion towards her, unless his prudence can be taken for granted.[2]

Even after the Reformation, the Council of Trent between 1545 and 1563 reaffirmed categorically that sexual pleasure is dangerous and incompatible with the things of God and repeated the virtues of virginity and celibacy. Thus fundamentally, Augustine's and Aquinas' thinking on sexual life and concomitantly attitude towards women, was endorsed and encouraged by what is considered historically as the Counter-Reformation.

It must be said to the credit of Martin Luther that he was able to challenge the traditional thinking of the Church on sexual life although he himself was the child of the medieval age. He questioned the

---

[2]   Cole, *Sex in Christianity and Psychoanalysis*, p.88.

superiority of the monks and the nuns because of their vowed virginity and celibacy and that they overcame the power of concupiscence. But Luther's understanding of the Original Sin is quite similar to Augustine. Original Sin or the Fall brought the "epileptic and apoplectic lust" of sinful sex and subjection of women to man. According to him, woman is the agent of generation, the bearer of children and the remedy of man's lust.[3]

That much respect Luther had for woman! Once he put it as "Woman was made either to be a wife or a prostitute." This discussion on the attitude towards women entertained by some of the stalwarts of the church is indicative of their great convergence and continuity with some minor discontinuities or divergences on this vital issue. According to a meeting of the Roman Catholic Synod in Rome in 1982, a Bishop categorically asserted that the concept of equality between women and men is a "communist notion". There are numerous people in responsible positions in Protestant and Roman Catholic Churches who persist in their belief that woman is the second human life to be created but first to fall.

At this juncture it will be useful to recall that for a long time in Europe women were treated as a moveable property - as a chattel. Their role was predetermined as a wife, mother, and housekeeper only. During the medieval time, the phenomenon of witchcraft was widely prevalent and witches were always invariably identified with the female. That was how one million women were persecuted during that time. It will be interesting to recall the words from the Handbook on the persecution of witches written by two dominican inquisitors in the fifteenth century called, *Melleus Maleficarum*,

> When a woman thinks alone, she thinks evil...I have found a woman more bitter than death, and a good woman subject to carnal lust... They have slippery tongues. ...Since they are weak, they find an easy and secret manner of indicating themselves in witchcraft. They are feebler both in mind and body. It is not surprising they should come under the spell of witchcraft... As regards intellect, women are like children... And it should be noted that there was a defect in formation of the first woman since she was formed from the bent rib, the rib of the breast which is bent in the contrary direction to man... Women have weak memories, she is a liar by nature... Let us

---

[3]   Ibid., p. 108.

consider her gait, posture and habit, in which she is vanity of
vanities... Woman is a weedling and a secret enemy. For the
sake of fulfilling their lusts they consort even with devils.

Such is the estimation of women by 'religious' monks of the fifteenth
century! How much of this prejudice is still obtaining in our time?
Obviously, the Dominican inquisitors took for granted the Thomistic
definition of woman as a "misbegotten male".

Etymologically, from the word feminine, it was shown that apostasy
or faithlessness was inherent in the very nature of woman. It must be noted
that the West has come a long way from that dark period and women are
experiencing some sense of liberation although Equal Rights Amendment (ERA) is of recent origin and wife-beating is still an issue in
Australia. The General Synod of the Church of England decided on 11th
November, 1992 with two-thirds majority to ordain women into the
priesthood. That will enrich our creeds, the scripture and the Church. But
in June of the same year the Supreme Court of the U.S.A. has restricted
women's right to abortion.

Traditional Attitude towards Women in India

In the Indian context the attitude and action towards women have not been
significantly different or better. It is said that during the Vedic age,
women enjoyed enormous freedom and power. Names of Sita, Savitri,
Damayanti and Draupadi are constantly cited as exemplary characters to
be emulated. On deeper reflection, we discover that these women were
models of submission and obedience. With nostalgia Indians recall the
names of Laxmi Bai, Rani of Jhansi, Ahilya Bai Holkar and others who
displayed the prowess and possibilities of women. In this century we
remember with joy and gratitude the life and work of women like Pandita
Ramabai, who worked for young widows and Saroj Nalini, the founder
of the women's Institute Movement. Yet we know very well that both the
śruti and the *smṛti* literature of Hinduism have not advocated the rights
and equality of women. On the contrary, they have considered them as
slaves to be exploited and oppressed. It is categorically stated in
Manusmṛti,

The wife should ever treat the husband as God, though he be
characterless, sensual and devoid of good qualities.... A
woman has no separate sacrifice, ritual or fasting. She gains

a high place in heaven by serving the husband... That woman
who prides in her father's family and disobeys the husband
should be made by the king a prey to the dogs in the presence
of a big assembly of people... If the wife disobeys the husband
when he is given to bad habits or becomes a drunkard or is
suffering from physical ailment, then for three months she
should be deprived of her valuable clothes and jewels and kept
away.[4]

These quotations from one of the most important and well-known
documents of the Hindu tradition are indicative of the thrust of thinking
about womanhood. Similar thought is expressed in ancient writings in
India. One of them states, "Women should follow the word of their
husbands. This is their highest duty." In another text it is written,

There is no higher world for the woman than that of the
husband. She who displeases the husband cannot go to his
world after death. So she should never displease the husband.

Obviously such texts testify to blatant discrimination and domination
over women nurtured and encouraged by thoughtful people of the time.
This is indicative of the fact that ancient India legitimised discrimination
against women through religious texts and thus society derived its
sanction for it. This generated a general negative attitude towards women
and was crystallised through structures like *sati*, child marriage, enforced
widowhood, *devadasi* and *dowry*. Such systems explicitly and visibly
systematised and institutionalised subordination and subjugation of
women in the Indian society. In recent time amniocentesis and ultra-
sonography have been widely used to indulge in female foeticide. Sex
selection through sperm-sorting is now being practised and successfully
used for test tube babies or In Vitro Fertilisation (IVF) to have only sons.
As a result the sex ratio in India stands at 927 per 1000 males. Earlier
female infanticide was also quite common. In Haryana it is 865 per 1000
males because of foeticide. Hindu Succession Act and the Hindu Women's
Right to Property Act, 1937 have an anti-women bias. Such discrimination and consequent deprivation have been internalised by the women
themselves through the centuries. In the process such systems have been

---

[4]   *The Laws of Manu* Trans. G. Buhler (Oxford Clarendan Press, 1986), V 147-
       V 166, pp. 195-197. See also IX 3, 78, 81; VIII 371; IX 230.

passively accepted as external and objective. Thus the very consciousness of women have been domesticated and they have become 'defuturized' using the category of Letty Russell. Women began to consider their inferior status in society as god-given and not man-made and therefore not amenable to challenge and change. They have become mute beings dominated by reaction and reflexive behaviour. They lost their sense of self-identity and self-hood, became dehumanised and consequently lost all respect and dignity. Concretely, it meant that the women of India were deliberately denied their social, economic and political powers and privileges. They were turned into a commodity - to buy and to sell.

The *Devadasi* system is thoroughly exposed and evaluated in a study undertaken by the Joint Women's programme. This system is widely prevalent in the adjoining districts of Karnataka and Maharashtra. The dedication of the *devadasis* takes place in many of the temples in that region particularly at the main Yellamma temple at Saundatti. The study clearly showed that it is a phenomenon with its rites, forms of recruitment, initiation procedures and myths of justification. This region has turned into the main market for prostitutes who migrate to Bombay. Thus there is a nexus between untouchability and prostitution in this system.[5] It is significant to note that under the existing law it was only the woman caught in prostitution who was punishable while the man or the men were free.

Mahatma Gandhi long ago highlighted the problem of child-marriage and quoted from the Census to show the high number of child widows in this country. In 1921 there were 9066 wives under the age of 1; in 1931 there were 44,082 which is an increase of nearly five times while the population increased only by one-tenth. He quotes a similar figure to indicate the corresponding increase of child widows for the same period.[6] Thus Gandhi addressed himself on women's issues explicitly and unequivocally.

The Committee on the status of women in this country has found that the impact of the transition from tradition has been to exclude an increasing number and proportion of women from active participation in the productive processes. In 1911 as many as 2.2 million women were

[5] Banhi, *The Devadasi Problem*, 1981/2. In Andhra Pradesh among the Domarra Tribals they are known as *Venkatasanis*

[6] M.K. Gandhi, *Women and Social Injustice* (Ahmedabad: Navjivan Publishing House, 1942). As early as 1925 Gandhi called for a "Constant and continuous agitation" against the evils perpetrated on women" (page 31).

engaged in trade and commerce; in 1971 this number came down to incredible 0.5 million. Faced with the modern manufacturing industry, cottage industry employed only 1.3 million in 1971 as against 4.6 million in 1961. In industry as a whole, the employment of women came down from 6.2 million in 1911 to 3.3 million in 1971. It must be remembered that the female population of India was only 124 million in 1911 as against 264 million in 1971.[7]

Recently it is calculated that women constitute only 28 per cent of the country's work force in the organised sector. Discriminatory thinking and practices against women persist in the Indian society although the Indian Constitution guarantees equality of sexes.

Thus at a conference of the Indian Association of Women's Studies it was said that the Women in the contemporary world "are at the mercy of the power-brokers of global politics since they belong to the third world." In 1991 they affirmed that the women are ignored in policy-making and marginalising their role in society.

India is also a signatory to the United Nations Charter affirming the equal rights of the sexes. Indian representatives also participated in a meeting of the U.N.O. where a Declaration was made on the Elimination of Discrimination. Both the Mathura and Maya Tyagi cases crystallised the problem of the definition of rape in our legal book. The onus of proof lies on the part of the woman. Justice V.R. Krishna Iyer had commented that the corpus jury of this country was discriminatory and the Parliament in its masculine innocence had not paid any heed to putting man on an equal footing of guilt with women on the issue of rape. Therefore the former Chief Justice of India, Y.V. Chandrachud, was of the opinion that the burden of the accused to establish that the girl was a willing and consenting party. Another Chief Justice of India, P.N. Bhagwati, had been at the forefront of equality of women from a legal perspective. But the tradition of discrimination against women is very strong in India even till today. 20,000 rapes are committed every year in India. One study shows that there is one rape every 54 minutes in India. It rose from 7,767 in 1987 to 9,793 in 1991.

India continues to be a tradition-ridden society where the women are submerged in the "culture of silence". It is a culture of dominance and dependence. It is not surprising that the Government of India in 1986

---

[7]   Urmila Phadnis and Indira Malani, ed., *Women of the World: Illusion and Reality. Fortune* magazine shows that even in the West, in the top 200 companies, women seldom reach the highest positions of power.

formulated a policy on education in which they added a section on "Value Education" and stated,

> ... to make education a forceful tool for the cultivation of social, ethical and moral values... such value education would help eliminate *obscurantism*, religious *fanaticism*, violence, superstition and *fatalism*.[8]

On 4th September in 1987, an eighteen year old Rajput girl, Roop Kanwar, was burnt alive and on the 16th of the same month lakhs of people glorified her death as *sati* and opposed the ordinance against it. Those people asserted categorically, "*sati* was an integral part of Rajput culture and the Hindu *dharma*."[9] The sati-death prompted Prof. Madhu Dandavate, to state that,

> In this recent incident what emerged out of the ashes was the mutilated dignity of Indian womenhood. The vast crowd that thronged displayed their deep roots in obscurantism. The conscience of politicians was crushed under the dead-weight of decadent tradition. The government's sensitivity was paralysed by upsurge of medievalism as the great soul of Raja Ram Mohan Roy lay buried under the ashes of the widow.

It may be recalled that it was Raja Ram Mohan Roy who waged a battle against this pernicious practise of *sati*, burning the widow at the funeral pyre of her husband, in the beginning of the nineteenth century. In 1829 this nefarious practise was abolished by law during the time of Lord William Bentick. Raja Ram Mohan Roy was assisted in his effort by the great Serampore missionary, William Carey who came to Bengal in 1793.

On 7th November of 1987 Dr. Ramaswamy's wife, Sashikala, condemned dowry-death, legitimised by religion and sanctioned by culture. It may be mentioned that according to the report there were 1,319 dowry-deaths in 1986; 1,912 in 1987; 2,209 in 1988; 4,001 in 1989

---

[8] *National Policy on Education*: 1986, The Government of India, p. 22.
[9] *India Today*, October, 1987, p.38. See in this context the result of an Empirical case Study by Promilla Kapur, *Love Marriage, Sex and Indian Women* (Delhi Orient Paperbacks, 1976), Ch. five and M.P Joseph's article on "Suttee: A critique from an Ethical Perspective" in the *SATHRI Journal*, 1/1993, pp. 65-95.

indicating an upward trend - around two a week. This statistic could indicate two facts — either there were more dowry-deaths in the country *de facto* or that increasingly more such cases are being reported and registered. But it certainly goes to show that dowry-deaths or bride-burning are on the increase and its openness and consciousness are more in evidence. That augurs well for the future of women in India. But such incidents are quite rampant in spite of the Prohibition of Dowry Act, 1961 and subsequently Dowry Prohibition (Amendment) Act, 1984.[10] It must be said to the credit of Gandhi that he challenged and sought to change the interpretation of scriptural texts that legitimize discrimination against women. He had said in 1936,

> ...all that is printed in the name of scriptures need not be taken as the word of God or the inspired word. But every one cannot decide what is good and authentic and what is bad and interpolated.[11]

In 1926 he had stated, "It is irreligion, not religion, to give religious sanction to brutal custom (child-marriage). The *Smritis* bristle with contradictions." Again in 1925 he had written, "Sanskrit texts of doubtful authority cannot be invoked to sanctify a practice which is in itself immoral." In this way Gandhi challenged the religious tradition of India which permitted such evil practises with regard to women. He was against traditionalism which is the dead faith of those now living. Increasingly many women and Women's Organizations are coming forward to liberate their fellow sisters from social, political and economic bondages. But it is very sad that in a recent interview, the BJP Mahila Morcha President, Ms Mridula Sinha said, "Everything will be fine if women learn to adjust." This is indicative of the depth of the problem with regard to the liberation of women.

An Ethical-Theological Basis for Women's Liberation

The negative or distorted attitude of the church Fathers towards woman-

---

[10] Banni, *Women and the Law*, 1981/1. Kapila Hingorani, An Advocate in the Supreme Court of India has clearly delineated the evils of dowry (Vide pp. 29-40). Only one-fourth of dowry death cases are actually registered.

[11] Gandhi, *Women and Social Injustice*, p.15. See also pp., 31-32. See Ch. VII, pp. 92-94 of the same book.

hood can be traced back to their interpretation and concomitant understanding of the Bible. Obviously they did not have the benefit of modern
hermeneutical tools and exegetical skills to encounter the Scriptural texts
particularly those which sounded derogatory towards women. We must
recognise the historical conditionedness of the writers of the books of the
Bible. The ancient church Fathers could not make use of the historical-
critical method or Form criticism to interpret and comprehend the
Scriptural texts. The Bible is the product of the patriarchal society.
Therefore Phyllis Bird maintains that it is essentially a man's book where
the women appear for the most part as adjunct to men, significant only
in the context of men's activities. Thus the language of the Bible is male-
dominated and the writers belonged to the androcentric pattern of family
life which bestowed exclusive rights in the political, legal and economic
life of the people.

The story of Lot's decision about his two virgin daughters (Gen.
19:8ff) and of Jephthah's vow to God which later led to the sacrifice of
his only daughter (Jud. 11:29-40) indicate that a woman's duty was to
completely submit to the will of the father or husband. The notion of
women as property could be directly traced from the Judaic patriarchal
family structure (Ex. 22:16).

Under the Old Testament law, the wife was no more than a possession.
The neighbour's wife could be coveted like his ox, ass or any other
possession (Ex. 20:17; Deut. 5:21). Even Ruth was finally bought along
with the field that Boaz redeemed (Ruth 4:5 and 10). A newly-wedded
wife if she did not show the sign of virginity was considered to having
violated the honour of her father and her husband and thus deserved death
by stoning. The man who had been with her in the act of fornication was
free from death (Deut. 22:13-21). But in the case of adultery, both man
and woman must be killed according to the Torah. The man deserved
death not because he is equally guilty of sin in the act as the woman but
because he had violated the exclusive right of the woman's husband (Lev.
20:10). Again it is only the husband and not the wife who can charge
infidelity in the partner and thereby demands his spouse to submit to the
ordeal of testing (Num. 5:11-31). Only man could initiate a divorce and
it is referred to as putting his wife away as if she was an animal with some
kind of an incurable disease (Deut. 24:1-4). Deut. 24:5 prescribes that
man should not be eligible for military service for a period of one year
after taking a wife. But in this situation the happiness of the husband is
paramount. Woman was considered as unclean because of the taboo
related to menstruation (Lev. 15:19-24) and child birth (Lev. 12:2-5).

Every Hebrew male regarded himself as carrying the seed in his loins. He was to plant the seed and a woman's womb was considered as a kind of an incubator. Her role in the processes of reproduction was essentially passive and subsidiary. Such attitudes and actions against women made them subservient and subordinate in the Hebrew Society.

To these actual and conceptual understanding of women in the Hebrew Culture was added the distorted interpretation of the Creation Myths (Gen. 1 and 2). Through both the stories the authors indicated the relationality, complementarity of the two sexes and their bi-sexual character - both being equally partakers of God's divine nature and grace. Genesis 2:18b has been variously translated as "a *helper* fit for him" (R.S.V.); " a suitable *companion* to help him" (Good News Bible): " A *partner* for him" (New English Bible). Obviously this differentiation is considered necessary and good. This is not warranted by the texts. Therefore it is not possible to concur with Thomas Aquinas who had stated, "the image of God is found in a secondary sense in women." Earlier St. Augustine had stated in his treatise, of *Holy virginity*, that only man is made in the image of God, which is a negation of the Biblical witness.

In St. Paul's writing similar negative attitude towards women is found. The social and cultural conditions influenced him and his rabbinic background endorsed this view. A Jewish man would daily pray that he was grateful to God that he was not created a woman. Women were not permitted to read from the *Torah* and for them it was better to burn the *Torah* rather than place it in the hands of a female. Paul was reared and nurtured in such a tradition. It is not surprising to read the derogatory remarks about women (I Corl. 11:12-16; Eph. 5:22-31; I Tim. 2:11-15; Col. 3:18-19). Obedience and submission was the watchword for women according to Peter and Paul. Yet Paul was able to transcend his historical conditionality and affirmed the principle of equality,

> For through faith you are all sons of God in union with Christ Jesus. Baptized into union with him, you have all put on Christ as a garment. There is no such thing as a Jew and Greek, slave and freeman, male and female; for you are all **one** person in Christ Jesus (Galatians 3:26-28).

Although Paul belonged to a male-dominated society he was able to grasp or have a glimpse of the vision of Christ.

When we turn to Jesus of Nazareth, we are astonished at his open and positive attitude towards womanhood in general and woman in their specificity. There is a surprising element of iconoclasm towards the traditional subjugation and subordination of women in Jewish life. Jesus's own disciples were amazed to see him holding a long conversation with a Samaritan woman in public,

> Just then his disciples came. They marvelled (surprised) that
> he was talking with a *woman*, but none said, "What do you
> wish?" or, "Why are you talking with *her*?" (John 4:27).

Thus Jesus not only violated the standard norm of the time when he asked for water from a Samaritan woman but also talked to her at length in public and thus offending the sense and sensibilities of the people of his time particularly his own disciples. For the sake of justice being done to the women folk, Jesus was ready to be angry and aggressive wherever necessary and desirable. In the story where a woman is condemned for adultery(Jn. 8:1-11), Jesus questions radically the misrepresentation of the Jewish judicial system that easily victimised the woman taken in adultery but the man is permitted to go free. There is no accusation against the man in this story. Prostitutes felt free in the presence of Jesus's not because he was easy with them but because he did not look at them as sexual objects to be exploited. Unlike other rabbis of those days, Jesus had quite a number of women friends and disciples like Martha and Mary (Luke 10:38-42; Jn.11), Mary of Magdala and others (Matt. 27:55-56; 28:1; Luke 8:1-3; John 19:25). Jesus particularly took note of the faithfulness of poor widows (Lu. 21: 1-4) and love and loyalty of woman of dubious character (Luke 7:36-50).[12] Obviously he did not tolerate double-standards and hypocritical attitude of the society of his day and therefore he was particularly harsh on Pharisees. Some people believe that his model of ministry was demonstrated by women waiting at tables. Dorcas, Priscilla and Lydia showed the example of service. These scattered examples indubitably prove that Jesus held women in high esteem and gave them equal love and respect. And yet the Church through the centuries have significantly and systematically marginalised women in its substantive ministry and theological thinking. Therefore even till today God is always conceived in male terms although Prophet Hosea in

[12] *See Women of Courage: Asian Woman Reading the Bible* ed. Team of AWRC (South Korea: Asian Women's Resource Centre for Culture and Theology, 1992), Ch. 10, 11, 14 and 16.

the eighth century B.C. thought of God as female - as a mother (Hosea 11: 1-9). Thus a Roman Catholic theologian from Sri Lanka, Fr. Tissa Balasuriya rightly asserts,

> The churches have tended to be the last refuge of male dominance. They have given male chauvinism not only a practical expression, but also a theological and even a quasi-divine legitimation.[13]

In this context it is important and necessary to note the traditional role ascribed to Mary, the mother of Jesus and to the modern interpretation. She is usually portrayed as gentle, passive and a humble mother concerned about her son when he gets lost in the festival crowd. They extol her quiet devotion and piety. But Fr. Balasuriya maintained that is a travesty of Mary perceived in an individualistic spirituality - a false kind of conformism to the ruling values and powers in spite of their evils. In the *Magnificat* (Lu. 1:46-55), Mary is perceived as a politically-aware Jewish woman who suffers under the humiliation of her people and hopes that God in the person of the Messiah would bring about the much-needed transformation. This is indicative of her high degree of sensitivity. It is significant to note that Mary does not disappear from the gospels after the birth narratives. According to the records she is with Jesus at crucial moments of his life when something new is about to break in. Through pain-love[14] she realises that loyalty to the Kingdom of God is higher than and prior to the loyalty to parents and family (Matt. 12:46-50; Repeated in Mk. 3:31-35; Lu. 8:19-21). Mary would have felt the pangs of separation but her son taught her the ways of the Kingdom. Mary provided for Jesus and Jesus provided for Mary before his death at the cross (Jn. 19:25-27). It is interesting to note that for a long time in traditional Christianity, Madonnas have been portrayed in sculpture, painting and poetry in a passive and individualistic way. But in Poland Black Madonna represented the struggle of the Solidarity Movement which was essentially a struggle of the Polish workers for justice and human rights. Indeed Mary, the mother of Jesus provided a model of

---

[13]   Tissa Balasuriya, *The Eucharist and Human Liberation* (New York: Orbis Books, Maryknoll, 1979), p. 52. See the whole section on "The Liberation of Women", pp. 51-58.

[14]   C.S. Song, *Third-Eye Theology: Theology in Formation in Asian Settings* (London: Lutterworth Press, 1980).

creative cooperation with God in pursuit of human liberation. Therefore it is ironic that the early church was not sure whether to extol Mary's motherhood and thus acknowledge the merits of all motherhood or to praise wifelessness, asceticism and celibacy. This is the dilemma of the church and in society at large.

Conclusion

Women continue to be harassed and exploited in the Indian society. It has been revealed that 5,427 cases of rape were registered in 1982 in India which is an increase of 0.3% over the previous year. As we have mentioned before that such statistics are indicative of the surface of the problem of women in India. The fact of the matter is that there are more cases of rape which are not reported and secondly there are more cases of 'rape' within marriage than outside which will never be reported. The more substantive issue with regard to women is their powerlessness. According to 1981 census, the sex ratio at 933 women per 1000 men continues to favour the latter. Ninety per cent of women work in the unorganised sector which offers no regularised basis for fair wages and decent terms of work. According to Neera Kuckreja Sohini, only 25 per cent of women are literate and in at least 57 districts in India, female literacy is less than 10 per cent. In the face of this situation women are against women being regressive and opposing protective provisions for women. Therefore in the final analysis both men and women need liberation if the gender gap is to be bridged.[15] Rosemary Reuther rightly affirms,

> The center of such a new society would have to be not just the appropriate new social form, but a new social vision, a new soul that would inspire the whole. Society would have to be transfigured by the glimpse of a new type of social personality, a "new humanity" appropriate to a "new earth". One might call this even a "new religion", if one understands by this the prophetic vision to shape a new world on earth, and not an alienated spirituality.[16]

[15] Somen Das ed. *Women in India: Problems and Prospects* (Delhi: ISPCK, 1989). This is an inter-religious and inter-disciplinary perspective on the subject of women.

[16] Rosemary Reuther, *New Woman and New Earth*, p.211.

The Nobel Prize winner Mother Theresa represents one model of Womanhood. But the Nobel Prize winners for 1991, Aung San Suu Ki from Burma and for 1992, Rigoberta Menchu, a Mayan Indian from Gautemala, are the new models of *Women's struggle* for human rights for their people. Women are being liberated from their traditional roles. That is the sign of our time.

IV

Alienation and Struggle of the Dalits

Introduction

In the previous Chapter, I have isolated the issue of women in India and have attempted to crystallise their liberation struggle. But we must realise that in a country like India, a *Dalit* woman suffers from double discrimination. Therefore, it is important and necessary that we turn our attention now to the self-conscious struggle of the *Dalits* in India to be recognised as human beings, aspiring to attain social status, economic well-being and political power. In this chapter, I will study the problem in retrospect before we look at their prospects. For this it is imperative to locate the problem within its historical context in India. This will enable us to understand the present predicament and the future hopes of the *Dalits*.

Historical Context of the Dalits

From time immemorial a segment of humanity in India has been designated as untouchable but in fact they have been considered as *unapproachable* because they suffer from permanent pollution. There are 429 Communities among the untouchables themselves. For centuries they were called *mlechchas*. In 1932 they came to be called "Depressed classes" but Gandhi preferred the term, *Harijan* (children of God). The untouchables objected to this term as they did not want to be isolated in that way in as much as all are children of God. They themselves prefer the term *Dalit*, the suppressed or the oppressed.

Ancient Indians ordered and organised the social life according to *Varnadharma*. This corporate structure became the strong determinant of the life of the people. This horizontal division of the Indian population became hierarchical or vertical stratification. Originally it was an empirical and an expedient division of society to maintain the cohesion and harmony of the heterogeneous population. The social differentiation based on the division of labour began to find religious legitimization in the *śruti* and *smṛti* corpus of Hindu religious tradition. This can be traced back to the *Ṛg* vedic time in the *Puruṣa sūkta*.[1] The cosmological origin of the caste-system is repeated in the Upanishad.[2] The ancient law-giver of India, Manu, recalls and reaffirms the texts of the *śruti*. He asserts in his *dharmaśāstra*,

> But for the sake of the prosperity of the worlds he caused the *Brahmaṇa*, the *Kshatriya*, the *Vaishya*, and the *Sudra* to proceed from his mouth, his arms, his thighs, and his feet.[3]

Again in the *Bhagvad Gita*, the four-fold social structure receives its divine sanction when Lord *Krisna* unequivocally asserts, "The four caste-system was created by Me by the division of *guna* and *karma*. Although I am the maker of this, know Me as the imperishable non-doer."[4] Obviously the writer of the *Gita* was able to move beyond the hereditary understanding to a system based on qualities and actions. It is significant to note that in spite of this redeeming feature of the *Gita*, the fifth caste or the *mlechchas* (barbarians) remain outside the pale of Aryan society.

Modern anthropologists, sociologists and ethnologists have made extensive empirical studies about the nature and extent of the caste system in many of the villages and towns of India. Their general consensus is that the stratification is not as rigid as it was conceived in the past. On the contrary, the scholars discovered an active mobility within the system. It was also discovered that the term 'caste' is at best an ideal nomenclature. It is a kind of mnemonic or a taxonomic device, providing a readymade scheme of classification. *De facto* the system does not work on the *varna* model, but on the *jati* model.[5] Thus it was discovered that there are more

[1] Ralph T H Griffith, *The Hymns of the Ṛg Veda*. Trans. with a popular commentary, 5th ed. 2 Vol. (Varanasi: Vidyavilas Press, 1971), Vol II X, 90, 11-12, p. 519. Only reference in the *Ṛg Veda*.

[2] Robert Ernest Hume, *Thirteen Principle Upanishads, Brihad Aranyaka*, 1, 4, 11-13, p. 84.

[3] George Buhler, *The Laws of Manu*, trans. (New York: Dover Publication Inc., 1969), 1, 31, pp. 13-14.

[4] Eliot Deutsch, *The Bhagavad Gita*, trans. (New York: Holt, Rinehart and Winston, 1968), IV, 13, p. 56.

[5] M.N. Srinivas, *Social Change in Modern India* (Los Angeles: University of California Press, 1968), p. 27.

than 5,000 *jatis* in India, 1,886 Brahmins alone with about 2,999 attributes. There is a certain nebulousness as to the position in the *jati* system which is of the essence in operation as distinct from the system in conception. Therefore, the various castes did not function as one closed class or as one endogamous group. Such studies were indicative of the fragmentation or the fractionalisation of the Indian society.

The third significant discovery of such scientific studies is that for centuries there is a perpetual attempt on the part of the lower castes to come up in the social ladder. This process of upward mobility has been designated by Srinivas as

> the process by which a 'low' Hindu caste, a tribal or other group, changes its customs, ritual, ideology, and the way of life in the direction of a high and frequently, 'twice-born' caste.[6]

In this process the lower castes gave up animal sacrifices and drinking liquor and thus attempting to incorporate the "Little Tradition" into the "Great Tradition". It is in this context the study of the Dalits become significant. It has been found out that this all-embracing system includes the *Dalit* in this sense. One study, done over a thirty-year period, demonstrates explicitly, that the leather workers (*chamar*) of Karimnagar, a village near Agra, became ultimately slightly below the Kshatriya.[7]

Sanskritization or Brahminization is a reaffirmation and not a negation of the caste-system. The change and mobility that takes place is within the all-pervasive structure. Thus according to Srinivas himself, it brings about *a positional and not a structural change*. It does not challenge the system substantively but only questions the status in the hierarchy. Therefore, in spite of all the changes and modifications that have taken place within the social matrix, there is no radical break in the normative sense. We can safely maintain with Tyler,

> The system of *jati* is an expression of that universal Indian mode of thought which not only maintains that there is a relativity of human potentiality but also insists that differences

6   Srinivas, *Social Change in Modern India*, p. 6.
7   William and Charlotte Wiser, *Behind Mud Walls*: 1930-1960 - with a Sequel: The Village in 1970 (Los Angeles: University of California Press, 1971), p. 260.

among humans are attributable to inherent degrees of purity
and pollution.[8]

As a result of this Indian mode of thought, the spirit of elitism, hierarchy,
submission and consequent resignation is widely prevalent. Rather such
a spirit fundamentally is constitutive of the Indian ethos even till today.
Yogendra Singh rightly asserts,

> Hierarchy was engrained not only in the system of caste and
> sub-caste stratification but also in the Hindu concepts of
> human nature, occupational life cycles and the moral duties.[9]

In this situation, differential treatment is meted out to the various
castes according to the position in the hierarchy. In the process of its
evolution, the caste system institutionalised, systematised and legitimised
inequality and discrimination on the basis of birth and heredity. There
was a relative recognition of the various castes and sub-castes except the
Brahmin castes who enjoyed an eminent status in the hierarchy although
empirically other castes had risen to high positions of power. But by and
large the people in the lower castes particularly the *Sudras* and the *Dalits*
are always aspiring to be born in the high caste, in the next life. Thus the
doctrine of *samsāra* (cycle of births and deaths) is closely related to the
doctrine of *samskāras* (ritual practices of each caste). Obviously such a
situation created a great sense of insecurity and anxiety and this is
essentially constitutive of alienation.

Varnadharma engendered alienation. This alienation was of fundamental nature. This kind of a social order has maintained a passive peace
and co-existence, but in its thrust and direction it has been disruptive and
dislocating. It divided the society into numerous fragments and fractured
the life of the people both internally and externally. It alienated from
oneself, from others not in the same group, and from the total scheme of
life. This process of alienation is better understood if *varnadharma* is
seen in conjunction with *svadharma* and *gunas*.

Historically *svadharma* was conceived as the internal and subjective
principle which had to do with the individual life of the people. The

[8]   Stephen S. Tyler, *India: An Anthropological Perspective* (California: Goodyear
      Publishers Co., Inc., 1973), p. 148.
[9]   Yogendra Singh, *Modernization of Indian Tradition: A Systemic Study of
      Social Change* (New Delhi: Thompson Press, Ltd., 1973), p. 191.

ancient pundits conceived of these individual duties in terms of in-born or inherent traits or characteristics or *guṇas*. According to this kind of thinking people are endowed with three kinds of dispositions or tendencies from birth namely *sattvik* (truthfulness), *rajasa* (energetic or martial) and *tamasa* (darkness, dullness, indolence or ignorance). Through the centuries these fundamental traits came to be exclusively identified with a particular caste and so the Brahmins came to be endowed with *sattvika*, the *kshatriya* and the *vaishiyas* with *rajasa* and the sudras and the *dalits* (untouchables) with *tamasa*. This hierarchical thinking came to be introduced at this level. This co-relation was understood in a mechanical and static way and the high caste people in particular could not and did not perceive of these qualities in various combinations and permutations. This was another mode of relegation of the *dalits*. They seem to be pre-occupied with the concept of nature rather than nurture. Dr. Radhakrishnan himself wrote, "In the natural hierarchy there cannot be one moral standard for all."[10] This kind of thinking postulated the ethic of pluralistic morality as maintained by Benoy Kumar Sirkar.[11] It is true that all people are born with certain traits but with education and training it is possible for people to change their character and personality. The static equation between the various castes and the qualities subscribes to a passive and obsolete psychology. Human nature is not fated or deterministic as the theory of *gunas* suppose. In this context, there is a subtle kind of conditioning in the negative sense in which one is made to believe that she/he is not somebody which one in fact is. In this sense the *dalits* experience alienation in an intrinsic way — one is made to negate one's own essence or ontology. Through this process of domination of one kind of thinking, domestication of the *dalits* took place in the history of India. They are made to feel and behave in an inferior way and consequently obeisance and sycophancy is a way of life for the Indian people. As Radhakrishnan rightly asserted that nature and nurture should be coupled together to view the human.

The human-made alienation made the fifth caste as barbarians or *mlechchas*. They were regarded as outside the pale of Aryan society.

[10] Sarvapalli Radhakrishnan, *Eastern Religions and Western Thought* (New York: Oxford University Press, 1959), p. 367.

[11] Benoy Kumar Sircar, *The Positive Background of Hindu Psychology* (New York: AMS Press, 1959), p. 236.

They were considered as lowest among people.[12] The dalits suffered from permanent pollution because of this fundamental alienation invented by the ancient minds. No amount of rituals could cleanse and make them pure. Thus often they were viewed along with dogs and crows.[13]

The laws of *Manu* have stipulated stringent rules to order the character and conduct of the *dalits*. This alienation meant separation from the main stream of life and consequently they were expected to live outside the village. The vessels they used for cooking could not be used by others even after they have been burnt in fire. Thus they were entitled to use only earthen vessels. The laws of Manu prescribed and proscribed these and other demeaning rules for the dalits.[14] If a Brahmin killed one of them he incurred the same penalty as for killing a dog. The *mlechcha* were considered among the vilest dregs of the human species and needed to carry a pair of clappers to warn others of their approach. Therefore, they were not only untouchable but *unapproachable* because it was believed that their very shadow was polluting. Thus the nature and content of their alienation were quite evident in the history and tradition of India.

At this juncture we need to know what constitutes alienation. It is not self-evident. Fundamentally, alienation occurs whenever and wherever there is a negation of freedom and the exercise of responsibility. Freedom constitutes one's true essence. One can be considered a person only because one is free. Freedom belongs to the transcendence and mystery of the human person. We understand freedom as one's capacity to think and act voluntarily and volitionally in the ultimate sense. It is the power to be and to do.

The sense of freedom must be viewed in conjunction with a sense of responsibility. The normatively human has been conceived in terms of responsibility. Basically the concept implies sensivity to people and situations, interpretation of the situation, being accountable and taking cognizance of the total social context. Another scholar has rightly maintained that responsibility is the capacity to respond, to govern one's action in accordance with decision and purposes, to be accountable for

12 P.V. Kane, *History of Dharmasastras: Ancient and Medieval Religious and Civil Law* (Pune: Bhandarkar Oriental Research Institute, 1938), Vol. II, Part 1, pp. 138-154.

13 P. V. Kane, *History of the Dharmasastras*, Vol. II, Pt. 1, p. 81.

14 Buhler, *Laws of Manu*, X., 52-56, PP. 414-415. See also J. Auboyer, *Daily Life in Ancient India: From Approximately 200 B.C. to 700 A.D.* (New York: The Macmillan Co., Ltd., 1965), p. 30.

what one does are part of the human as against the animal mode. The obvious question is about the nature and extent of freedom and responsibility exercised within the *guṇas-svadharma-varnadharma* matrix, particularly for the *dalits*. It may not negate freedom and responsibility absolutely but inherently such a combination of concepts cannot maximise these fundamental values of human life. In such a situation, the human powers become atrophied, the *dalits* become 'thingified', used as means and not as ends in themselves and consequently this syndrome affects adversely the spirit and quality of the people in general and the *dalits* in particular. They are considered as objects and not as subjects endowed with possibilities and options. They are like fungus or cauliflower as Sartre would put it, rigidly determined by conditions of birth, heredity and environment. Life loses its authenticity and becomes a mere construct of the society. When the *dalits* internalise this human-made social stratification, this hierarchy becomes entrenched or ingrained. In the process, one is alienated from oneself, and concomitantly loses one's selfhood or personhood. It is the identity crisis for the dalits because one is confronted with preservation of one's humanity and individuality. In this scheme of life, human beings in general and *dalits* in particular are considered as prisoners of causality and determined by antecedent causes in the ultimate sense. In this sense, they are "thrust into existence" in the midst of all kinds of shackles which have rendered them slaves. That is the essence of alienation because there is a definitive loss of freedom and responsibility in all their ramifications. Fundamentally, we can affirm that the *guṇas-svadharma-varnadharma* configuration has alienated the *dalits* empirically. One became alienated structurally, systematically and intrinsically. The question is, can we attribute this alienated condition to the inherent meaning of *dharma*.[15] In this chapter we cannot go into a discussion about the concept of *dharma*. But it is important to mention that historically or using the spatial language horizontally, *dharma* functioned as the fundamental mode of alienation in India.

We can understand this process to a great extent within the categories of Peter Berger—externalisation, objectivisation and internalisation.[16] In the beginning, the Indian society was the product of the Hindu mind but

---

[15] This is discussed in my forthcoming book, *New Dharma: A Theological-Ethical Paradigm* (Delhi: ISPCK, 1993).

[16] Peter L. Berger, *The Sacred Canopy: Elements of a Sociological Theory of Religion* (New York: Doubleday and Co., Inc., 1969), pp. 4-8, 9-14 and 15-19.

gradually it attains to such facticity or objectivity that the Hindus become the product of the society, which they had originally planned and ordered. Berger calls this process as man's "great propensity for order" which is a kind of "prototypical human gestures."[17] But it must be remembered that originally and etymologically *dharma* is ontological in character — that which holds and upholds, supports or sustains. Over the centuries it lost its ontological thrust and acquired a deontological connotation, duties to be performed and rules to be obeyed and that is how *varnadharma* and *svadharma* came to be conceived.

Modern Struggle of the Dalits

Due to modernisation and the recent independence of India, the plight of the dalits is better known and they themselves are becoming conscientized. The process began in a significant way from the beginning of the century. Indians like Gokhale and Gandhi fought relentlessly for the upliftment of the people. Gandhi, among the few others, articulated the conscience of the Indian people on this issue. He called the untouchables as *Harijans* (children of Hari). For him this system was poisoning Hinduism and later said, "I do not want to be reborn, but if I have to be reborn, I should be born as Untouchable..." [18]

The Struggle of the *dalits* gained significant momentum with the advent of Dr. B.R. Ambedkar, who himself was one among them. He is the architect and the Father of the Indian Constitution. It was in the Constitution, in Article 17, that Untouchability was abolished in 1950. But unfortunately, in spite of all the provisions for safety and security of the Untouchables, atrocities against them are still rampant. Following is the statistic.[19]

---

[17] Peter L. Berger, *A Rumor of Angels: Modern Society and the Rediscovery of the Supernatural* (New York: Doubleday and Co., Inc., 1970), p. 53.
[18] Shri Chinmoy, *Mother India's Lighthouse: India's Spiritual Leaders* (New York: Rudolf Steiners Publishers, 1973), p. 86.
[19] Hariharan, "Asia's Untouchables", in *Atlas World Press* Review, January, 1976, p. 26, and The Week, Aug. 25, 1991.

Atrocities against scheduled castes

	1986	1987	1988	1989	1990
Bihar	1633	1271	1297	997	Aug 507
Gujarat	649	727	665	593	788
Madhya Pradesh	4421	2879	3764	4226	5210
Rajasthan	1481	1465	1572	1588	1373
Tamil Nadu	758	650	709	409	502
Uttar Pradesh	4697	4348	4755	5195	6096

For this reason, Michael Mahar had expressed pessimism about the improvement of the conditions and status of the *dalits*.[20]

The Dalit Panthers stand within the revolutionary tradition of Mahatma Phooley and Dr. Ambedkar. Jytirao Phooley has been called the "Father of the Indian Social Revolution". In the nineteenth century he started his movement for the education of untouchable girls and demanded radical reorganisation of Hindu society on the basis of individual liberty and social equality. He fought a relentless battle against Brahmins through many activities and writings. He called his organisation *Satya Sodhak Samaj*. Dr. Ambedkar assumed the leadership of the revolt of the Depressed classes in 1920s. He began to write about it in his paper entitled, *Mook Nayak*, and founded the *Bahishkrita Hitakarini* Sabha. He said that the caste system deadens, paralyses and cripples the people. It has ruined the Hindu race and has destroyed, demoralised and devitalised the Hindu society.[21] He discovered that at the root of the Hindu social system lies the *dharma* which is prescribed in the *Manusmrti*. Because of this nexus between a religious concept and the social system, he thought that it was necessary to destroy such a religion, if one were to abolish the caste system. Like Periyar and Phooley, Ambedkar blamed the Brahmins for the condition of slavery obtaining in the society. Once Ambedkar wrote to Gandhi about temple entry, "If the Hindu religion is

---

[20] Michael Mahar, *The Untouchable in Contemporary India* (Arizona: University of Arizona Press, 1972), pp. 421-429. John C.B. Webster in his book, *The Dalit Christians: A History* (Delhi: ISPCK, 1992) has confirmed this after twenty years. See also James Massey, *Roots: A Concise History of the Dalits* (Delhi: ISPCK, 1991)

[21] D. Keer, *Ambedkar - Life and Mission* (Bombay; Popular Prakashan, 1954), p. 261.

to be a religion of social equality, then an amendment of its code to provide temple entry is not enough. What is required is to purge it of its doctrine of *chaturvarna*."[22]

From this perspective we realise that the Dalit Movement preferred the British rule to Brahmin rule but Ambedkar took cognizance of the fact that only within the framework of a free state it would be possible to work for political power for the *dalits*. After independence he wanted to conceive of democratic nationalism in terms of anti-Brahminism. In 1936 Ambedkar founded the Independent Labour Party on the fundamental assumptions that Bharminism and Capitalism are twin enemies of the working class in India. He was closer to the Communists than the Congress Party. But he was also disappointed with the Communist Party of India because he realised the omniscient character of Brahminism. Dr. Ambedkar, like Phooley, emphasised mass education and direct action to restore the self-respect of the untouchables. He realised that a power struggle was necessary.

In recent times, the Father of the Dalit Movement is Shyam Sunder, who is a follower of Dr. Ambedkar. Sunder organised the party called "Bhim Sena". It came into existence in 1968 and was made up of militant and dedicated youth of scheduled caste origin. Sunder, like his worthy predecessors, wrote a book called *Mool* in which he advocated that they were the original inhabitants of India. He thought of an alliance with the Muslims. His demands were: Surrender of 25 per cent of the villages in each taluk with which they could form "Dalistan" within India: a separate electorate, a separate scheduled caste university, and a strong political organisation for the untouchables. The *Dalit Panthers* emerged as a force in 1972. But unfortunately, in Karnataka this movement went for a radical change, broken up into *Dalit Sangharsha Samity* (mainly of the intellectual Harijans) and the *Dalit Action Committee* (mainly of political-minded Harijans). Like the Anti-Brahmin Movement, the *Dalit* Movement is demanding a radical and revolutionary structural change within the Indian society. Only then will socio-economic changes be possible. They have maintained a very militant stand even till today as is evident in their regular journal called *Dalit Voice*.

It is tragic that even after so many years of effort, the status of the dalits

---

[22]   *Ibid*. p. 261 See also my article entitled, "Christian Response to some selected Movements for Social change in India in the 19th and 20th centuries." in *The Gospel Among Our Hindu Neighbours* ed. Vinay Samuel and Chris Sugden (Bangalore: Partnership in Mission, 1983). pp. 21-44.

remains the same. The Government of India had introduced the Reservation Policy for the Dalits. Mandal Commission had endorsed it and raised the quota to 59.5 per cent including the Other Backward Classes (OBC). This has been done to atone the sin of Untouchability in this Country. But in the hands of the politicians it has become a game - a vote bank.

In the midst of this dismal and disgusting situation, is a person like Swami Agnivesh, the Arya Samaj leader. He upholds the rights of the *dalits* openly. In 1980 he led a *padayatra* for the entry of the dalits into the Nathdwara temple in Rajasthan. Still there are 'holy temples' in the country that do not permit their entry and thereby violating the Directive Principle Article 38 which calls for social justice in the running of all "institutions of national life." Article 46 demands protection of *dalits* from social injustice. Obviously it is a long road to freedom and full freedom they must have. This is an opportune time for the liberation of the *dalits*. There is a rising consciousness among them. That augurs well for the future and offers a hope of a new day for them and for all people in India.

Theological-Ethical Response

God in Jesus Christ is a sensitive God - sensitive about age-old institutionalised, well-organised suffering and oppression of a vast segment of the Indian society called the *Dalits*. The God whom we believe in the Old Testament and the New Testament does not suffer from *ataraxia* or *apatheia*. The suffering servant in the Old Testament, Passion Narratives and particulaly the story from Gethsamene to Golgotha are reminders of God's involvement in or identification with human and historic suffering. God to be God in this context, cannot remain neutral as He/She sided with the slaves in Egypt against Pharoah long ago. God comes to liberate and save. As Christians, as human beings, it is our responsibility to work for the liberation of the Dalits at the socio-economic-political level without separating these three areas of human life. We have to work at a structural/systemic level. In this way we demonstrate our faithfulness and obedience to a faithful and righteous (just) God.[23] But we can redeem ourselves if we as Christians are liberated from caste prejudices having separate seminaries, churches and places of

---

[23] Much has been written on the subject. For detail see A.P. Nirmal ed. *A Reader in Dalit Theology* (Madras: Dept. of Dalit Theology, UELCI, 1991); *(continued on next page)*

burial. Only then we can think of the liberation of the *dalits* who form
a third of the 18 million Christians in this country.

²³   *(Continued from last page)*
      ed. *Towards a Common Dalit Ideology* (Madras: Dept. of Dalit Theology,
      UELCI, 1989); M.E. Prabhakar ed. *Towards a Dalit Theology* (Delhi: ISPCK,
      1989); *Religion and Society Journal*, September, 1990 on *Dalit Theology
      and the SATHRI Journal*, January - 1991 and *Asia Journal of Theology*,
      October, 1992.

V

The Issue of Communalism: Its Meaning and Implications

Introduction

Communalism is endemic to the Indian reality. This has given rise to divisive forces pulling people in different directions. Fissiparous tendencies have been let loose in the country in the name of religion, region, language and caste. Communalism is jeopardising the unity and integrity of the nation which is just over forty six years old. Such deep divisions are disrupting our common life and disintegrating the country. There is fractionalisation of the Indian society. Communal riots between Hindus and Muslims in Aligarh in 1978, Jamshedpur in 1979, Moradabad in 1980, Hyderabad in 1981, Meerut in 1982, Bhiwandi in 1984, Ahmedabad in 1985, Meerut again in 1987, Bombay and Calcutta in 1992-93 testify in a tragic way the implication of communalism. Thousands die unnecessarily as a result of these communal riots. Ram Janambhoomi-Babri Masjid issue sustains this dangerous attitude between the two major communities of the country. Demolition of the Babri Masjid by the *Sangh Parivar* on Sunday, 6th December, 1992 is an assault on the Constitution of India — on her secular character. It indicates the "Obnoxious criminalisation" of the political process in the country after forty-six years of Independence. The reality in India can be described in the following words:

> The political parties in our country are far below on the evolutionary scale. All parties, no matter what ideology they propound, multiply by splitting into two like amoeba, the earliest form of life that appeared on the earth. Indian politics

is positively in the amoeba stage and how much it has to evolve to become an effective instrument of social reconstruction and radical change is still an enigma engulfed in ignorance. The distance from the amoebic stage to the atomic one is aeons. And the vast qualitative difference between the amoeba-splitting and atom-splitting has to be grasped in proper perspective. If a split produces additional creative energy it is to be encouraged. The political situation in India calls for continuous ideological bombardment to eliminate the dead elements from the nuclei and to release new energy in abundance by fission. The methodology is first fission and then fusion. But what we have at present is utter confusion (from *Negations*, April-June, 1982).

What is said about the political parties in India, *mutatis mutandis*, could be applied very well to the communal issue in this country. In this chapter I would like to examine briefly the issue of communalism particularly from a theological-ethical perspective.

RSS-VHP-BJP: Context of Communalism

The Telegraph dated 21st December, 1990, received a letter to the Editor with a thumb impression. It was entitled, BJP took away my family from a rickshawpuller named Y. Ravana Reddy from the Muslim-dominated Zumirhat bazaar area of Hyderabad. His wife was stabbed to death and his only son was killed in quick succession. In fear he fled to Calcutta. As a Hindu he does not blame the Muslims of the area but the Bhartiya Janata Party for murdering his wife and son.

In 1963 Jawaharlal Nehru, the first Prime Minister of India, was asked how to handle the Communists if they came to power at the centre and he flared up, "Communists, Communists! Why are all of you so obsessed with Communists and Communism? The danger to India, mark you, is not communism. It is "*Hindu right-wing communalism.*" How prophetic he was thirty years ago. It seemed that the national movement prior to Independence was able to develop a multi-religious, pluralistic common consciousness. But obviously today it seems that it was only a veneer and that gloss has worn off. After forty-six years of Independence, the divisive forces are raising their ugly heads with a vengeance, changing the very character and composition of the Indian nation.

In 1939, fifty-four years ago, M.S. Golwalkar, the former Rashtriya

Swayamsevak Chief, declared in a book entitled, *We or Our Nationhood Defined*, "To keep up the purity of the race and its Culture, Germany shocked the world by purging the country of the Semitic race, the Jews. . . a good lesson for us in Hindustan."[1] From this fascist perspective, he had asserted that all those not belonging to the nation, i.e., Hindu race, religion, culture and language, naturally fall out of the pale of real national life. Those who cannot be such 'patriots' or 'nationalists' are considered traitors or even 'idiots'. The non-Hindus in India have to abandon their differences, adopt the religion, culture, and language of the nation and completely merge themselves in the national race or else continue as foreigners. He wanted the glorification of the Hindu religion and culture and if not non-Hindus will have to stay in the country wholly subordinate to the Hindu nation. This gave birth to the theocratic concept — Hindu Rashtra based on the Hindu religion as they perceived it. Earlier in 1923, Damodar Vinayak Savarkar propounded the idea of *Hindutva* (Hindu consciousness). RSS-VHP-BJP nexus has started its own "dharma Yuddh" on the basis of such a distorted thinking. Ramjanmabhoomi-Babri Masjid issue is a moment in that history. Such historical distortions and myopic visions are being relentlessly and ruthlessly pursued by people like Lal Krishna Advani, Murli Manohar Joshi, Balasaheb Deoras, Ashok Singhal and others. The configuration between religion and politics has its own logic and dynamism. They have made the people believe that India is not a free country but '*Kurushetra*' and they must follow Ram as a historical figure. Consequently, as a nation we are receding into pre-history and losing our priority about food, clothing, shelter, education and unemployment. Ashok Mitra, the well-known economist, has termed this kind of communalism as primitivism. He defines the latter as a "framework of attitudes which steers clear of any reasoned weighing of costs and benefits attendant to a particular act." In this context, the role of religion has been questioned.

In last five years (1989-1993) there has been a systematic upsurge of this ideology. As a result the BJP has gained from two seats in the Parliament in 1985 to 119 seats in 1991; from ruling one state in India to four states till the demolition and the declaration of President's Rule in these states. The one-dimensional ideology of *Hindutva* has gripped the consciousness of the majority community and the BJP is saffronising the consciousness of the people. For the present they have focussed on

---

[1]   M.S. Golwalkar, *We or Our Nationhood Defined* (Nagpur, 1938), pp. 27 and
       p. 52.

Ayodhya and have demolished the Masjid but it could move to Mathura, Varanasi and other places. Uma Bharti, Sadhvi Rithambara and other leaders of such a movement are using the traditional Hindu images, metaphors and symbols for building the national consciousness and not just to build a temple here and a temple there. Sudhir Kakar has analysed the situation from a psycho-social point of view.[2] For him Ayodhya represents an aggressive ethnicity as a reaction to modernising and globalisation. In this context, Indian History is sought to be rewritten, Hindu religion loses its catholicity and universality, and the Indian Constitution and the secular character is being questioned. The historian, Bipan Chandra has analysed the situation very well.[3] He maintains that there are stereotypes about Muslims in India and on this basis such people deny the possibility of Hindu-Muslim unity in the present because of historical memories of tyranny. Some people go to the extent that Hindus should seek revenge for the wrongs done in the medieval period. Recently, M.J. Akbar, a well-known journalist, has written a book entitled, *Kashmir: Behind the Vale*. In it he maintains that secularism lies at the root of Indian nationhood and we must uphold it conceptually and concretely. Swami Vivekanand said in 1893 "I am proud to belong to a nation which has sheltered the persecuted and the refugees of all religions and all nations of the earth."

Meaning of Communalism

In the narrow sense, communalism refers to that attitude and action which emphasize the claim of primacy and exclusiveness of a communal group delimited by religion, region, race and caste and demands solidarity of its members in thinking and doing. It is an attempt to absolutise the group to the exclusion of other communities as the Shiv Sena has done in Maharashtra or Bajrang Dal in Bihar and RSS-VHP-BJP, Akali Dal in the Punjab, DMK in Tamil Nadu, Telegu Desam in Andhra Pradesh and Muslim League in India are other examples of political parties which are basically communal. In the broader sense, it is defined as that philosophy

---

[2]   Sudhir Kakar, "Reflections on Religious Group Identity" in *Seminar* 402, February, 1993, pp. 50-55. See the detailed discussion in Tapan Basu et al. *Khaki Shorts Saffron Flags* (New Delhi: Orient Longman, 1993), pp. 12-55. See also *Seminar* 402, February, 1993 by N. Ram, "Hindutava's Challenge", pp. 23-27.

[3]   Bipan Chandra, *Communalism in Modern India* (New Delhi: Vani Educational Books, 1984).

which stands for the promotion of the exclusive interests of a particular caste or a particular ethnic or linguistic group. Thus it must be discussed, taking into account the various forms of communalism which are equally vicious and pernicious. There is an intrinsic relationship among them.

The Nature and Extent of this Issue in India

On the basis of both of these understandings of communalism, we are in a position to draw some implications. It is a partial or a sectional view of the communal reality prevailing in India. It is quite irrational and results in a conscious or an unconscious deception. It is essentially prejudicial and discriminatory in character. Communalism is parochial, divisive and dysfunctional to a healthy national life. It is basically reactionary as it results in fragmentation which is not conducive towards working for a just society. It is used as an ideology by the ruling class and power elites to whip up emotions in the name of caste, language, religion or region to capture political power. There is obvious communalisation of politics and politicisation of religion in India. There are forces and people both inside the country and outside who perpetuate the pattern of "divide and rule" because it helps them to monopolise power. At this juncture we need some clarifications about various terms we use with regard to this problem.

In a pluralistic society like India, ethnicity or ethno-nationalism is a reality. Ethnicity refers to any group of people having a common historical heritage such as race, culture, language, religion, or anything which binds people together as a *community*. It is an extended form of family or kinship. Associations are formed on the basis of caste or religion or language to promote the interests of the members. This is where we have to affirm the sociological reality of communities. We are all born and bred in a community — nurtured and nourished by it. In one sense we can say that community is written into the very constitution of the human or that community belongs to the very being of the human. From this point of view we have to promote and pursue actively our communal life and not indulge in individualistic enterprises which negate the very sense of wholeness. We are communal creatures and must affirm our communitarian character and identity without loosing the sense of togetherness.

Some scholars think that though communalism is parochial to the extent that it excludes and rejects other communities, but several factors such as interaction with other segments, spatial mobility and new ideas impinging and as a result, the narrow, parochial communalism gives way to a process which is broader and potentially secular. This process could be termed as communalisation. At this level we have to emphasize diversity in the midst of unity. Emphasis on unity should not jeopardise the richness and diversity of our people. Divisions based on communalism have to be overcome but diversity must be preserved and promoted in democratic and secular ways. Obviously we cannot work on the facile assumption that India is one, homogeneous and monolithic. Therefore a call for unity should not be an attempt to threaten or destroy diversity. Diversity must become the very essence or condition of the unity which we espouse. In and through this mutual enrichment of communities in India, there is an engendering process through which a new identity is affirmed and a new India takes shape.

It is possible to use *communalism* as a progressive tool by the oppressed and the exploited communities in India to protect themselves from their oppressors and assert their rights. Ezhavar used Sree Narayan Paripalan Yogam, the Harijans and the Neo-Budhist movement, EVR Periyar movement in Tamil Nadu and the present Dalit movement are some of the examples of a more positive kind of communalism aiming towards justice and liberation. To a great extent mass conversion to Christianity or to Islam as a social protest or the Veerasaiva movement in Karnataka are other examples which are positive and valuable in character. We are talking of people who have been domesticated and rendered dependent through centuries and such movements have resulted in the conscientization of such people. That is a hopeful sign for India. Therefore it is important to distinguish between such positive and valuable forms of communalism as against the negative forms which are basically exclusive, and a closed system of thinking and not an open-ended process. It is basically destructive and disruptive of the larger community character and interests.

Religious Communalism in India

Today in India we are faced with the problems of Islamic fundamentalism, Hindu revivalism and Christian conservatism. To this has been added Sikh extremism and consequent terrorism. These forces together promote and practise communalism in this country. Sankaracharyias, Maulvis and some Bishops bless such forces and legitimise such religions. Politicians and political parties exploit such communal feelings to their advantage and win votes. They encourage such fascist, fanatical and intolerant forces.

Religious communalism has created unnecessary politicisation and unhealthy polarisation. They are sterile and irrelevant rendering our national life fragmented and broken. Such forces have not benefitted the growth of a fuller and richer life, for the people. Such politicisation and polarisation are positively harmful negating the wholeness of human life. In 1978-79 the *Freedom of Religion Bill* by an independent member of the Indian Parliament, Om Prakash Tyagi, is an example of this from the past in post-Independent India. It sought to politicise religion in the name of freedom. It was a deliberate attempt to deny the rights of the religious minorities in secular India. It was an attempt to make an issue out of a non-issue in a poor country like India.

More recently in 1986, *Muslim Women* (Protection of Rights on Divorce) *Bill* was introduced and passed in the Parliament. It is another attempt to institutionalise discrimination against women in general and Muslim women in particular. It has excluded significantly Muslim women from the purview of Section 125 of the Criminal Procedure Code. Shah Banu has stirred the hornet's nest. This would have been a good opportunity to introduce reforms in ancient religious codes like the *Sharia* which would approximate to modern condition and context. Instead the politicians yielded to the pressures from fundamentalists and 'talaque' continues to be easily available to Muslim man. These are the forces that divert and dilute the attention of the people from more central issue confronting the nation. These attempts also militate against the secular character of the country which is interested in keeping religion and politics in tension where in various religions of the country contribute to the creativity of the political life. Religions must help to shape the political life giving it a focus and direction.

We cannot condemn Muslim fundamentalism, Hindu revivalism or Sikh extremism if we indulge in Christian communalism. In the past it was practised in terms of mission compounds and today in terms of "mission-compound mentality", "crusading mentality", and superiority complex making absolute and exclusive claims. Communal clashes in Kanya Kumari district crystallised this problem very well. The RSS masterminded the clashes most effectively but the Christians were also responsible. The Christians wanted to demonstrate their political strength through various religious events — unity processions, inviting Brother Dinakaran to speak at Nagarcoil particularly at that time of tension. There is also a rumour that the church hierarchy had ordered not to admit Hindu students in Christian schools and Colleges. The *Last Temptation* of Jesus and Salman Rushdie's *Satanic Verses* have stirred the communal hornet's nest among Christians and Muslims respectively.

There is a concerted move on the part of Muslims to oppose common civil code. Our government has suddenly woken up to the problem. The President of India, talked about the abuse of religion and said, "Experience has shown that the communal and fundamentalist forces, aided and abetted by external elements are challenging our basic values of nationalism, secularism, democracy and socialism." The former Prime Minister, Rajiv Gandhi, hinted at a legislation for separating religion from politics. He said, "It is time to concretise these issues...and not leave them in a nebulous state but specifically initiate in motion certain steps to separate politics from religion." That augurs well for the secular vision of this country and live together in unity with our religions and regional differences. The Bill is being debated at present.

Apartheid System in South Africa

At the global level, the issue of communalism expresses itself in terms of racial segregation on the basis of colour. In 1991 the Italian fashion firm, Benetton, advertised a white child as an angel and a black child's hair looked like two horns of the devil. At this point I would like to focus on racism as communalism with a particular reference to South Africa. The social system obtaining in South Africa is called *apartheid* which literally means colour apart. It is a form of racial discrimination actively and directly supported and sustained by the very Constitution of that country. Under this law, a vast majority of the population of 28 million blacks particularly 7.5 million Zulus, 4.5 million coloured people and about 1.2 million people of Indian origin are openly segregated by the minority 6.5 million white people. This system over the years has resulted in economic deprivation and political powerlessness of the non-whites. It is a situation of dominance and dependence. The non-whites have been denied of their fundamental rights — rights to dignity and equality. They cannot determine their own dignity in their own country. The Referendum which Pieter Botha had won, had given a limited power for the coloureds. It has effectively divided the non-whites in South Africa and have diffused their united cause. The apartheid system is an affirmation of a master-slave relationship in the modern world. It has given birth to its own kind of communalism based on colour. Thirty one out every 1000 whites; 10 out of every 1000 Indians while only 2.5 blacks out of 1000 go to university in that country.

Historical Background

At least for about last one hundred years there has been an effective and an identifiable resistance movement against this pernicious system. Mahatma Gandhi set sail for South Africa in April, 1893. He became the "Coolie barrister" in that country. He had learnt that in the Transvaal a very stringent enactment was passed in 1885 which deprived the Indians of all their rights. According to it, the Indians could stay in that country only for menial jobs. It was slightly amended in 1886. The Indians could own land in that country only in locations set apart for them. They had no franchise. Gandhi was thinking of returning to India but some leaders of the Indian community wanted him to stay in South Africa and launch a protest movement against these kinds of inhuman laws and so he wrote, "Thus God laid the foundations in my life in South Africa and sowed the seed of the fight for national self-respect.[4] During his stay there he founded the Natal Indian Congress, fought for the rights of the wage-earners and indentured labourers particularly opposing the tax law imposed by the white authority. In those days the non-whites had to get registered in their own country with thumb impressions even if they were literate. General Smuts, who was the Prime Minister of South Africa, was very happy at the departure of Gandhi!

After Gandhi's departure, Michael Scott arrived from the United Kingdom and continued the struggle against this overt and institutional form of racial segregation. In 1946 the Pegging Act was passed, further aggravating the predicament of the non-whites in South Africa. Dr. Malan who had taken over from General Smuts as the Prime Minister of South Africa, was more adamant and intransigent. He refused to be moved by the appeal of Scott. As a result Scott mobilised the world opinion for the plight of the non-whites, and the United Nations Organization passed a resolution asking for a watching brief over South Africa.[5]

After Scott's departure, Trevor Huddleston arrived on the scene. Immediately he became concerned about the racial problem in South Africa and assumed the leadership of the non-violent struggle. He wrote

---

[4] Mahatma Gandhi, *Autobiography* (Washington D.C. Public Affairs Press, 1948), p. 140.

[5] Scott has documented these facts in his book, *The Time to Speak* (New York: Doubleday and Company, 1958), See also Martin Luther King Jr. *Letter from Birmingham Jail* (New York, Harper and Row, Publishers) for a similar problem.

in 1956, "Christian love is so searching, so demanding and so revolutionary in its force that it has no kind of relationship to the thing which is so
often called by its name... There are people who want to live comfortably
with injustice and intolerance."[6] *Bantu Education Act* was passed during
his time in South Africa. This Act sealed the possibility for the *Bantus*
to pursue education without discrimination. They were neither equipped
with the necessary conceptual tools nor given the practical skills in their
schools. Huddleston opposed this Act in 1955 and was arrested and taken
to court. The judge asked Huddleston, "Is it the function of a Priest to defy
a magistrate?" Immediately he retorted, "Is it the function of the minister
of religion to remain silent in the face of injustice?" Huddleston, like
Gandhi and Scott before him, became frustrated and wrote, "But South
Africa Like Jerusalem is blind."

Another person who became actively involved in this situation of
institutional racism was the tribal Chief, Albert Luthuli.
He had remained passive for a long time but at the age of fifty-one, he
began to wage a war against the apartheid system. The local people had
suffered three hundred years of white dominance. During this time,
Verwoerd was the Prime Minister and he talked about "separate growth"
and "peaceful coexistence". He even talked about "good neighbourliness"
but this was really an attempt to hoodwink the indigenous people. The
government of South Africa persisted in their policy of denying political
power to the people. At this juncture, Albert Luthuli became the President
of the African National Congress. Riots broke out in 1952. The Congress
launched the Potato Boycott to make the white people aware of injustice
being perpetrated in that country. In 1960 Luthuli burnt his Pass which
he had to carry like a Passport in his own country. The Government
banned the African National Congress in 1960. In the midst of this
attitude of the racist regime, Luthuli continued to say that he will not
jeopardise the South Africa of tomorrow by precipitating violence today.
But the structural violence in the form of the apartheid system continued
unabated. Luthuli wrote in frustration, "... the vast majority like Pharoah
have hardened their hearts."[7] It is not surprising that Charles Hooper

---

[6]   Trevor Huddleston, *Naught for your Comfort* (New York: Double Day and
       Company, 1956), p. 236. See also Martin Luther King Jr., *Why We Can't Wait*
       (New York: Harper and Row, Publishers, 1964), p. 85.
[7]   Albert Luthuli, *Let My People Go: An Autobiography* (London, Collins Press,
       1962), p. 130. See Martin Luther King. Jr., *Strength to Love* (New York:
       Harper and Row, Publishers, 1963), p.14.

wrote in 1962. "If the man of peace does not prevail, give us the man of blood."

The Prime Minister after Dr. Hendrick Vorwoerd, Vorster, followed the same policy of segregation but with a "sweet reasonableness" (billik heid). He welcomed a trade delegation from Malawi. They talked about 'neighbourliness'. At the same time two Bills were passed in the House during the time of Vorster aimed against the coloured people (mulattos). So we know the nature and content of this "good neighbourliness"!!

The Church in South Africa

The segregated society found its legitimation from the church in South Africa. The Dutch Reformed Church approves the apartheid system. It gives a theological affirmation to a sociological reality in South Africa. It has evolved a theology of racial discrimination based on a doctrine of double predestination. The common people are made to think that the non-whites have descended from Ham about whom we read in the Old Testament. Under the auspices of the church, one conservative professor, Andrianus Drost Pont, wrote against two white liberal theologians namely Albert S. Geyser and Rev. C.F. Beyers Naude. According to him these theologians are "sold to the devil".

The Christian Institute of South Africa is an inter-denominational and multi-racial Information and Conference centre at Braamfontein in Johannesburg. Rev. Naude was the Director of this Centre for a long time. It is an oasis of racial harmony in the desert of racial discrimination. He had become the General Secretary of the South African Council of churches and had stated categorically, "Apartheid cannot be reformed. It has to be removed once and for all".

Recently some South African church leaders like Bishop Tutu and Dr. Allan Boesak have become actively and aggressively involved in the fight against this diabolical system. Bishop Desmond Tutu is the Anglican Bishop of Johannesburg and he is also the General Secretary of the South African Council of Churches. At the 6th Assembly of the WCC he had asserted, "The WCC is not anti-South Africa, it is anti-injustice". The Nobel Peace Prize winner said, "I am opposed to all forms of violence — the violence of an unjust system as apartheid and the violence of those who seek to overthrow it. But there may come a time when it is justified to overthrow a system of violence." The Revd. Dr. Allan Boesak is the President of the World Alliance of Reformed Churches. He has founded the anti-apartheid coalition called the United Democratic Front in South

Africa. He had declared at the Vancouver Assembly in 1983, "In-equality is still sanctified by law and racial superiority is still justified by theology. Today, with the blatant support of so many Western Governments, apartheid seems stronger than ever and the dream of justice and human dignity for South Africa's black people more remote than ever."[8]

The present Situation: The above statement of Dr. Boesak is endorsed by the Commonwealth Eminent Persons Group (EPG) that visited South Africa. They came to learn directly and personally about restriction of movement, arbitrary arrests, detention without trial, torture and death, ongoing forced removals and re-location in resettlement camps. After this the British Foreign Secretary, Sir Geoffry Howe, himself visited and could not deny these things and yet Margaret Thatcher remained silent and Ronald Reagan had talked about "constructive engagement." Both the United Nations and the Non-Alligned Meet (NAM) have called for comprehensive mandatory economic sanctions against the racist regime of Pretoria. Simultaneously, some countries of the world have come forward to help the "frontline states" bordering South Africa who have been affected directly or indirectly by this system. The multi-cameral South African legislature with Asians and 'coloured' ministers of state being appointed, has helped only to crystallize the problem and the real intention of the former President, P.W. Botha. Political power remains securely in white hands as constitutionally entrenched. These cosmetic changes strengthen and re-affirm the apartheid system. In the meantime, Nelson Mandela of African National Congress has been released from long incarceration but more recently the Black leader, Chris Hani, has been brutally murdered by the white racists in that country. South African President F.W. De Clerk realizes that racism is well entrenched in that society as it is in the U.K., U.S.A. and Europe. But the Blacks are looking forward to the first multi-racial election in South Africa in 1994.

A Theological-Ethical Reflection

Communalism in these parochial and prejudiced forms, distorts the gospel and betrays the basic message of Jesus. He came to announce the coming of a community which is fundamentally and qualitatively different from but continuous with our communities. It distorts the very

---

8   *Gathered for Life*, Official Report, VI Assembly, World Council of Churches, Vancouver, Canada, 24 July-10 August, 1983, pp. 222-223.

meaning of Sin and Salvation. Nairobi Assembly of the WCC had declared in 1975, "Racism is a sin against God and against fellow human beings. It is contrary to the justice and love of God revealed in Jesus Christ. It destroys human dignity of both racist and the victim." In 1983, the Vancouver Assembly affirmed,

> ... to oppose apartheid in all its forms, to support those who struggle against this sinful system of injustice and to denounce any theological justification of apartheid as a heretical perversion of the Gospel.[9]

The above statement applies equally to those who absolutise their groups.

On 25th September, 1985, 151 theologians from various denominations issued a theological comment on the political crisis in South Africa called 'kairos Document'. In it they reaffirmed the 'Prophetic theology' and stated, "God appears as the liberator of the oppressed. He is not neutral. He does not attempt to reconcile Moses and Pharoah, to reconcile the Hebrew slaves with their Egyptian oppressors, or to reconcile the Jewish people with any of their later oppressors. Oppression is sin and it cannot be compromised with; it must be done away with."

St. Paul affirms, "In Christ there is neither Jew nor Greek, there is neither slave nor free, neither male nor female for you are all one in Christ" (Gal. 3:27-28). Therefore God is forming a universal Community transcending the lesser communities based on colour, caste, region or religion. We are called to actively participate in God' vision for humanity. Believing in an inclusive and open community based on *Koinonia*, Christian cannot indulge in such communalism mentioned above or the kind of injustice done to the *dalits* as mentioned in the previous chapter.

As Christians we believe that the human race is one in origin and in its essential nature. Texts in the Bible testify to God's desire for a community of universal love based on a relationship of equality and mutuality (Gen. 5:1; Mk 7:24-30; Acts 10:28-30). In our speech and action, we have to approximate to the Kingdom of God which is characterised by freedom, justice and love. Therefore in India with her tremendous pluralism, we cannot simply talk about co-existence of communities but a *pro-existence* where there is mutual enrichment and development—learning to grow into the other. That is the challenge and

---

[9]   *Gathered for Life. Ibid.*, p. 152.

responsibility we have under God in Jesus the Christ. Communalism in its various forms is an open and a direct affront to God's vision for the future of humanity. The God of justice calls us to fight such forces and dismantle such a system that divide and destroy communities of people. Therefore in positive terms, it is imperative to promote and encourage pluralism as a gift of God. We have to affirm categorically the plurality of reality, both human and divine. Black and white, Brahmin and Dalit, men and women have to fight historic and existential injustice and live together as one differentiated community. Ultimate unity and oneness is the goal of all religions - Hindus, Christians, Muslims and others. The unity is based on equality and dignity of all people. God is not neutral in this situation.[10] God takes side with those who are oppressed like the *dalits* in India, the blacks all over the world and the minorities.

10   James H. Cone, *A Black Theology of Liberation* (New York: J.B. Lippincolt Co., 1970), pp. 121-138.

VI

Building a Communitarian Consciousness: A Biblical-Theological Perspective

Disruption of Community Life in the World

Related to the changing national life, is the seismic, sea-changes taking place at the global level particularly in the former U.S.S.R., East Europe and Germany. In some sense it is cataclysmic but in many ways it is quite catastrophic. After seventy-three years of open, explicit ideological confrontation, phenomenal transformations are taking place. East Europe has opened up and liberalised. Berlin Wall has come down and Germany has been unified. The 'U.S.S.R.' has significantly changed its character and composition, nature and scope. The United States seemed to have triumphed and the American ideology has conquered. As we are living in the last decade of the twentieth century and preparing for the twenty-first we are plunged into a unipolar world with a single axis. Community presupposes a dipolar world with a double axis. Single superpower is not congenial for building a wider community. This one ideology will shape and transform theology. Monopoly cannot be the basis for corporate life.

Collapse of communism in the 'U.S.S.R.' and in East Europe should not lead us to euphoria and excitement as it is happening in the Western World. There are some Western nations who are indulging in triumphalism which is reminiscent of the old 'crusading' mentality and messianism. This disease has afflicted much of the history of the Western world at large and of the church in particular in terms of colonialism, neo-colonialism and the missionary movements. The present phenomenon is a form of neo-colonialism in the making, which is quite subtle and pernicious. But I am glad that there are some prophetic voices, both in the East and West, that warn us of the impending danger. The ideological changes that are taking place very rapidly before our eyes call for sober reflection and critical analysis. What kind of issues are crystallising and what kind of conclusions are we to draw? What kind of shift is being made and ought to be made in those countries? We rejoice and express our full solidarity with those millions for overthrowing dictatorship/authoritarianism and for enjoying a measure of social freedom/democracy. But precisely at this point they have to work out carefully and painfully the nature and scope of this new-found freedom. Obviously, the leaders of the countries in East Europe and some past leaders of the 'U.S.S.R.' had betrayed the Marxian vision and hope. This is not a moment of triumph of Adam Smith over Karl Marx. Rather John Galbraith rightly remarks that a re-reading of Adam Smith as well as Karl Marx is necessary in this changing scenario.

From the perspective of community life, we must reject any subtle shift from socialism to capitalism—from State control to private control—from a communal world to a privatised, individualistic world that does not take cognizance of the plurality of reality. Richard Hazlett and Dean Turner in a book entitled, *Benevolent Living: Tracing the Roots of Motivation to God*, maintain that free enterprise of the free market system has also failed. They quote approvingly Kenneth Boulding, who had written in 1954,

> Market behaviour and market institutions—that is commer-
> cial life—frequently leads to the development of a type of
> personality which mistakes the abstractions of commerce for
> the realities of existence, and hence loses much of the richness
> and complexity, say of the marital relationship. There must be
> economy in human relationship if *large* fabrics of society are
> to exist at all.[1]

After nearly forty years, we hear a new voice, Vaclav Havel, a recent President of Czechoslovakia, in his 1990 New Year's message states,

---

[1] Richard Hazlett and Dean Turner, *Benevolent Living: Tracing the Roots of Mountains to God.* Foreword by Charlie Hartshorne (California: Hope Publishing House, 1990), pp. 21-22, See also pp. 13-33.

The worst of it is that we live in a spoiled moral environment. We have become morally ill because we are used to saying one thing and think another. We have learnt not to believe in anything, not to care about each other, to worry *only about ourselves* . . . Let us teach ourselves and others that politics ought to be a reflection of aspiration to contribute to the happiness of the *community* and not of the need to deceive or pillage the *community*.

Both Boulding and Havel are pleading for the recognition and actualisation of the deeper need of humanity in terms of a communitarian consciousness. A Hungarian person has recently remarked, "I have survived forty years of communism, but I'm not sure that I'll survive one year of capitalism." From a community perspective we have to seriously consider the value and validity of privatism, market economy and concentration of wealth and consequent power which are all perceived as 'liberalisation'. It is an important issue from the development point of view as we live in a broken and divided world—the rich North and the poor South. But more significantly such pervasive monopoly has and will manage to manipulate the minds—thought and life of people in the name of freedom. We must understand that the world market economy can "eat up the substance of *society*" (community) or in the words of Jurgen Habermans, it can colonise the *lifeworld*". It is a form of totalitarianism which is equally bad if not worse. One form of totalitarianism cannot be replaced by another which is more subtle and vicious. This cannot be a sure foundation of community life. It cannot promote active interaction between the worlds and forge a new, inclusive community. State collectivism should not be substituted by a shallow, unhealthy competition and rugged individualism.[2] Such individualism militates against evolving a bigger, inclusive community.

This recent ideological 'victory' of capitalism is essentially a Western 'victory' and this could be misconstrued as a Christian 'victory' against the 'evil empire'. Such an interpretation cannot be conducive towards communitarian thinking and collective living. At this critical juncture in human history, it is worthwhile to recall the meaningful distinction made by the German sociologist, Max Weber, between *gemeinschaft* and

[2]   Robert, Bellah, "The Role of the Church in a changing Society, in *Currents in the Theology and Mission* June, 1990, p. 190 and see also Vol. 17, No. 4, August, 1990 on "Common good"

gessellschaft. Both communism (socialism) as practised in East Europe and the former U.S.S.R. as well as capitalism as in the West, have actively promoted the latter vary often at the expense of or to the exclusion of the former. The latter concept exemplifies the external, physical aspect of society which is the 'given', static dimension. Gesselschaft can, at the maximum, perpetuate co-existence. But the multi-religious, pluralistic world in which we live demands pro-existence, living for and with people of all regions and religions. The concept of *gemeinschaft* can be congenial to promote such a purposive, conscious community. Obviously, the present ideological trends threaten or hamper fostering such a hope and vision.

Such an ideology is impacting powerfully on the theology of our time. Rather the former is reinforcing or strengthening the thrust of the latter. Privatisation in economics is supporting or reaffirming privatistic (individualistic), non-relational theology. Liberalisation basically means freedom of the few against the many millions of poor people particularly in Asia, Africa and Latin America. Freedom, in this context means to be left alone or getting away from other people as many would want in the West and also in the East. This ideology cannot promote the theology of involvement and engagement but of isolationism and escapism from the fundamental problems of poverty and liberation. Therefore I believe, that Hindu communalism at home is very well aggravated and accelerated by Christian fundamentalism. In such a situation, the doctrines of Sin and Salvation, Mission and Evangelism continue to be interpreted in a narrow, exclusive and individualistic way. Such a thinking continues to harbour dualism or dichotomy between body and soul, individual and the social (community). Distortions cannot help in the formation of the kind and quality of community we are dreaming of. Dualism can only produce its own distortions both conceptual and practical. Above all such an ideology cannot develop communitarian consciousness particularly the inclusive, inter-racial and inter-religious one. It wants to remain homogenous in this heterogenous world. So-called liberalisation cannot bring liberation for the many millions in the world. For the reasons stated above, we need a theological-ideological basis for building an inclusive community. In this brief paper we cannot go into detail but we can give some indications

---

3   John Macquarrie. *Three Issues in Ethics* (New York: Harper & Row Publishers. 1970), p.65.

Building a Community from a Biblical Perspective

John Macquarrie has affirmed. "The history with which the Bible deals is the history of communities rather than of individuals."[3] It must be noted that in the beginning there was some exclusive character of this community—the chosen people. But there was the constant impingement of other communities—Babylonians, Assyrians, Persians and others and thus giving to it an inter-racial, inter-religious, inter-regional character and content. The simultaneous creation of Adam and Eve is indicative of the communitarian character of humanity from its inception (Gen. 1:27)—"It is not good that the man should be alone" (Gen. 2:18a). Therefore the sexual distinction is not just physiological. It is the basis of community. I have already mentioned about it.[4] This bi-sexuality indicates variety, diversity and differentiation. Thus the community that we envisage is not one 'type'. This is the fundamental lesson of the biblical testimony. We have to discern this from the pages of the Bible. The basic language of the Bible is collective, corporate. No attempt is made to isolate, emasculate. On the contrary, truth emerges at the intersection of encounters and engagements. It begins with the old Israel, uses the metaphor of the New Israel, moves to the concept of the Church as the Body of Christ and finally there is the vision of the Kingdom of God and of new creation of heaven and earth. Consequently, the Jewish understanding of God (YHWH) had to grow and expand. At one time they conceived of God in an exclusive, narrow and monopolistic way. But later through extensive experience and exposure they began to recognise and acknowledge the universal Lordship (Sovereignty) of God. They began to realise that in the economy of God's salvation all people are included.

The incarnation is the revelation of the relational God who encounters and claims all kinds of people. God is actively engaged in forming larger, inclusive community—"I tell you, many well come from east and west and sit at table with Abraham, Issac and Jacob in the kingdom of heaven" (Matt. 8:11). Thus it is surprising to discover Jesus' affirmation and appropriation of the Gentiles, the Roman centurion, the Syrophoenician woman (Mk. 7:26), the Samaritan woman (Jn. 4:7-26), Samaritan man in his parable (Luke 10:33-37) and others. No attempt is made to reject such people on the basis of their racial or religious affiliations. In this sense Jesus is multi-racial and multi-religious or more appropriately trans-

---

4   See page 15 of the book.

religious and community-oriented. Jesus was a Jewish rabbi who rose above parochial and petty considerations of the Pharisees and other orthodox people of the time. Peter and Paul were able to capture the spirit of Jesus when they affirmed, "Truely I perceive that God shows no partiality, but in every nation any one who fears him and does what is right is acceptable to him" (Acts 10:34-35) and "There will be tribulation and distress for every human being who does evil, the Jew first and also the Greek... For God shows no partiality" (Rom. 2:9 and 11). God has no religion and Jesus did not come to establish a religion but a community. He came to show a way of life and share the good news of God's salvation. There is no way we can imprison Jesus in one region or religion. Jesus is the basis of a multi-racial and multi-religious community. He came to fulfill and enrich religious heritage of all people. Thus the Bible from the beginning to the end is an inter-racial and inter-religious document attempting to approximate to a multi-religious community. Jesus came to practise and promote such a perspective and build a new community which is not homogenised and monolithic. Discernment enables us towards a differentiated community. For Jesus, community is not only thought (idea or concept) but deed—the Word was enfleshed.

The Bible makes us relational, communitarian and thus-worldly. In the light of the Scripture, Christianity cannot be conceived as individualistic, non-relational and other-worldly. On the contrary, the ancient apostolic affirmation was organic in character. Let me give few examples from the Epistles. Firstly, we are acquainted with the Biblical language of *growing into* (Eph. 2:21-22). It says "As every structure is aligned on him, all grow into one holy temple in the Lord" (JB). New English Bible translates it as, "... the whole building is bonded together." J.B. Phillip translates it as, "properly fitting into its neighbour." And finally the RSV translates it as, "joined together." If we read few more verses of the Chapter we are struck by the architectural, organic metaphors and symbols. It affirms community with diversity and differentiation. It talks about, "breaking down the dividing wall of hostility or partition" (Eph. 2:14) Thus the community which is advocated is not a mathematical unit or an arithmetical one. This is referred to as the "Body of Christ" which needs building up with all its richness and possibilities (Eph. 4:12). We discover a similar vocabulary used in Colossians 2:19,

> and holding fast to the Head, from whom the whole body,
> nourished and knit together through its joints and ligaments,
> grows with a growth that is from God.

This is an example of knitting and of the biological growth. It makes abundantly clear that the community for which we aspire is not given or pre-determined. There is growth and evolution.

Secondly, there is the Pauline language of *"building up"* in I Corinthians 8:1. As Christians we have to engage in building up a community with love and care. In this sense we cannot be exclusive and narrow-minded. This language is repeated in II Corinthians 13:10 where he clarifies and strengthens the original point of building up and not be negative or nihilistic—"not for tearing down." This is indicative of the fact that community-formation particularly with a multi-religious, multi-racial mentality is painful and difficult. This positive, open attitude is again asserted in, "therefore encourage one another and build one another up, just as you are doing" (I Thess. 5:11). The old English used a good word for it, *edification*. The other translations are, hearten one another"; "fortify one another". Obviously, this is related to the concept of the *Body of Christ* with its diversified membership, with its unique character and composition.

Thirdly, the related concept of the epistles is *upbuilding* in Ephesians 4:16-16. In this passage it is mentioned that for upbuilding (stronger concept than just building) the community there is a need for all kinds of special (expert) people. The nature of the upbuilding is indicated in terms of "equipments of the saints"; "mature manhood"; and "stature of the fulness of Christ." Thus upbuilding gives solidity and stability to the community. Upbuilding demands responsibility and freedom. In Romans 14:19 Paul affirms categorically, "Let us then pursue what makes for peace and for mutual upbuilding". In another letter, Paul says, "... strive to excel in building up the church" (I Cor. 14:12b). The fundamental goal set by Paul for the early Christians was to strengthen or reinforce the effort of community-formation.

Fourthly, the common language in all the epistles is *built into*. This is mentioned in several places in different contexts (Eph. 2:22; Col. 2:7; I Pe. 2:5). All these four powerful phrases were used by the ancient apostles to capture the communitarian thrust of Jesus. We are indeed struck by the organic, relational language of the primitive church. Obviously, there were dissensions and divisions in the early church but what is more important was the distortion of the gospel. The former is essentially sociological in character while the latter is very much theological-ethical. Paul, Peter and others were eager to advise the Christians to transcend their sociological conditioning and affirm the theological perspective in attitudes and actions.

Building a Community from a Theological Perspective

Faith and fellowship are intrinsically related. Christianity is a community creating reality. Community and Christ belong together. He came to forge a new larger community, transcending our own small, racial , regional or religious communities. Jesus came to foster a new relationship. We cannot truncate and fragment God's vision *of* and *for* community—the Kingdom of God. Thus Dietrich Bonhoeffer states "There is in fact one religion from which the concept of community is essentially inseparable, and that is the Christian religion."

As there is no self without the world, so also there is no human being apart from and to the exclusion of other human beings. As we cannot indulge in any new forms of Gnosticism or Manichaenism, we cannot reduce the human being to a monad. His/her very existence is communal in character. Community belongs to the very being of the human as John Macquarrie has put.[5] Earlier Martin Buber conceived of the human as "I-Thou". He had said, that is the primary compound.[6] In this sense "social contract theories are distortions of the human self. In our modern time, individualism exists in terms of certain philosophies like Existentialism and in the Cartesian formulations. As the body is the basis and the subject of personality in the thinking of Feuerbach, so also Aristotle long ago defined the humans as a 'social being'.

God is community. He/She is not in isolation, cut off from reality, particularly human. He/She has a creational, redemptive relationship with the world and the humans in and through the Incarnation. The Incarnation is the purposive interpretation and interation of the divine-human. Thus Jesus is the paradigm for the "I-Thou" relationship. Now it is for us to extend and expand the Buberian thought to "We" relationship without destroying the dignity and the otherness of the other. It is for us to move forward and forge the inter-racial, inter-religious community.

Community is not just an idea but a deed. For this we have to summon the Holy Spirit to help us—"Come Holy Spirit, forge your larger community." Holy Spirit is the ground of our meeting, the current of communication and the go-between-God as John V. Taylor maintains.

---

5   Macquarrie, *Three Issues*, op. cit., p. 61.
6   Martin Buber. *I and Thou* (New York: Charles Scrimber's Sons, 1957); (Originally appeared in German in 1922) Later this concept was developed further by Richard H. Niebuhr, *The Responsible Self: An Essay in Christian Moral Philosophy* (London: Harper & Row Publishers, 1967); pp. 69-89.

He/She will bring about mutual recognition and interpenetration.

At this juncture it is important to remember that the main theme of the last Assembly of the World Council of Churches in Canberra, Australia was, "Come Holy Spirit, renew your *whole creation*." It is significant that after several Christological themes, the W.C.C. has ventured on this subject. It is good that the W.C.C. is deliberately and definitively moving away from Christocentricism which has been reduced to Christofascism by many adherents. It has moved to a more theo-centric theme which is conducive towards a larger community. More significantly, this was an attempt to proximate to the original theological affirmation - God as Trinity and thus affirming the plurality of reality, both divine and human reality. The divine reality approximates to the sociological reality. He/She is not a personal possession or a subjective property. He/She is both subjective but more important an objective phenomenon in the world producing new possibilities. It is good that Christians become all embracing in their affirmation and actions particularly given the ecological disaster and the environmental collapse. But this concern for the whole of creation or the biosphere should not be at the cost of or to the exclusion of the larger 'communosphere'. From the latter perspective, it is good that the W.C.C. began its ecumenical journey with the concept of "Responsible Society" in 1948. Later it was modified and expanded to the "Responsible World Society" to "just participatory, sustainable Society". Therefore we can presume that the Seventh Assembly's prayer or petition includes, "Come Holy Spirit, forge your larger community." But a prayer is not an escape. We cannot leave it to the snake as Harvey Cox has reminded us taking his clue from the book of Genesis. It is for us to make this possible with the power of the Spirit. Surely, the *ochlos* must be located within the larger *oikos*.[7] But we must remember that the word, *oikos*, primarily refers to the household or a family of people. Even the word, *oikoumene* means the land that is inhabited. We must keep our focus clear without losing sight of the total context.

This modern and revised emphasis on the doctrine of the Holy Spirit is a good transition to the total Godhead. We cannot disrupt or distort the divine as we have done with human beings and communities. We cannot subscribe to a Christology that is exclusive, narrow and above all aggressive. It is the resurrected, eschatalogical Christ that we have to accept and practise (I. Cor. 15:17). Jesus has said, "God is the God of the

---

[7] *Christian Mission in Theological Perspective.* Prepared by the Board of Mission of the Methodist Church (New York: Abingdon Press, 1967), p. 123.

living, not of the dead" (Matt. 22:32). We have to locate the Christ within
the trinitarian framework and reconceptualise Christology. Indeed it is
desirable and necessary to make the significant shift from the Ptolemaic
to the Copernican to the Einsteinian world. We live in a dynamically
changing world or a world of change. Essentially, God is a God of change
or a changing God. We cannot conceive of plurality of reality, both
human and divine as immutable and static. Now we are convinced that
mass is not as solid as we thought. Rather it changes into energy ($E=Mc^2$)
and thus the absolute character of substance is abolished. The language
of static substance or of nature has to be replaced by the language of
relation or relativity. The Bible affirms not only God's love and creation
of the world (Gen. 1 and 2; Jn. 3:16) but his/her radical enfleshmment and
consequent engagement (Jn. 1:14). It is important to apprehend God's
radical immanence-incarnation-Immanuel in the midst of his/her transcendence. This is God's fundamental quality or character. Thus one
scholar has stated, that Jesus' incarnation is the "infinite commitment to
finite." and therefore Christology is not a point of reference but a *pointer*
to the open future. Tom Driver goes on to assert. "Christ must be
reconceived in relativistic terms".[8] In the light of this discussion, Christ,
as traditionally and historically conceived cannot be considered as
Centre, Model, Norm or "Once and for all." We live in a world of
changing centre, models, norms and paradigms. Certainly, we have to
learn from them but to move on as pilgrim people. We cannot get 'stuck'
to the historical Jesus. We have to relate consciously and critically Christ
to our multinational plurality as well as to the socio-economic-political
reality. Christ within the trinitarian creed cannot be static and monolith—
the Christ of the past and the Christ of the future who is ahead of us—
"Before Abraham was, I am" (Jn. ;58). We have to look beyond Christ
to the power of the Holy Spirit. This will provide a basis to the formation
of an inclusive community.

Holy Spirit is primordial—the elemental force or energy, the
undifferentiated, all pervading power. As we have mentioned before He/
She is the revitalising energy. The work of Christ has to be viewed in
terms of the *parakletos* (Jn. 14:16 and 26; 15:26:16:7).

---

[8]   Tom F. Driver, *Christ in a Changing World: Toward an ethical Christology*
      (New York: Crossroad, 1981), p. 62. See also D.W.D. Shaw, *Who is God*
      (London:SCM Ltd., (1968), Chs. 1 and 2 and Daniel L. Migliore, *Called to
      Freedom: Liberation Theology and the Future of Christian Doctrine* (Phila-
      delphia: The Westminster Press, 1980) ch. 3.

Trinity is profoundly and fundamentally rational and relational. Martin Buber had said, "In the beginning is the relation." Therefore Driver writes, "Every dyad turns out to be a tryad." He illustrates this point from the importance and impact of the peripheral vision and gestalt psychology. Any knowledge is the interaction among the knower, the known and the context of knowing or common, contextual field or ground of knowing. Applying this to the trinitarian formulae, we must view the three persons not as independent, self-contained persons in the modern sense of the word. They are considered to be co-divine, co-equal, and co-eternal. It is interesting to recall St. Augustine who wrote.

> And if the charity whereby the Father loves the Son and the Son loves the Father, displays beyond the power of words, the communion of both, it is most fitting that the *spirit* which is common to both should have the special name of charity.

Believing in this statement, we cannot subordinate or prioritise any component part as was done in Nicene Creed (Filioque Clause). Trinity is a democratic principle and not hierarchical or linear. There is rather mutual dependence and recognition in the triune principle. In our new Christological formulation, it is imperative to emphasize the fundamental communitarian mode of life expressed in solidarity. It also indicates variety and diversity. Theology in general and Christology in particular cannot occur in isolation. We find similar emphasis in other religions particularly in Hinduism in terms of Trimurthi-*Brahma, Vishnu and Shiva*. Trishul or the trident is a symbol of the tri-unity. Thus it provides, *mutatis mutandis* a good basis for developing a community. Trinity is community.

We can develop further this communitarian thrust on the basis of the principle of *perichoresis*, developed by the Cappadocian Fathers of the early church like Gregory of Nyssa and Gregory of Nazianzus. It is possible to recover that emphasis for the establishment of the larger community. Perichoresis is an affirmation of collegial hierarchy and rejection of the vertical hierarchy in the Trinity. The trinitarian concept accepts the basic principle of *primus inter pares* (first among equals). Thus there is unity in diversity or diversity and richness is endorsed and encouraged in the midst of unity and oneness. This unity together with diversity is explained in terms of sun, its rays and heat; intrinsic relationship in the family; three petals of a leaf; time conceived as past, present and future; an object having length, breadth and depth; size, shape, weight, colour and hardness cohering in a stone; a plant with its roots, stem, flower and fruit. Therefore, perichoresis or circumincession is the mutual interpenetration of the three 'persons' or 'personalities'. Thus there is sufficient theological grounding for forging a community.

Conclusion

Christianity must move us to community action. Christ is more than our apprehension or formulation about him. He cannot be contained or conscripted by Christianity. Christ does not belong to us in an exclusive sense. We belong to him. In Christ, God is in relationship with all people. God does his work in his own way and in his own time (in the fulness of time) "For my thoughts are not your thoughts, neither are your ways my ways, says the Lord" (Isaiah 55:8). At the core of our belief is this mystery and sacredness before which we all stand recognising that he has not left himself without any witness (Acts 14:17) and in many and various ways God has spoken in the past (Heb. 1:1) and he continues to speak and act. He is reconciling all people everywhere (II Cor. 5:18) and summing up all things in him (Eph. 1:10, Col. 1:20). We will hold on to Jesus realising that he is vulnerable. [9] Communitarian thought and community life is the only option before us. Let us choose that life and live.

---

[9]   Somen Das, *Weakness of Power and Power of Weakness: Seeking Clarity, Credibility and Solidarity* (Delhi: I.S.P.C.K., 1990), Chs. III and IV.

VII

Euthanasia and Medical Ethics

Introduction

In this chapter an attempt is made to deal with the medical issues and euthanasia in particular in the context of human rights. There was a private Bill pending before the Lok Sabha entitled. "Mercy Killing Bill, 1980", (Bill No. 14 of 1980), introduced by Shri. M.C. Daga, M.P. The Bill aroused a lot of comments and criticisms. It raised the substantive issues pertaining to euthanasia from the perspective of human rights. It also raised the more primordial issues about life and death, pain and suffering, dignity and integrity of a person. That is what I seek to discuss in this Chapter. In 1988 the Seventh Biennial Conference of the World Federation of Right-to-Die Societies highlighted the issue through an active inter-disciplinary interaction of the medical, legal and ethical experts. Prolonged death of B.T. Ranadive, veteran communist leader, the Emperor Hirohito of Japan and Raj Kapoor of Bombay Hindi film raised the issue also. Ranadive asked for euthanasia. But it was denied.

It may be worthwhile to remember that some people have sought for the amendment to the U.N. Declaration of Human Rights which would include, "the right of incurable sufferers to voluntary euthanasia", referring to Article Five of the Declaration which states that, "No one shall be subjected to torture." The Articles Three and Eighteen declare that, "every one has the right to life, liberty and the security of person..." We need to know what this means in terms of euthanasia. We need to know whether the right to life does necessarily mean the obligation to live especially, when continued existence in extreme situations of illness could be demoralizing and dehumanising as it happened in the case of Marshal Tito of Yugoslavia. For this reason the book, *Final Exit* by Derek Humphry became the best-seller in 1991 as it advocated suicide for the terminally ill. The Michigan pathologist Dr. Jack Kevorkian became famous because he helped a women suffering from Alzheimer's disease to commit suicide in 1990. This raises serious moral issues.

At this juncture it is important to note that this issue of euthanasia and other medical issues have become crucial and critical because of the tremendous advances made in the medical science in our time—in terms of bio-medical technology, surgical skills and chemotherapy. The very boon of modern life seems to have been reduced to a bane in certain cases. Before we proceed any further it is important to define euthanasia which is made up of two Greek words, *eu* and *thanatos*. Etymologically it means easy or gentle death, and not killing which I think is a misnomer. Therefore, euthanasia has been defined as a "theory that in certain circumstances, when owing to disease, senility or the like, a person's life has permanently ceased to be either agreeable or useful, the sufferer should be painlessly killed either by himself or by another."[1] More appropriately it would be better to talk about enabling or facilitating a person in such conditions to have a gentle or merciful death. It is interesting to note that long ago, during the inter-testamental period there was a recognition of the role of the doctor. It is good to read the Deuterocanonical or the Apocryphyal scriptural section like Ecclesiasticus or Sirach 28:1-15. Verse one says, "Honour the doctor for his services, for the Lord created him", and verse 14 clearly states, "to give them (doctors) success in relieving pain." This is a reminder of the earlier Hippocratic Oath, one of which says, that the doctor must engage himself in preserving life and to relieve human suffering. The same principle is enshrined in the Declaration of Geneva, 1948, the International Code of Medical Ethics, London, 1949 and the Declaration of Helsinki, 1964.[2] In spite of these professions and affirmations there seems to be an inherent contradiction and incompatibility between relieving pain and preserving life.

Human Rights Consideration in Euthanasia from a Theological Perspective

The fundamental affirmation we need to make is that we believe in a creator-God who found his creation good. God has created us and given us life. There is a definitive and a decisive relationship between God,

---

[1] H.J. Rose, "Euthanasia", *Encyclopedia of Religion and Ethics* V. pp. 598-601.

[2] George V. Lobo, *Current Problem in Medical Ethics*, (Allahabad, St. Paul's Publication, 1980), pp. 211-213.

nature and the world of people. God intends the welfare or well-being of this creation. God posits a great value to it. Both in his intellect and activity God preserves and sustains the well-being of this creation. God is the author of life and maintains it. From this perspective we need to assert the right to live.

Human Rights—The Right to Live

As we have realised that our life is a gift from God. God is the ground of human life and the proper reference point for all human action and thought. We are ultimately subjected to him. At this juncture it is important to ask several pertinent questions like what is life? What is human life? How is it to be sustained? At what costs?

We have asserted that God is the creator. But we must realise that he is not only the creator and preserver of human life but also its promoter, creating new possibilities for greater well-being. This is very well demonstrated in the medical science in particular. God created conditions for enhancement of life which make our life abundant. This should be enough of an indication that God is not interested in the quantity or the length of days but essentially the quality of life (Jn. 10:10). Of course quality has to be pre-conditional to the quality but not in an absolute sense. It is here that we need to understand the meaning of *humanum*. Essentially one is a relational being—in relation to God and persons. The concept of the *imago dei* (image of god) is indicative of this relational character of the person. So when we talk about the worth and dignity of the human person, we must realise that it is derivative to a great extent. Bonhoeffer spoke of the alien worth of the individual. Paul Ramsey asserted,

> The value of human life is ultimately grounded in the value God is placing on it... Man's sacredness is not composed by observable degrees of relative worth. A life's sanctity consists not in its worth to anybody... No one is ever much more than a fellow fetus; and in order not to become confused about life's primary value it is best not to concentrate on degrees of relative worth we may later acquire... Man's essence is his existence before God and to God, as it is from him. His dignity is "an alien dignity; an evaluation that is not of him but placed upon him by the divine decree."[3]

---

[3] Paul Ramsey, "The Sanctity of Life", in *The Dublin Review*, 1967, pp 10-11. See also his book, *Fabricated Man: The Ethics of Genetic Control* (London: Yale University Press, 1970).

Better than Ramsey, I think that Karl Barth had been able to hold the dialectic between affirmation and negation of human life when he stated,

> Human life—one's own and that of others—belongs to God. It is his loan and blessing... Therefore respect is due to it, and, with respect, protection against each and every callous negation and destruction. Obedient abstention from such destruction, and therefore the obedient protection of life, will naturally include knowledge of its limitation. It is not divine life, but creaturely. It is not the eternal life promised to man, but temporal... Thus the protection of life required to us is not unlimited nor absolute. It is simply the protection which God wills to demand of man as the Creator of this life and the Giver of the future eternal life... It simply refers to the fact that human life has no absolute greatness or supreme value, that it is not a kind of second God... But since human life is of relative greatness and limited value, its protection may also consist *ultima ratio* in its surrender and sacrifice.[4]

From these two lengthy quotations we realise that the right to life is not absolute. We cannot idolise human life as it is. We cannot dogmatically affirm the sanctity of life. We must be able to make a distinction between lives or among lives. Human life, is undefinable because it is partly measurable and partly immeasurable. In the light of what God has done and is doing through Jesus Christ we cannot subscribe to a physicalist view of life. The *summum bonum* is not merely the biological life. For this reason we cannot be concerned with the somatic good of the human organism only but one's spiritual well being. Jesus had to come and redeem this human life and give it a meaning. When we talk of the human we must mention the qualities which constitute the human. Freedom, self-consciousness and self-possession are some of the qualities in addition to the ability to think, feel and relate. Therefore it is rightly said, "Human life and human death must be comprehended personally and interpersonally as well as bodily-biologically."[5] So we do not value existence *per se* but what is valued about it. In the midst of this

---

4   Karl barth, *Church Dogmatics*, III/4, trans. A.T. Mackay et al. (Edinburgh, T. & T. Clark, 1961), pp. 397-398.
5   Harmon L. Smith, *Ethics and the New Medicine* (Nashville: Abingdon Press, 1970), p. 165.

ambivalence about right to life, we must maintain a basic posture of respect for human life. Gustafson has written,

> ...respect for life does not necessarily indicate the preservation of human physical life at the cost of unbearable pain to individuals, and even to families around them. Nonetheless an attitude of respect is primary, for life is received from a power that wills its well-being.[6]

As we are discussing about the right to life on the basis of human worth and dignity because one is created by God, we must realise that the human beings must decide about this right on the basis of deliberation. This right is not self-evident. One important quality of being human is the sense of responsibility. One has to be accountable to God and realise the potentialities for well-being which is already present in nature and history. Humans are co-creators, partners with God, approximating to various possibilities. In a real sense human actions have to be responsive and responsible to God's actions upon us. The good is not fixed and immutable but it has to be explored and established consciously. This involves risks—that is the bane or boon of human existence. From this perspective, the humans are under no obligation to accept passively and submissively degrading or degenerative death as Jonathan Swift, the great satirist and Irish clergy had to face. Such disproportionate effort to support life at all costs focuses too much time, attention, energy and resources on oneself and on others.

Human Rights—The Right to Die

It is interesting to note that the Roman Catholics who have been generally against euthanasia or abortion, make a distinction between Ordinary and Extraordinary methods. According to them, ordinary methods are medicines, treatments, and operations which offer a reasonable hope of benefit, and which can be obtained and used without "excessive expense, pain or other inconveniences." On the other hand, extraordinary means are those resources and appliances which would involve "excessive

---

6   James M. Gustafson, *The Contributions of Theology to Medical Ethics* (Marquette University: Theology Department, 1975), p. 60. See also Arthur J Dyck, *On human Care: An Introduction to Ethics* (Nashville: Abingdon Press, 1977), Ch. IV, pp. 72-91.

expense, pain or other inconveniences and not offer reasonable hope of benefit." It is very difficult to distinguish between these two methods because they would very much vary according to time and place. But whatever the problem involved, it is significant to note that the Roman Catholics cannot think of maintaining human life absolutely at all costs. There is a tacit recognition of the patient's right to die. This is made little bit more clear by the principle of Double Effect enunciated by the Roman Catholics. This means that the death or the killing should not be the direct intention of the doctor but of mitigating pain and suffering which may indirectly or consequentially lead to the patient's death. By whatever casuistry the Roman Catholics may try to justify euthanasia, basically they are affirming the quality of life which means conscious control of death, as man has tried to control birth and life.[7].

There is a profound dread of death even in normal circumstances. But we must conceive of death and life in a continuum. It is a process and a development. Life or death is not an event or a sudden happening. There is death in life and life in death or through death. This is the paradoxical character of the continuum. Christians need to view death in the light of sin and a call to enduring life in Christ Jesus. Therefore, we must see it positively and with hope and if and when necessary be able to assert the right to die. It is not the terminus but a transition to some other kind of life as we believe in the resurrection of the dead. So we have no reason to fear death and try frantically, through all kinds of expensive and time-consuming means, to prolong so-called life or really to prolong death which has already set in. We must recognise that death is inevitable but the manner of death need not be.

In the context, it is useful to discuss briefly about human suffering. We know very well that human beings are frail and finite creatures. He/she partakes of this creaturliness. We know that Jesus Christ suffered and died. And we believe that this suffering has a redemptive value and purpose. We are aware of bearable suffering that teaches us or even purifies us. But we also know of uncreative, useless and hopeless suffering that does no good either to the sufferer or to the persons who have to silently observe or prolong such a suffering. Human suffering is not a virtue by or in itself. Consequently, humans have learnt to control such a suffering at birth, in life and one must do the same during death wherever necessary. One need not suffer. Very often it is either

[7]   Joseph Fletcher, *The Ethics of Genetic Control* (New York: Anchor Press, 1974) p. 157.

rationalised or explained away in terms of God's will or in the name of nature. Such an attitude is really a dereliction of duty. It really means to deny mortality and to submit to some kind of fatalism or even determinism. In such a context of pain and sufferings we are suggesting "one's inalienable right to die."

Human Rights—Right to Die with Dignity

We have already indicated some of the qualities that constitute the humanum. To be considered as a person or a personality it is important to have these characteristics. When these become diminished or virtually absent in a human being one has the right to die when these are in tact. A World Federation of Right-to-Die Societies have been formed all over the world in last ten years (1983-1993) and the Hemlock Society was established in 1980 to advocate Euthanasia.[8]

This means that at our death we do not want to live in a puppet-like condition, without self-consciousness or self-hood — when we are sedated, comatose and become a betubed object, manipulated and subconscious if not subhuman. Such a "medicated survival" takes away the personal dignity and integrity of the patient along with the interper sonal values of relationships. We cannot encourage living death, when the meaning of life, the right to life has been lost. Therefore, it is rightly stated,

> Every man in this world has surely the right to die in peace and comfort, it would be an invidious contradiction of our honour

---

[8] Number of books are available on the subject. Some of them are Derek Humphry and Ann Wickett, *The Right to Die: Understanding euthanasia* (New York: Harper & Row Publishers, 1986).
Robert L. Risley, *Death with Dignity: A New Law Permitting Physician, Aid-in-Dying* (Oregon: Hemlock Society, 1989).
Gerald a Larue, *Euthanasia and Religion: A survey of Attitudes of the world Religions to the Right-to-Die* (Oregon: Hemlock Society, 1990)
Stanley M. *Rosenblatt, Murder of Mercy: Euthanasia on Trial* (New York: Prometheus Books, 1992)
Robert M. Veatch, *"Brain, Death and Slippery Slopes"* in The *Journal of Clinical Ethics,* Vol. 3, No. 3, 1992, pp. 181-187.
Ann Wickett, *Double Exit: When Ageing Couples Commit Suicide Together* (Oregon: Hemlock Society, 1989)
Patrick Nowell-Smith, "Euthanasia and the Doctors - a rejection of the BMA's Report in *Journal of Medical Ethics,* 1989, 15, pp. 124-128.

if pride in technical ability made our patients fear us at death. When is the body dead. If the heart can be restarted the patient is technically still alive, even though the brain can be irretrievably lost to contact with the world again. Sometimes, when one knows the patient will die later anyway, a man should be allowed to die in peace.[9]

From this perspective, there is a Christian masochism in that attitude which deliberately advocates physical suffering as a sure means to "sharing in the sufferings of Christ." To maintain dignity in death, it is not good to prolong bodily functions long after the human organism has ceased to be intentionally, self-directingly and purposively viable. Smith has put it in a stronger language when he states,

> It deserves asking whether we can say without equivocation that doctors who refuse to allow an accident victim to die (for example, one whose brain is destroyed) are not aggressors against the well-being of the patient's family and all their resources so long as the patient's death is artifically postponed? Or that hundreds of hours and millions of dollars expended in the care of mechanically metabolized human organisms, for whom there is no real medical hope of recovery, do not constitute in some sense an assault upon the common good?[10]

Basically he is advocating dying with dignity and the violation of this right as very serious. It may be recalled that long before Smith, Karl Barth, the champion of respect for life had said,

> Yet in this connection the question arises whether this kind of artificial prolongation of life does not amount to human arrogance in the opposite direction, whether the fulfillment or medical duty does not threaten to become fanaticism, reason folly, and the required assisting of human life a forbidden torturing of it. A case is at least conceivable in which a doctor might have to recoil from this prolongation of life no less than

---

[9]   Vincent, Edmunds, *Ethical Responsibility in Medicine* (London: E & S. Livingston Ltd., 1967), p. 56.
[10] Smith, *Ethics and the New Medicine*, p. 156.

from its arbitrary shortening. We must await further develop-
ments in this sphere to get a clear general picture. But it may
well be that in this special sphere we do have a kind of
exceptional case. For it is not now a question of arbitrary
euthanasia; it is a question of the respect which may be claimed
by even the dying life as such.[11]

What would he have said now after thirty five years when we have
more sophisticated machines and chemicals to prolong human death? In
this sense, it seems that human mastery over life and death has become
demonic and dehumanising bereft of human dignity.

Understanding of Human Rights

At this juncture it is essential to look at the nature of human rights we are
talking about.

We need to consider the question of context with regard to human
rights. I believe that much of the content of human rights will dependent
on and determined by the *context* in which they are nourished and
nurtured. The content of human rights cannot be divorced from the
context. For this reason we must realize that no individual right is
absolute and unconditional. This also means that human rights have a
double character. In one sense it is given while in another sense it has to
be discovered and formulated in each historical milieu. From this point
of view, we cannot know human rights *a priori*. Our responsibility is to
contextualise or relativise human rights without forgetting their universal
and universalisable dimension. Some scholars have given emphasis on
the given character of human rights without sufficiently considering their
contextual character.

Connected with this concern for contextualisation, we must realise
that we cannot afford the luxury of indulging in vague generalisations and
sterile abstrations. If we are genuinely concerned about human rights we
have to start from the particular—see human rights in micro-terms of
actual situations and moments as in the case of a dying patient. We cannot
afford to neglect the tremendous diversity and complexity of issues in the
world. We cannot any more work on the facile assumption that the issues
are the same, homogeneous and monolithic. This is what happened if we
accent unduly the universalistic character of human rights. We have to

---

[11]   Barth, *Church Dogmatics*, Vp:/ OOO/4, p. 427.

take seriously the variables even within one issue. As soon as we become specific, we become acutely aware of the difficulty of knowing in advance the human rights of a dying person. I am not therefore advocating the rejection of human rights but their abridgement or expansion, on a priority basis. Basically this is indicative of the fact that we need some kind of a higher norm on which we can establish human rights of a patient. I believe we have to talk about distributive or transforming justice (to use the language of Paul Tillich) as the highest norm.

I have raised for issues. Firstly, I have raised the issue of a the universal and the particular with regard to human rights. As soon as we give greater emphasis to the particularistic approach to human rights we raise questions with regard to the *Human* and *Rights*. From this perspective we cannot talk about the human and of rights in general, in the abstract. It must have a measure of specificity to make sense or meaning for the patient. Related to the first and the second issues, I would like to raise the issue of the absolute and the relative nature of human rights. Are they disjunctive or is there a dialectical character to human rights? In the context of euthanasia we need to be aware of these dimensions of life and death.

Euthanasia in the Context of Public Health Care in India

While we are struck by the awe-inspiring discoveries and inventions which can prolong life or death indefinitely, there was a report about a "Capital Scandal". Cholera and gasteroenteritis killed 300 people and hospitalised 80,000 in New Delhi. In 1993 nearly one thousand died in one state of W. Bengal according to Official Reports. We are becoming aware of the silent scourge of our time called AIDS (Acquired Immuno Deficiency Syndrome). ICMR estimates the number of carriers of Human Immuno Virus (HIV) at 6,37,000 in Indian urban areas alone. Nearly ten lakh Indian carry the Virus. Worldwide it is 14 million people. flies, mosquitos, open drains and garbage are responsible for this situation. Immediately following this report, was the news of adulteration of oil affecting 2,500 people in Calcutta.

According to the Doctors this resulted in "ascending toxic neuropathy" and the people suffered from residual symptoms of paralysis.[12] T.B., Small pox, Malaria and Diarrhoea continue to afflict millions of people

---

[12]   *Indian Express,* August 15 and 31, 1988.

in this country. Days of epidemics are not yet over.

In the midst of this health-care situation, the World Health Organisation reported that 25 million people die from water-borne diseases in the developing countries every year. 460 million Indians do not have safe drinking water. According to another study 70% of the inland water in India is unfit for human consumption. As a result the country loses 73 million working days, costing the exchequer Rs. 600 crores every year. India accounts for a third of the five million children who die in the developing world every year from diarrhoea. Common diseases mentioned above and typhoid, hookworm and guinea worm account for as much as 80% of our health problems. 98% of residents of Varanasi suffer from some form of stomach ailment or other. River Ganges continues to be the most polluted river in the world in spite of the cleaning efforts. Modern urban life has generated its own quantum of sulphur dioxide in addition to smoke and dust. This is the scenario of health-care in modern India.

In the midst of this anomalous situation the medical industry in India is promoting a drug culture. We have come to learn about the malpractices of pharmaceutical giants. Migraines tablets have been peddled as "appetite stimulants" and anabolic steroids have been promoted for the treatment of malnutrition in children. Preparations banned in 1983 are still available in the market. There are about 16,000 drug firms in the country and 100,000 brand names! Every fifth drug is sub-standard in the open market. It is a Rs. 3500 crore annual business. Just about 25 multinational companies control the pharmaceutical industry. Three-fourths of our population has to go without medicines. There is no quality control, no rational drug policy after 46 years of Independence—No unbiased drug information. The pharmaceutical lobby enjoys *laissez faire* freedom pouring a glut of unwanted (80% are redundant) drugs into the market in myriad forms of pills, capsules etc. Thus much of the problem in health-care is drug-induced, particularly after 'liberation' and decontrol.

This drug culture is sustained and strengthened by big hospitals which essentially cater to the affluent industrial society based on urbanised health system. The emphasis in these places is not on preventive, promotive medicine but curative services. 87 per cent of hospital beds are congregated in urban areas while 70 per cent of the Indian population is still rural. These hospitals are not only urban based and biased but also huge in size. There are three hospitals of over 1000 beds and eleven hospitals of between 500 to 1000 beds in Bombay and most of those are within a radius of five miles. The basic health-care model recommended by the Bhore Committee has not been implemented. Social discrimination, economic deprivation and the lack of political will prevent the nation to take seriously what Justice Lentin and the joint report of the Indian Council of Social Science and the Indian Council of Medical Research had recommended. Therefore Antia, Director of the Foundation for Research in community health, Bombay, rightly asserted,

> Small is beautiful is highly relevant in the field of medicine for individual human care and attention are the essence of medical practice. Imposing hospitals with the latest gadgetry not only fail to function in our culture but by their very nature are dehumanising institution where everything matters but the patient.

Similar sentiments were expressed about big hospitals in India catering to the wants of the rich and the few. These are called high-tech or NRI hospitals that advertise heavily, grow around commercial, affluent centers, have no relation to the health-care needs of the city, its environment, the rural mass and the government does not have a monitoring cell.[13] This concern has been expressed by the former President of the Indian Medical Association, Dr. V. Parameshvara, and the President of the Karnataka chapter of the IMA, Dr. Raju Reddy. This situation is aggravated by these big hospitals encouraging diagnostic laboratories. Over or unnecessary investigation is an unhealthy trend. These labs pay commission to the doctors amounting to Rs. 1000 to Rs 1500 for a scan and 80 per cent of them have been found negative. A recent study revealed that money-hungry middlemen are exploiting kidney donors and helpless patients with Terminal Renal Failure. A kidney is sold for Rs. 1 lakh. There is no law to check the kidney business which is a six thousand crore industry just in the city of Calcutta. Thus organ transplant is a blessing in the modern world but it is a multi-billion dollar business across continents. Transplantation of Human Organs Bill, 1992 has been passed but it has many loopholes. Such is the broader context of health-care within which we need to take cognizance of the issue of euthanasia.

The elite, specialised doctors, big hospitals and drug lobbies together have created an ethos which can be categorized as Iatrogenesis, using the

[13]   *Indian Express,* September 2, 1988.

helpful category of Ivan Illich. This is the sick-making powers of diagnosis and therapy. According to him, "The medical establishment has become a major threat to health." We have to assert the civil right to equitable health-care and eliminate the medical monopoly. Health-care has come to mean sickness-care thus falsifying the conception of sickness and health. This is called "medicalization of life" or "expropriate the power of the individual to himself" or herself. Illich has stated,

> In a complex technological hospital, negligence becomes "random human error" or "system breakdown", callousness becomes "scientific detachment", and incompetence becomes "a lack of specialised equipment." The depersonalization of diagnosis and therapy has changed malpractice from an ethical into a technical problem.[14]

In this context Illich would agree with Paul Ramsey that there are things we can do which we ought not to do, which is a necessary condition for preventing humanity from total abasement by technical control in the whole medical realm. This is equally or more true in the context of the above discussion on euthanasia in particular. Thus we need to turn to specific criteria that could help us in our decision.

Ethical Criteria for Health-Care

I may begin by maintaining with Nelson and Rohricht,

> While health is not the totality of human wholeness, it is a basic component. While physical healing is not the same as personal healing, it is intrinsically related. And while creative medicine will not usher in the reign of God, it can contribute significantly to that fuller realization of our common humanity, which is both a gift and an achievement.[15]

I have already indicated the broken world in which we live and the ambiguity of problems facing the medical world. For this reason it is

[14] Ivan Illich, *Limits to Medicine: Medical Nemesis: The Expropriation of Health* (Calcutta: Rupa and Co., 1977), p. 30.

[15] James B. Nelson and Joanne Smith Rohricht, *Human Medicine: Ethical Perspectives on Today's Medical Issues* Revised and Expanded Edition (Minneapolis: Augsburg Publishing House, 1984), p. 216.

important to articulate clear criteria. Gustafson has formulated medical, ethical, economic and political criteria which intersect and have a cumulative effect on the medical practice and promotion.[16]

Firstly, there are six medical criteria—frequency of a disease in a community, diseases that are life-threatening (mortality), morbidity or severity of those diseases that impair normal human functioning and significantly lower the quality of life, illness that strike persons of all ages, sequence of the disease process at which therapy is likely to be effective over a long period of time and the state of bio-medical research that will benefit patients. These criteria are relevant and meaningful for the promotion of health care in general and in the context of our discussions on euthanasia in particular.

The ethical criteria according to Gustafson are four related patterns of moral reflection—distinctive justice and its fine-tuning in equity; calculations of possible outcomes of certain choices in terms of a variety of "benefits and costs"; the question of the moral limits of research i.e., whether there are investigations that ought not to be undertaken for moral reasons regardless of their potential benefits for others; and the common good, e.g., how can concerns for the well-being of the larger whole be taken into account? In the light of these criteria particularly, about justice and firmness, Gustafson refers to the process of aging and asks, "Has the calling of biomedical research been expanded considerably if one alters the primary criterion from the elimination of threats to health and life to the amplification of the life span?" He comes to the conclusion, "Given health problems of many of the poor in the United States and of countless others throughout the world is it just to proceed with this research?"[17] I wish Gustafson had put it positively and categorically.

There is a moral repugnance at the introduction of economic efficiency as a criterion—human health and life cannot be quantified in monetary terms. But in this broken and divided world, there are painful distributional choices. Gustafson has rightly affirmed,

> Incremental choices that do not take account of the efficient
> use of the limited total resources generally face the questions

[16] James M. Gustafson, *Ethics from a Theocentric Perspective: Ethics and Theology* Volume Two (Chicago: The University of Chicago Press, 1984), pp. 350-360.

[17] Gustafson, *Ethics from a Theocentric Perspective*, Ibid., p. 265

of cost at some stage; they do not avoid it but delay its consideration.[18]

Therefore Gustafson argues that economic efficiency becomes morally relevant. There is no virtue in wasting finite resources and there is a merit in attempting to increase the beneficial outcome at the lowest possible cost.

The final type of criteria is *political*. We have already mentioned that there is a definite lack of political will to promote and strengthen basic health needs for all and not permit elitist doctors, hospitals and drug lobbies to monopolise medicine and in the process distort the very meaning of health and healing. In the area of euthanasia it is imperative to pass legislations that would help doctors in the hospitals to do the necessary. Organisations like the IMA, ICMR-ICSSR, National Drugs and Pharmaceutical Development Council and the Christian Medical Association of India together could bring pressures on political leaders on this issue and encourage authentic understanding of medical care which is much more than physical survivability. It must categorically affirm that miracles of modern medicine cannot deliver humanity from its finitude and morality.

Conclusion

Basically, in this chapter we have called into question the very concept of human rights with regard to death and dying. We have asked the question, "What is human?" in the context of patients dying slowly but surely from some terminal illness like cancer, irreversible injury like brain damage or incurably infirm leading to irremediable loss of consciousness. We have attempted an answer and said that in such situations very often the human is lost. Secondly we have called into question the traditional understanding of rights, which are fixed and prescribed and can never be violated like the right to life. The basic postulate of natural law is to avoid evil and to do good. Increasingly these have become compatible. Doing good sometimes may mean doing 'harm' like euthanasia.

This means that as human beings we have a vital role to play both in life as well as in death. We cannot flinch from our responsibility. We are called to be God's worthy stewards or deputies and must exercise our

---

[18] Gustafson, *Ethics and Theology*, Ibid., p. 269.

God-given freedom with awesome responsibility. The human is created "little less than God" (Ps. 8) which means that we have to have the highest degree of accountability for the well-being of the whole creation. We can either frustrate or further God's purpose and intention by what we do or fail to do. God has opened the way for us into the future. God is with us in our struggle—in our predicament. This is more so with the issue of euthanasia. We can never be certain in our actions because we are finite and fallen. It is a twilight world or a borderline situation where we do not know clearly the good or more important which is the greater good. There is a serious conflict of values and we are called to make a choice in the midst of this terrible ambiguity. This is inherent in any moral decision of our time and more so with the termination of life. Karl Rahmer said,

> One ought soberly and courageously to consider, according to a supra-individual morality, what sacrifices would be expected of the humanity today on behalf of humanity tomorrow, without being too quick to speak of immoral cruelty, of the violation and exploitation of the dignity of man today for the benefit of man tomorrow.[19]

---

[19]   Karl Rahner, *Theological Investigations,* IX (New York: Herder and Herder, 1972), p. 224.

VIII

Political Life Promoting
Justice and Peace

Introduction

In this chapter, I hope to explain and evaluate something of our political life particularly in India. We are aware that politics makes and breaks human life in terms of justice and injustice. According to Aristotle, we are all political beings meaning that we belong to the 'polis' or city. It clearly indicates the limitations implied in the use of the word by Aristotle. Obviously, in his political scheme he excluded the slaves and 'barbarians'. Today, the word is used more comprehensively meaning that which fundamentally orders and organises life in the society. From time immemorial there have been leaders of various sorts. Kings and emperors, *rajas* and *maharajas* adorn the pages of history with their deeds and misdeeds. We cannot conceive of a time in history when there has not been some kind of a leader. But the question before us is the quality and character of leadership — the kind of leadership that promotes peace based on justice.

It is not possible for me to go into all the aspects of politics and government. For our purpose we will broadly divide this chapter into two main areas namely, forms of Government and social justice and forms of relationship between States and Religion.

I. Forms of Government

We are all born into some kind of a political life. It is the warp and woof of human existence. Basically, government is the organisation of people under authority. In the west, there has been Machiavelli who wrote *The Prince* which was finally published in 1532. In India, there has been Kautilya's *Arthasastra* written during the reign of Chandragupta Maurya

(322 or 325 B.C.). Both these Treatises deal with the system of Government. Both of these documents offer blue print for dictators, Evidently they are not guides for efficient democratic form of government. But they clearly indicate that some form of government shapes and forms our thinking and determines our doing. It affects our life deeply. It enables us to do something while it prevents us from doing something else. We cannot escape politics. It is not something peripheral or external to our being and doing. For this reason it is imperative that we pay attention to it and discern the forces at work in the political life and make the right choice of government that would support, sustain and promote human justice and maximise human possibilities for their growth and development.

As I have mentioned earlier, that people have always lived under some system of government or political authority however crude and simple it might have been. The concept of "social contract" presupposes that there was a time in history when people lived without some form of government. That is a myth. On the contrary, by his very nature humans need to be controlled and organised for the common good. In this sense, a government is an instrument of coercion enacting laws and enforcing them on a population. But its work is not only to uphold law and order but to positively establish justice and bring about the common welfare. That would be the dual role of any authentic government.

A government has to do with control and organisation which means it exercises authority and power. For our purpose we will study some significant forms of government in terms of power and raise questions like "who is in power?" "What kind of power and how is it exercised?" "How does one come to assume power and how does one stay in power?" Answer to such questions decide which is relatively the best form of government. From this point of view we can broadly divide the multifarious systems of government under two main categories namely, the ones that bring about the concentration of power and the others which basically believes in the devolution of power. The first category we could designate as 'Oligarchy', and the second category as 'Democratic'. Let us take a cursory glance at the various forms of oligarchy.

(A) Oligarchical Forms of Government
Basically, oligarchy is a form of government in which the power is vested in a few-persons or a dominant class or clique. It is essentially a government by the few. In the earlier times and even till today in certain countries a ruler is conceived to have descended directly from the gods

or even considered as incarnation of some diety—regarded as "vicegerents of God" or "the anointed of the Lord". They are not elected by the people as such but pretends to have been chosen by God himself. Consequently, such rulers think that their power and privileges are derived from above. This is how the concept of "the divine rights of kings" came into existence. In such a context, an individual or a group of clever people could get together and make themselves masters of the race in the name of God. This is the form of oligarchy which is technically known as **theocratic**, literally meaning the rule of God. Under such a form of government slavery or serfdom becomes a possibility. It is really a seizure of power by a privileged or a dominating group. Power becomes concentrated and entrenched, and vested interests are rampant. A clear example of such a form of government in our time would be Iran where Ayatollah Khomeini combined in his person the leadership of the religious system in Iran and also its government. This has been designated as "mullacracy", which is an indigenised form of theocracy. Fundamentally, such a form of government is a negation of democracy in which a strict separation is maintained between religion and state. RSS-VHP-BJP wants the country to become theocratic-Hindu Rashtra!

The other expressions of oligarchy would be *plutocracy* and *aristocracy*. Plutocracy is a form of government in which the wealthy class enjoys supreme power and privileges. Aristocracy is the government of the best or of the elite, the upper class. Such expressions of oligarchy are not blatantly common but they are very much present even in democratic forms of government. The other most common and obvious expressions of oligarchy are *monarchy* and *dictatorship*, which are widely prevalent even in the modern world. monarchy literally means "sole ruler" and the word suggests exclusive or absolute power, indicates social rank and sets him apart from others. This apartness is registered in the mode of successions. It is essentially a system of hereditary rule. Today in our time a country like Japar has this form of government in which the Emperor is still considered as chosen by God. But it is mitigated by the democratic structures of politics in the country. Other countries like Denmark, Spain and even England have a monarchy but the kings and queens of today enjoy only nominal or formal power. But monarchy still persists as an anachronism.

The most vicious and a contemporary expression of oligarchy is *dictatorship*. It is usually an individual who enjoys a kind of transcendent authority. It is an unrelieved personal authority exercised very often to the detriment of people's aspirations and ambitions. Such a government imposes on the people an irresponsible personal power which is decisively supported and sustained with the active collusion of a ruling class or clique. Originally, dictatorship was not a permanent form of government but only a temporary suspension of the regular government to deal with any emergency situation. But such exceptions have become the regular feature of some countries. This kind of government leads to totalitarianism which means that the individual backed by the caucus, controls and manipulates the whole economic, and cultural life of the society. The result of such a government is that a proper distance and distinction between state and community is blurred and reduced to one reality. The community cannot have a life of its own. Therefore it is rightly stated,

> Dictatorship alone makes its sheer will the sole justification of the authority. At all stages of society men have been concerned with the source of authority, finding it in the community or in the will of God or in sanctified tradition-Dictatorship sweeps aside all such concern. Its own being is the only answer it permits.
>
> Dictatorship ignores the community. The order it sets up is not harnessed to the communal frame of order. It arrogates to itself complete independence from that frame. Its own law is always that of the hour. There is no law, or basis of law, beneath it. The will of the dictator is untrammeled by legal processes. No law has any higher status than his mere decree.[1]

This lengthy quotation brings out clearly and sufficiently the problems and difficulties associated with such a form of government. Such a leader is *ad hoc* and erratic in his behaviour towards the citizens. People are taken for granted and they are not systematically and rationally taken into account in the administration of the state. There is a real disregard for law but it can gain quasi-constitutional character. In the past we know about Oliver Cromwell, Robespierre and Napolean and in this century we are well informed about Mussolini, Stalin and Hitler who were dictators

---

[1] R. M. MacIver, *The Web of Government*, Revised Edition (New York Macmillan Publishing Co., Inc., 1965) p. 168 See also Harry F. Ward, *Democracy and Social Change* (New York: Modern Age Books, 1940) ch. IV-VII and Sheldon S. Wolin, *Politics and Vision* (Boston: Little, Brown and Co., 1960).

par excellence. In our own time this form of Government has assumed alarming dimensions in many countries of Asia, Africa and Latin America. Till recently we had military dictatorships in the Philippines, South Korea, Pakistan and such other countries. Movements for the restoration of democracy have become significant in this context. We are aware of Fascist Italy and Nazi Germany with their black-uniformed elite guards, secret police system (SS), brown-shirt storm troopers (SA) and secret state police (Gastapo). Goebbels and Himmlers are the products of such a system of government. It is a system that essentially remains external to the social framework. The ruling elite maintains a feudalistic character and the subordination of the individual to the state takes place. Dictators demand unconditional obedience and unswerving discipline. In this circumstance, the lives of the people become generally characterised by suspicion, fear and submission. People find it difficult to grow to their full potential as human beings. They are treated more as subjects of the state rather than subjects determining their own destiny. They are treated as mere citizens with duties to perform rather than human beings with fundamental rights to enjoy. Such is the fate under such a form of leadership.

For our purpose, we can now summarise the basic characteristics of dictatorship under six points:

1. Elevation of the Executive above the Legislature
2. Consequent assimilation of the decree to the law
3. Insistence on political orthodoxy
4. Suppression of opinion unfavourable to the regime
5. General exaltation of the state
6. Creates a graded hierarchy of power

(B) Democratic Forms of Government

In simple terms, democracy literally means a government *of* the people, *by* the people and *for* the people. The definition makes clear the source and origin of power, the means and methods of this power and the purpose and objective of such a power. Essentially it is the rule of the people or the power of the people. Therefore, in such a State, it is people that enjoy sovereign power. Fundamentally, it is *lokniti* and not *rajniti*.

It was in the seventeenth century that Jean-Jacques Rousseau had pointed out that "force does not create right" and that "the strongest is not strong enough to be always masters unless he transforms strength into right"—The Social Contract theories of Thomas Hobbes and Rousseau attempted to deal with this problem of power and authority in the 17th and 18th centuries but in the process Hobbes created a *Leviathan* which is frightening. John Locke's *Treatise on Government* was published in 1690. It was he who expounded the idea of a representative government. This is the meaning of democracy as a people's rule. Even in the city-states of Greece and Rome, they did not or could not have direct democracy, meaning that all the people would rule. Rather what is common in history is indirect rule of the people through their representatives.

The most significant element of administration which was discovered explicitly is the principle of "checks and balances" which would not permit any particular interest group or individual asserting its or his complete dominance. For this purpose three essential organs of the government namely, the executive the legislature and the judiciary functions separately. They are distinct but not disjunctive. In addition to these three, the press and the opposition act as sentinels of democracy. The press must be able to voice and form public opinion which would have an impact on the government. The opposition must be there not simply to seize power but provide a responsible critique of the Government's policies and programmes. "Eternal Vigilance is the price of liberty" is the affirmation.

It must be admitted that the pyramid of power is not completely eliminated under democracy but there is the possibility of more mobility and flexibility within and between the grades. There are differentiation (of groups), diffusion (of interests) and delegation (of responsibilities) within a framework of democracy. Power is made responsible to the people and there is a high degree of accountability. There is a realisation of the organic wholeness of all people as citizens constituting the state. In this sense the government is an agency of the people set up by them and responsible to them. Consequently, democracy by its very nature is a government by the *consent* of the governed. For this purpose, Universal Adult Franchise is introduced where the people exercise power through the ballots and not bullets. Abraham Lincoln had said, "no man is good enough to govern another person without that other's consent". At this juncture we need to affirm the fundamental values enshrined and embodies in democratic forms of government. Let us look at them briefly.

Firstly, primary presupposition of democracy is *equality*. All are equal in the sense that they are entitled to equal opportunities and possibilities. Everyone is capable of fulfilling his/her potentials given the requisite environment and education. No *one* person can be regarded as inferior or superior in an inherent sense. Class, caste, colour and creed create discrimination and segregation among people. These are human constructs or artifacts which we must be ready to question, challenge and change for the good of all people.. The good life cannot or should not be a monopoly of any one group. Democracy must ensure equal distribution. Such an affirmation of equality acknowledges the dignity and worth of every person.

Second undergirding of democracy is *freedom*. This means that people are free from constant encroachments or interferences in their social and personal life. The state cannot usurp the whole life of the individual. But freedom also means free for fuller human life attaining fulness and enrichment. This would include *justice* in terms of social, political and economic life. Democracy must ensure this kind of freedom. It has been rightly stated,

> Man requires freedom in his social organisation because he is 'essentially' free, which is to say, that he has the capacity for indeterminate transcendence over the processes of and limitations of nature. This freedom enables him to make history and to elaborate communal organisation in countless variety and in endless breadth and extent.

The recent pro-democracy movement of the students in China indicates this point very well.

The third presupposition and principle of democracy is the recognition of the *double character of the human*— innate goodness and also an inherent desire to be selfish and self-centred or sinful. This paradox is very well expressed by Reinhold Niebuhr, "Mans capacity for justice makes democracy possible but man's inclination to injustice makes democracy necessary."[2] Therefore for this reason, we cannot be unduly optimistic or idealistic or unduly pessimistic and realistic with regard to human life and action. Democracy is an implicit acknowledgement of this dual nature of people. We must recognise our infinite possibilities but also our dire limitations as finite and fallen creatures prone to pride and arrogance. it is a confession that "power corrupts absolutely." In a

---

[2]   Reinhold Niebuhr, *The Children of Light and Children of Darkness* (New York: Charles Scribmers Sons, 1944), p. xiii see the discussion on *"The Transfiguration of politics"* in Paul Lehman *The Transformation of politics* (New York: SCM P. Ltd. 1975). Ch. 11, pp. 238-290.

true democracy, therefore, it is possible to avoid the dangers of arbitrary and absolute power which can be checked and corrected. This brings us to the fourth significant value.

If we are to safeguard democracy and uphold justice in that context, we need to be *responsible*. Accountability is the hallmark of this form of government. The Governed have the responsibility to constantly control the absolute propensities of the ruler. In this context, we must realise that voting and election cannot be the be-all and end-all of democracy. It is important for the electorate to be enlightened and educated thoroughly about the programmes and policies of the government, bringing them under constant critical scrutiny. Therefore, extensive pre-election preparations are very necessary to make democracy viable and valid. Post-election watching and guarding the elected is also significant in this context. Consequently this means that in the final analysis, much depends on human responses to make democracy workable and effective. It does not happen by fiat or fate but by conscious and concerted endeavours of the people to ensure justice. In this sense democracy can never be fully and perfectly established. It must go through a process of maturation and development. It is a process and not a finished product—it is the process of participation of the people in the decision-making, which can make democracy successful. In the light of this discussion, we can briefly look at the democratic government as it functions in India.

(a) Democracy in India

India is considered as the largest democracy in the world in terms of its population rather than the quality and character of its government. Some of the best aspirations and hopes are enshrined in the Indian Constitutions. We have enacted a parliamentary democracy after the Westminster model. But the dreams and hopes of our founding fathers and mothers are in shambles, considering the plight of the people who are in deplorable condition. The vast majority of the Indians, nearly 60% of the population, are below the poverty line, hovering between life and death or between survival and extinction.

That is the Indian reality which we have to confront and change. The question before many people is whether our form of government is conducive to bringing about justice for those teeming millions who are perpetually marginalised and submerged in a "culture of silence". Last forty-six years have demonstrated that the big monopoly houses have increased their profit-making and thereby enhance their assets while for the poor, this freedom means that they are free to starve or die. The recent

Economic policy of the Government of India indicates the problem of Democracy and freedom. It has given freedom to outsiders to interfere directly in the policies and programmes of the Government. In such a context, many people ask whether India is fit for democracy or whether democracy is suitable for a poverty-stricken country like India with her manifold language groups. Her very seize makes the working of democracy difficult. With its 60% illiterate people it is easy to buy votes. Therefore we do not have "one man one vote" but in fact one man ten votes. The elections are regularly rigged and the electorate manipulated. The very expenditure at each election is forbidding in a poor country like India. India provides the best example of the scope and limitations of democracy—both its possibilities and dangers.

The above questions which have been raised are legitimate. But we must remember that precisely within the framework of freedom one can assert one's human rights—wage a relentless battle against oppression and exploitation. Therefore it is indeed a false choice or a misplaced debate between food and freedom. One cannot be sacrificed or divorced from the other. the two are intrinsically related. One needs food to make life possible while one needs freedom to make our material life meaningful and happy. So we cannot talk about food or freedom rather *food with freedom*. Democracy becomes formal and irrelevant if it does not bring about fuller human life in terms of our social, political and economic justice. It must be said to the credit of our poor people that in our recent history they have shown that they are not prepared to have food at the cost of freedom and equality—to the detriment of human dignity and respect. This was well demonstrated during the Emergency period in India (1975-77). Jaya Prakash Narayan captured this mood very well in his *Prison Diary*. his commitment to democracy was crystalised here.[3] It is important to remember that political scientists like Rajni Kothari and Romesh Thapar have emphasised democracy. Thapar has thus opposed dynastic democracy in India and called for authentic diversification and devolution of power to the *Panchayat*. They rebelled against such State oppression. Such is the story in South Korea, Philippines and Poland where their affluence is at the cost of highest human values. They consider that as the diminution of their dignity as human. **Glasnost**

[3] Jaya Prakash Narayan, *Prison Diary* (Pune: Abhay Prakashan, 1977. See particularly pp 11-13,43, 88-89, 107-108, 112-115, and 122-124. There was a similar struggle for democracy in China which resulted in Tiananmen Massacre in 1989.

(openness) and **perestroika** (restructuring) of Mikhail Gorbachev have made the Soviet democratic in character.

Finally, we can affirm that in spite of the dangers of democracy in India, it is the people of India that can make it work effectively and thereby making it a positive instrument of justice. Such is our hope and vision. For this purpose, democracy would imply some limitations on the rich and the 'haves' for the benefit of the poor and the 'have-nots;. We cannot absolutise freedom. It has to be conceived relatively. This means freedom is for the limitation of freedom for the sake of justice. I would say with W. Churchill, "Democracy is the worst form Government, only there is none that is better." It is to awaken the *loka-shakti*.

II. State and Religion

In the history of the world, the relationship between the State and Religion (religions) has been conceived in four distinct ways. Firstly, there have been countries and even now there are nations where religion is above the State, where the government gives patronage to one particular dominant religion. There is a profession of a State religion as it frequently happens in Roman Catholic and Muslim countries of the world. Very often the power of the State is subsumed under the power of the religious head. The two are either confused or identified. Such a relationship sometimes assume *theocratic* form which we have already discussed.

Secondly, this relationship in some countries makes the state all powerful and religion is relegated to an inferior status. The government is either indifferent to religion or tries to control and manipulate religion to its advantage. In such a situation the religious demands and aspirations are stifled and freedom is very much undermined.

Thirdly, there are countries in the world like UK where a particular religious denomination is in alliance with the State. Even till today, the Archbishop of Canterbury sits in the House of Lords. Today of course he has a nominal status like the monarchy in England. Because of its democratic structure neither the queen nor the Archbishop is able to exert much influence on the State but the fact is that such institutions exist.

Fourthly and finally, there are many countries in the world where they maintain a critical distance between State and Religion. This means basically four things. Firstly, such a State is not definitively and decisively a religious or a theocratic State. Secondly, the State does not have a religion of its own but this should not mean that it is anti-religious or atheistic. It maintains a certain amount of neutrality. Thirdly, no special favours or partiality is shown by the State towards any particular religion however strong and powerful a religious group may be. And finally, this entails that in such a context, an individual or a religious group is free to profess, practice and propagate his or her own religion. There is complete religious freedom and any religious group can grow into a viable and effective voluntary agency in such a State. This is called a *Secular State*. The founding fathers and mothers of India wanted this country to be a secular state and inscribed it in the Constitution. We need to champion the cause of secularism and make it an article of our faith. What are the fundamental values of a secular state?

Obviously, the stalwarts of India's independence had a great vision and a broader perspective. They realised that India with its numerous religious communities could not opt for the other three types of relationship between State and religion. The first two alternatives are rather exclusive and aggressive, bringing about division and fragmentation of the population on the basis of religions. India with its long history and heritage of *tolerance* and *co-existence* could not conceive of State and religion in opposition or the state controlling religious activities, giving priority and precedence to the dominant religious group. India is a pluralistic state, meaning that there is a tremendous diversity of religious beliefs. This diversity should not divide or lead to fanaticism or fundamentalism. I have discussed about this in chapter five. It should enrich and enhance the possibilities of all communities in India. India has a composite culture and it should be sustained and upheld.

In a secular state there is an open and a happy recognition of all religions on an equal basis. The minorities are respected and honoured. Full freedom is given for their development and growth. It is also an acknowledgement of the fact that various religions can enrich and enliven each other for the sake of the common good. In such an atmosphere each religion is able to flourish and fulfill its destiny and direction. We need to know briefly why such a separation of the state and religion is important for the people, particularly in India.[4]

Firstly, the state has authority and power and demands allegiance and obedience but the religious groups have a higher loyalty to some cosmic

[4]   See John C. Bennet, *Christians and the State* (New York: Charles Scribner's Sons, 1958); James Hastings Nichols, *Democracy and the Churches* (Philadelphia; The Westminster Press, 1951); Harvey Cox, *The Secular City* (New York: The Macmillan Col, 1965); John Macquarrie, *God and Secularity* (Philadelphia: The Westminster Press, 1967).

power or principle which is called God or the Kingdom of God. From this point of view, the two cannot be identified or religion cannot be superseded because of their different sense of loyalty. *Secondly*, the state is primarily concerned with the national welfare and community while religious concerns and goals transcend national boundaries and barriers. All religions aspire to embrace the whole world and conceive of a world community and not merely a national community. Its desires and hopes are global in character. *Thirdly*, for the state the maintenance of justice and security is the highest priority but for religions, they also ardently believe in these priorities but are conditioned and tempered by love and compassion. We know very well that justice in the court of law may not be appropriate or even approximate to higher justice. For this we need love as the criterion. This is the imperative. *Fourthly*, we know that the State exercises coercive power while religions must examine and evaluate the various forms of coercion. They may not agree and consent to the kind of coercion practised by the state. Religion must have the power and freedom to disagree with *all* that the State does. We must not permit patriotism to turn into a form of idolatry of the State. This brings me to the *final point* about the secular State. It is important for religion to maintain a distance and distinction from the State. It must play a *prophetic role* in the life of the nation and for the sake of the good of all. In the process it is possible for religion(s) to oppose the state and provide critical, creative correctives for the sake of higher justice. It must have the freedom to challenge and seek to change the *status quo* wherever possible and necessary. This freedom and separation from the State are not for the purpose of exclusive, arrogant and selfish claims of religion. It is to promote and enhance human life in its authenticity and wholeness.

III. Threats to Secularism in India

I have already mentioned that the Indian Constitution, in its very Preamble affirms the secular character of the nation. Yet we know of the recent encroachments and erosion of this character both from the State itself and from some religious bodies and political parties in India. In the last five years RSS-BJP has posed a real threat to our secular Constitution and character. They have called it *minoritism* and want it to be deleted from the Indian Constitution itself. In the past the "Freedom of Religion" Bill mentioned in chapter five was a Private Bill. The country and the people were exposed to some peculiar arguments and contradictions. Such a Bill was really an affront to the conscience and minds of the people.

Religious equality and religious freedom were guaranteed by our Indian Constitution and the stalwarts of our freedom movement. Precisely this principle and high ethical ideal were being negated by this Bill. It sought to nullify the safeguards enshrined in the document. The Bill was really an attempt to take away this religious freedom in the name of Freedom of Religion which was therefore a misnomer. Numerous religious minorities in this country were threatened and it offered a point of rallying. It was an occasion for new resolutions and commitments. There was a greater sense of unity and purpose among the religious minorities. Though the sense of unity prevailed but the Bill died a natural death. But it is important to note that in a secular country like India, Om Prakash Tyagi in particular, sought to politicise religion unnecessarily leading to an alienation of communities. Such an attack on religion very often leads to extremism. It is a deliberate attempt to undermine Article 25 of the Indian Constitution. It may be recalled that it is also enshrined in the Charter of the United Nations, Article No. 18 for which India herself is a signatory. In such a situation it is difficult to deal with the virus of communalism so rampant in our society. Secular state should be able to check obscurantism, superstition and communal fanaticism. On the contrary, a Bill of this nature only strengthens and reinforces such diabolical forces. We must remember that in a country like India with its religious diversity and pluralism, no *one* religion ought to be selfish, exclusive, aggressive and closed. No *one* particular religion can or should monopolise power and possibilities. Respect for all religions demand mutual understanding and enrichment. Aggressive attitude on the part of the majority will strengthen or reinforce minority complex or "mission-compound mentality." This brings us to the moot issue of the Bill-Conversion.

We know very well that Christianity has been a missionary religion from its very inception. (Matt.28:19; Mk.16:15; Luke.24:47). This missionary enterprise brought its benefits in terms of medicine and education in particular. Schools and Colleges, hospitals and clinics have been established in the name of the Founder of that religion. In last one hundred years, Hinduism has become a missionary religion having established its institutions all over the world. It has acquired a world-wide status and stature. Basic to the idea of conversion is that the votaries of a particular religion believe that they have something or somebody to share with others—something to tell which they consider to be good, true and beautiful. This is part of the freedom guaranteed in the Indian Constitution. It says that each religion has the right to preach, propagate and practise its own faith. No one should interfere with this right. Of course very often conversion had meant becoming denationalised and even de-historicised in a particular sense.[5] We must realise that in the name of freedom we must not practise force or fraud which has been the case in some cases. This freedom must be enjoyed by all religious groups and institutions. No form of fundamentalism can be tolerated from which ever quarters it may originate. If this type of communalism grows it would be difficult to maintain the unity and integrity of this great inter-religious nation. Clashes occurred in Kanya Kumari and Kerala. Such incidents highlight the significance and value of the secular. We must not permit either Christian or Islamic or RSS fundamentalism to vitiate and poison the atmosphere of this nation. On the contrary, it is imperative that various religious groups are enabled to live and work together—to co-operate and collaborate with each other for the socio-economic transformation which is the need of the hour. That should become the common cause and our common task. We strongly believe that a secular state is most congenial for such an activity. M.J. Akbar in his book, **Kashmir: Behind the Vale** has asserted that the Secular framework is the only hope for India. We may end this section in the words of Haroid Laski,

> A state church (or religion) is bound to receive privileges in some shape or form; and no citizen enjoys genuine freedom of religious conviction until the state is indifferent to every form of religious outlook from Atheism to Zoroastrianism.

With our long tradition of tolerance and co-existence, this should be considered possible, desirable and necessary.

---

[5]   See Mahatma Gandhi, *Young India*, 10-20th August, 1925, 29th September, 1927; *Harijan*, 30th May, 1936. He had said, "If the Christians would live their lives according to the teaching of Jesus Christ, there would be no Hindus left in India."

IX

Violence and Non-Violence: Re-Appraising Gandhi's Understanding of the Sermon on the Mount

In this chapter an attempt will be made to evaluate the idea and use of violence and non-violence from the Gandhian perspective. Issues like adivasis, women, the dalits, and communities of other people have become explosive, caught between violence and non-violence to bring about liberation and justice. Even euthanasia is considered as a form of violence. Violent crime in India has increased from 8.2% in 1953 to 14.6% in 1990 according to the Prime Minister himself. 1992-93 bomb blasts and discovery of explosives in Bombay and Calcutta indicate the violence of our time. The murder of Rajiv Gandhi in India and President Ranasingha Premadasa in Sri Lanka raise afresh the nature and practise of violence. Serbian aggression against Muslims in Bosnia continues.

The film on Gandhi by Richard Attenborough had evoked attention and renewed interest in the life and work of Mahatma Gandhi. He is considered by millions as the Father of the Indian nation, a social reformer and a pioneer of the use of non-violence in the political-public sphere. His influence is far-reaching and his impact world-wide. Therefore it is not surprising that Martin Luther King Jr. is referred to as the Gandhi of the United States, Danilo Dolci as the Gandhi of Sicily and Adolfo Pere Esquivel as the Gandhi of Argentine. This obviously means that Mahatma Gandhi has become normative for many nations and people.

Gandhi himself has acknowledged his immense indebtedness to many people and books. He was informed, influenced and inspired by personalities like Leo Tolstoy, David Thoreau and John Ruskin and by the Gita, Koran and the Bible. He began to read the Bible from 1886 while he was in London for his legal education. He did not enjoy reading the Old Testament but the New Testament had a different effect on him. In his study of the Bible it was the Sermon on the Mount that had an enormous impact. He explicitly acknowledged its influence on his life and thought.

In this chapter I propose to show his interest in and interpretation of the Sermon on the Mount. Secondly, I would like to demonstrate this interpretation in terms of his understanding of violence and non-violence. Finally, I would like to evaluate his understanding of the Sermon and show its relevance and significance.

Gandhi's Appreciation of the Sermon

From the Beatitudes he would have been attracted to Matt. 5:5 and 9 which says, "How blest are those of a gentle spirit; they shall have the earth for their possession." And "How blest are peace-makers; Gods hall call them his sons." These verses have been conducive to his formulation of the idea of non-violence. Matt. 5:38-48 influenced him very much because these verses speak against retaliation and malice and affirm categorically love and forgiveness as the way of life. From this perspective, he conceived of the two masters mentioned in Matt. 6:24 as violence and non-violence. The other verse which he quoted very often in his writings is Matt. 7:21 which states, "Not everyone who calls me "Lord, Lord" will enter the kingdom of Heaven but only those who do the will of my heavenly Father." The idea contained in Matt. 7:16-20 was used by Gandhi, in his articulation of the concept of non-violence. Finally, the verse that helped him to put the Sermon in a wider perspective was Matt. 5:17 which explicitly asserts, "Do not suppose that I have come to abolish the law and the prophets; I did not come to abolish, but to complete." From this verse he derived the principle of continuity and extension of truth through at all time. On this basis he refused to negate the variety of religious traditions and experiences. The various verses quoted above from the Sermon appear frequently in his writings, in *Harijan* and *Young India* which has made a great impact on his life and philosophy. Of course he would have read such similar verses in Hinduism, Buddhism, Jainism and in other religions. These together had a cumulative effect in his enunciation of the concept of non-violence.

Such verses made him affirm non-violence and negate violence explicitly.

Gandhi's Concern to Interpret

It must be mentioned to the credit of Gandhi that he had his own interpretation of the verses mentioned above. He did not conceive of them literally. He applied his own historical-critical method to understand and appreciate them. *Interpretation* was an important principle for Gandhi. He refused to accept any verse as it is. Therefore he said,

> The message of Jesus, as I understand it, is contained in his Sermon on the Mount unadulterated and taken as a whole; and, even in connection with the Sermon on the Mount, my humble interpretation of the message is in many respects different from the orthodox.[1]

In another context he reaffirms his insistence on interpretation.

> "If then, I had to face only the Sermon on the Mount and my own interpretation of it, I should not hesitate to say, 'Oh yes, I am a Christian...'"[2]

Although his interpretation was different from the orthodox he was able to say,

> Then I can say that Jesus occupies in my heart the place of one of the greatest teachers who have made a considerable influence on my life. Leave the Christians alone for the present. I shall say to the Hindus that your lives will be incomplete unless you reverently study the teachings of Jesus.[3]

He himself tried to unify the teachings of Gita, the Light of Asia and the Sermon on the Mount. Through his readings of the various sacred

---

[1]   Young India, 8-12-1927, quoted in M.K. Gandhi, *What Jesus Means To Me* compiled by R.K. Prabhu (Ahmedabad: Navjivan Publishing House, 1959), p. 11.

[2]   M.K. Gandhi, *The Message of Jesus Christ* ed. Anand T. Hingorani (Bombay: Bharatiya Vidya Bhavan, 1963), p. 44.

[3]   M.K. Gandhi, *ibid.*, p. 42.

texts he came to the conclusion that renunciation was the highest form of religion.[4] In spite of this attempt to unify various teachings, it was the New Testament in general and the Sermon on the Mount in particular attracted him most. He said,

> It was the New Testament which really awakened me to the rightness and value of passive resistance. When I read in the Sermon on the Mount, such passages as 'Resist not him that is evil'...I was simply overjoyed...[5]

He not only advised his Hindu friends to read the Sermon but also the Indian Christian to read it likewise. He had felt that much of Christianity which is practised is a negation of the Sermon on the Mount particularly in terms of crusades, wars and the violence of his time. For him the law of love is enshrined in the Sermon which he called the *Law of Abandon* which brings out very well the voluntary and vulnerable character of love. In *Young India*, he wrote,

> It is that Sermon that endeared Jesus to me and even if it is proved that Jesus never lived still the Sermon on the Mount would be true for me.[6]

By now it is apparently clear that Gandhi gave priority to the precept of Jesus rather than his person. It was Jesus' ethical thought that was paramount for Gandhi. Therefore the Law of Abandon which he derived from the Sermon on the Mount was foundational to his conception of non-violence. Then it is not surprising that on his visit to Rome he was able to say,

> I saw there at once that nations, like individuals, could only be made through the agony of the Cross and in no other way. Joy comes not out of the affliction of pain on others, but out of pain voluntarily borne by oneself.[7]

[4] M.K. Gandhi, *An Autobiography: The Story of My Experiments with Truth*, trans. Mahadev Desai (Boston: Beacon Press, 1957), p. 69.
[5] M.K. Gandhi, *Speeches and Writings of M.K. Gandhi* (Ahmedabad: Navjivan Publishing House, 1959), p. 130.
[6] M.K. Gandhi, *The Message of Jesus Christ*, p. 66.
[7] M.K. Gandhi, *Ibid*. p. 68

Here we realise that although Gandhi could not significantly move from the precept to the person of Christ, yet he seriously took the idea of atonement embodied in the Cross. So it is rightly stated by S.K. George,

> Christianity has got to recapture this fundamental element in its teaching. A religion which has the Cross for its centre and its symbol ought never to forget that it was pang-born and that the values it stands for can only be conserved and enshrined in the heart of a world it seeks to save by the willing endurance of pain. It is this great lesson that is being emphasised anew by that true servant of God: Mahatma Gandhi.[8]

Even the great American evangelist, E. Stanley Jones was compelled to admit,

> Never in human history has so much light been shed on the Cross as has been through this one man and that man not even called a Christian. Had not our Christianity been vitiated by our identification with un-Christian attitudes and policies in public and private life, we would have seen at once the kinship between Gandhi's method and the Cross. A non-Christian saw it instinctively.[9]

It was the Sermon on the Mount that inspired Gandhi in this direction and appealed to Christians to become worthy of the message that is embedded in it. He told a group of YMCA people in Colombo, Sri Lanka, that they should drink deep of the fountains that are given in the Sermon on the Mount and serve God, the Compassionate, Tolerance incarnate. Now we need to understand the hermeneutics that were involved in his interpretation of the Sermon on the Mount.

Hermeneutics of Gandhi

I have already mentioned that Gandhi was prepared to give his own interpretation because he did not accept the sacred scriptures as the pure

---

[8] S.K. George, *Gandhi's Challenge to Christianity* with Foreword by S. Radhakrishnan and Horace Alexander (Ahmedabad: Navjivan Publishing House, 1947), p. 29.

[9] E. Stanley Jones, *Mahatma Gandhi: An Interpretation* (Lucknow: Lucknow Publishing House, 1948), p. 137.

word of God, unconditioned by history and people. He wrote in 1927,

> And I, therefore, admit, in all humility, that even the Vedas,
> the Koran and the Bible are imperfect word of God and,
> imperfect beings that we are, swayed to and from by a
> multitude of passions, it is impossible for us even to understand
> this word of God in its fulness.[10]

Later he wrote in *Harijan* corroborating his earlier statement,

> I exercise my judgement about every scripture including the
> Gita. I cannot let a scriptural text supersede my reason. Whilst
> I believe that the principal books are inspired, they suffer from
> process of *double distillation*. Firstly, they come through a
> human prophet, and then through the commentaries of inter-
> preters. Nothing in them comes from God directly.[11]

From the above quotation it is clear that Gandhi believed in the
inspiration of the Scriptures but not in their inerrancy or infallibility. He
exercised his own reason and judgement to comprehend the various
Scriptures, including the Bible. And so he could not accept everything
in the Gospels as historical truth. On the contrary, Gandhi accepted the
conditionality of the sacred Scriptures. Once he was asked, "Are you sure
that no great result has come through your own study of Jesus?" To that
question he replied,

> Why? There is no doubt that it has come, but not, let me tell
> you, through theology or through the ordinary interpretation of
> theologists. For many of them contend that the Sermon on the
> Mount does not apply to mundane things, and that it was only
> meant for the twelve disciples. Well, I do not believe this. I
> think the Sermon on the Mount has no meaning, if it is not of
> vital use in everyday life to everyone.[12]

He seems to be vaguely aware of some of the interpretations that were
prevalent during his time. It may be interesting to note that writing about

[10] M.K. Gandhi, *What Jesus Means to Me,* p. 31 (Young India, 22-9-1927).
[11] Harijan, 5-12-1936 quoted in *Ibid.,* p. 32. See also ch.III, p. 30 of the book.
[12] M.K. Gandhi, *Christian Missions: Their Place in India* (Ahmedabad: Navjivan
      Publishing House, 1941), p. 278.

"Women in the Smritis" Gandhi had categorically mentioned that lot of so-called scriptures are bad and interpolated and said,

> There should, therefore, be some authoritative body that would revise all that passes under the name of scriptures, expurgate all the texts that have no moral value...[13]

From this we realise that Gandhi was willing to subject all sacred scripture to critical scrutiny and make morality and ethics the basic principle of interpretation. It was this perspective that guided his thinking and doing all his life. This criterion he makes explicit when he states,

> If you interpret your texts in the way you seem to do, you straightaway condemn a large part of humanity unless it believes as you do. If Jesus came to earth again he would disown many things that are being done in the name of Christianity. Is it not he who says, Lord, Lord, that is a Christian? And cannot he who has not heard the name of Christ Jesus do the will of the Lord?[14]

He did not view the Sermon on the Mount so much Christologically but ethically. From this perspective, he was able to cull out some clear principles for his conception of non-violence. To that we turn our attention now.

Principles of Non-Violence from the Sermon

Mahatma Gandhi advocated certain fundamental principles on which he based his concept of non-violence. These principles pertain to the human, to society and to the world in general. He derived these principles from various religious sources. The Sermon on the Mount was not an exclusive source or resource for these principles. For our purpose I will elaborate on some of these principles.

Firstly, according to Gandhi, non-violence has a definite theological dimension in the sense that a non-violent crusader must have a living faith in God. In the *Harijan* of 1939 he announced the various qualifications

---

[13] M.K. Gandhi, *Women and Social Injustice* (Ahmedabad: Navjivan Publishing House, 1956), p. 15.

[14] M.K. Gandhi, *Christian Missions*, p. 159.

of a satyagrahi. He had said that a *satyagrahi* does not depend for his strength on external means. His strength comes from within, from his reliance on God. He went on to assert,

> A *satyagrahi* imbued with such faith will inspire the whole people by his example and may induce a heart change even in the oppressor, who freed from fear will the more readily appreciate his simple faith and respect it.[15]

Obviously such a demand puts a severe limitation on non-violence. Gandhi himself recognised, "In the long run non-violence cannot work in those who do not have a living faith in the God of love."[16] To him the hero of non-violence must be like a piece of clay in the hands of the divine potter. This belief in God is basic to Bible in general and the Sermon on the Mount in particular. The Bible is certainly one of the sources for such an imagery or metaphor.

Secondly, Gandhi based his non-violence on the principle of the goodness of every person. Through non-violence we need to appeal to this innate goodness. In Hinduism a person is considered to be a part of divinity. In Christianity, every person is considered to be made in the image of God, *Imago dei*. As children of God every person possesses potentialities and possibilities which need to be recognised. Gandhi once said, "Man as animal is violent but as spirit is non-violent. The moment he awakens to the spirit within, he cannot remain violent. Either he progresses towards *ahimsa* or rushes to his doom."[17] Gandhi recognised the sinful character of the human but emphasised his goodness. This is the pre-supposition of many of the verses in the Sermon. Increasingly, this aspect is being accentuated by Christian theologians like John Macquarrie. He affirms,

> But I do not think of sin as having utterly destroyed the *imago dei* or as having totally extinguished the drive towards authentic humanity. There is in man original righteousness as well

15   M.K. Gandhi, *Satyagraha: Non-Violent Resistance* (Ahmedabad: Navjivan Publishing House, 1957), p. 295.

16   Paul Regamey, "*The Mystique of Non-violence*", in Thought, Autumn, 1966, p. 381.

17   Thomas Merton, *Gandhi on Non-Violence*, (New York: New Direction Paper, P.K., 1966), p. 28.

as original sin, a tendency to fulfillment which is often impaired but never quite abolished; for if it were, the very consciousness of sin would be impossible.[18]

Although we affirm the goodness of every person we must take seriously what Paul Regamey says,

> This power is nothing but a dream, a wish, finally a trap if truth is not all-powerful active love, bestower of grace and strength. Of course some 'unbelievers' may have enough confidence in the fundamental goodness of men to hope that it can overcome by itself egotistical interests, wickedness, hatred and violence. And so certain 'unbelievers' of good-will who believe in man can enlist in the ways of non-violence themselves.[19]

In addition to the above, we must take seriously the warning given by Reinhold Niebuhr when he asserts,

> The order of human existence is too imperiled by chaos, the goodness of man too corrupted by sin and the possibilities of man too obscured by natural handicaps to make human possibilities solid bases of the moral imperative.[20]

I think Gandhi himself realised this problem in the midst of the struggle for independence but he refused to negate this principle. We must realize that the application of non-violence very often prompts moral complacency rather than contrition. Non-resistance may shame an aggressor into goodness but it may also prompt him to further aggression.

---

[18] John Macquarrie, *Three Issues in Ethics* (New York: Harper and Row, Publishers, 1970), p. 91. See also his book, *The Concept of Peace*, p. 18. See also his *Jesus Christ in Modern Thought* (London: SCM Press, 1992), Ch. 4, pp. 31 and 371.

[19] Paul Regamey, *Non-Violence and the Christian Conscience* (London: George Allen & Unwin Pub., 1966), p. 55. Read on Gandhi in Hannah Arendt, *On Violence* (New York: Harcourt, Brace & World, Inc., 1969), p. 53. It may be mentioned that David J. Koniger considers *Satyagraha* as the "global form of life". See his book, *The New Universalism: Foundations for a Global Theology* (New York: Mary Knoll, Orbis Books, 1992), Ch. 4, pp. 150-162.

[20] Reinhold Niebuhr, *An Interpretation of Christian Ethics* (New York: Charles Scribner's Sons, 1956), p. 54.

Such is the bane of human life!

Thirdly, Gandhi based his conception of non-violence on the principle of the redemptive power of love. The Sermon on the Mount inspired him in this direction. It was this belief which prompted Gandhi to say, "Even Nero becomes a lamb when he faces love."[21] He had strongly maintained that every *satyagrahi* must overcome evil by good, anger by love, untruth by truth, and *himsa* by *ahimsa*. He staunchly believed that every fallen person could be saved by love. Obviously Gandhi had an implicit faith that the aggressor will melt at the sight of suffering. Here again we need to recognise the entrenched and intransigent character of sin and evil in the world. We must recognise the impersonal historical forces which disrupt all human efforts towards goodness and justice. As such it is rightly stated,

> The weakness of the spirit of love in solving larger and more complex problems becomes increasingly apparent as one proceeds from ordinary relations between individuals to the life of the social group.[22]

The reality of our time does not reflect always the triumph of redemptive love in the economic, political and social spheres. The fundamental issue is to demonstrate the power of redemptive love through non-violent resistance. Gandhi showed it in some measure in his struggles but it cannot be absolutised. One writer maintains,

> A saintly abnegation of interest may encourage the ruthless aggrandisement of the strong and the unscrupulous. These facts are so plain that every effort to introduce suffering, love as a simple alternative to the complexities and ambiguities of social justice, must degenerate into sentimentality.[23]

Fourthly, Gandhi's conception of non-violence is based on the principle of parity between ends and means, the tree and the fruit

---

[21]   Quoted in Harvey Seifert, *Conquest by Suffering* (Philadelphia: Westminster Press, 1956), p. 270.

[22]   Reinhold Niebuhr, *Moral Man and Immoral Society* (New York: Charles Scribner's Sons, 1953), p. 74.

[23]   Reinhold Niebuhr, *Faith and History* (New York: Charles Scribner's Press, 1949), p. 184.

enunciated in the Sermon (Matt. 7:16-20). Gandhi had an unflinching faith in the dictum, "The means must justify the end." For him the means and ends are two ways of conceiving the same actuality. They could be distinguished only temporally. Both means and ends partake of a continuous process. Gandhi had said, "The means precede the end in time but there can be no question of moral priority.[24] According to him, they are convertible terms as means is the end in the process and the ideal in the making. The end must inevitably come out of the means. He insisted on the purity of means to achieve a noble end. Only this renders such actions authentic and authoritative. But we must realise that in the midst of the human predicament in terms of economic, political and social injustice, we cannot deliberate on the means when the end is immediate and urgent. Therefore Saul Alinsky said, "He who sacrifices the mass good for his personal conscience has a perverted conception of what is meant by personal salvation." The urgency of the end and the cause to be achieved are the criteria for the use of means. But it must be conceded that it is very difficult to establish this objectively and critically. In the midst of the human dilemma it is not always possible to incarnate the end in the means. When we decide to be rigid and legalistic about our use of means we may delay justice and defer righteousness.

From this brief study of the basic principles of Gandhi we realise that he took seriously the various injunctions contained in the Sermon on the Mount. He was fully conscious of the demands and the commands of Jesus with regard to violence and non-violence. But it seems that he did not recognise with sufficient seriousness the theological affirmations contained in the Bible as a whole. He seemed to have over-estimated the human, idolised human society and exaggerated the verities of life. He does not seem to understand the irrational character of the human which thwarts him in seeking the approximation of justice. It is not surprising that Gandhi said, "I do not think Hitler and Mussolini are after all so very indifferent to the appeal of world opinion."[25] Deliberate massacre of six million Jews in Germany fifty years ago negates Gandhi's wishful thinking.

Later he had added rightly that the Germans as a nation are not any worse than any other people because all people are tarnished with the

---

[24] Quoted in Joan Bondurant, *Conquest of Violence: The Gandhian Philosophy of Conflict* (Berkeley: University of California, 1958), p. 173.

[25] M.K. Gandhi, *Non-Violence in Peace and War*, (Ahmedabad: Navjivan Publishing House, 1944), p. 200.

same brush. Obviously, he was not prepared to make distinctions even during the time of crisis. The two world wars in one generation and the Holocaust in Germany have proved that the logic of history has less power than the illogicality of the human. Therefore Albert Camus has rightly said, "So rebellion arises from the spectacle of the irrational coupled with an unjust and incomprehensible condition." Failure to recognise this demonic element in human nature made Gandhi utter, "Even if Hitler was so minded, he could not devastate 700,000 non-violent villages. He would himself become non-violent in the process."[26] I chose to illustrate the above point with the example of Hitler to indicate the depth of depravity in the human. Therefore while **agapaic** love is not irrelevant, its relevance is conditioned by the sinful and demonic elements that are present in history. Thus it is wisely stated by Reinhold Niebuhr,

> The doctrine of original sin must be taken seriously. Through it one may understand that no matter how wide the perspectives which the human mind may reach, how broad the loyalties which the human imagination may conceive, how universal the community which human statecraft may organise, or how pure the aspirations of the saintliest idealists may be, there is no level of human, moral or social achievement in which there is not some corruption of inordinate self-love.[27]

It is true that Gandhi recognised the diabolical forces rampant in his society and waged a relentless battle against them. But it must be realised that non-violence resistance does not always bring about the necessary changes. Now the question is whether Gandhi himself recognised and acknowledged the limitations of pacifism. In the light of his readings of the Holy Scriptures particularly the Bible, I believe Gandhi was a practical pacifist and not a rigid absolutist.

Truth-Seeking as Gandhi's Mission

The word 'non-violence' has entered the English language as the translation of the Sanskrit word, *ahimsa*. Etymologically, *himsa* is the desiderative form of *hani* meaning to kill or to damage. So *himsa* means

[26] Quoted in Harvey Seifert, *Conquest by Suffering*, p. 150.
[27] Reinhold Niebuhr, *The Children of Light and the Children of Darkness* (New York: Charles Scribner's Sons, 1944), p. 17.

to wish to kill. *Ahimsa* means renunciation of the will to kill or damage. It is a kind of persuasion which may be by reason or by persuading others through one's suffering. It is interesting to note that Gandhi did not designate his movement as a non-violent or *ahimsa* movement but *satyagraha*. In this section I would like to indicate that Gandhi was not an absolute pacifist but a man who was open and flexible because he was basically a worshipper of truth.

To Gandhi non-violence was not an isolated phenomenon or an insulated principle. To him it was part of a larger scheme of life and therefore he called it *satyagraha*. So *ahimsa* was placed in the context of *satyagraha*. This word was first coined by him in 1906 during his residence in South Africa. Somebody had suggested *sadagraha* and Gandhi modified it to *satyagraha*. It is a compound of two Sanskrit nouns: *Satya* (truth) from *sat* (being) and *agraha* (firm grasping). *Satyagraha* has been translated differently by different scholars. To Corman it is "steadfastness for truth" or Mme C. Drevet thinks it to be "the attachment of truth and the strength of the soul which inspires truth". According to Gandhi himself it is, "the indefectible grasp of truth". In short Gandhi would characterise *satyagraha* as 'truth-force' or 'soul-force.' Fundamentally, Gandhi was in search of truth both in his public and private life. He entitled his biography as *The Story of My Experiments with Truth*. A person dedicated to the quest of truth cannot be dogmatic. He opens himself to the winds of truth from wherever it blows. His fidelity to the ancient vedic prayer becomes perspicuous. But it also becomes clear that he goes beyond the Sermon on the Mount to understand the message of the Bible. He seems to be giving his tacit approval to the Biblical verse which says, "Your shall know the truth, and the truth will set you free" (Jn. 8:32). He was seeking the guidance of the spirit of truth mentioned John 16:13. Consequently, it is not surprising that Gandhi came to the conclusion that *Truth is God* and God is Truth. To him these terms are reversible. He was essentially a seeker of truth which has multifarious expressions in terms of freedom, justice and equality. The most persistent note in Gandhi is the recurring theme that non-violence is truth-seeking. This cannot be an expression of absolutes and substance but of relatives and process. As such Bondurant says that by enthroning Truth on the highest pedestal, Gandhi thus truly became catholic, and lost all traces of separateness from every other honest person who worshipped gods other than his own.

He could not absolutise non-violence because of his allegiance to truth. When questioned about his many inconsistencies about non-violence, Gandhi retorted,

> At the time of writing I never think of what I have said before.
> My aim is not to be consistent with my previous statements on
> a given question but to be *consistent with the truth* as it may
> present itself to me at a given moment. The result is that I have
> grown from truth to truth.[28]

When the Congress Party passed a militant resolution in 1939, he
commented that he could not serve the cause of non-violence if he
deserted his best co-workers just because they could not follow him. He
remained with them hoping that their departure from non-violence would
be confined to the narrowest field and would be temporary. As a practical
idealist he could not work on the basis of an *a priori* principle. He
approximates to the Niebuhrian perspective when he says,

> Life is governed by a multitude of forces. It would be smooth
> sailing if one could determine the course of one's action by a
> general principle whose application at a given moment was too
> obvious to need even a moment's reflection. [29]

He was prepared to deliberate and discuss before arriving at an
'ought'. He was prepared to exercise his rationality with freedom and
responsibility to arrive at a normative decision and action. Basically this
constitutes ethics and morality. Decision-making cannot be reflexive, it
has to be a *reflective* process and this is what Gandhi affirmed. Consequently, he had no hesitation in saying if there was a national government,
he could conceive of occasions when it would be his duty to vote for the
military training of those who wish to take it. He felt that if a person fights
with his sword single-handed against a horde of dacoits armed to the teeth,
he would say that the man is fighting almost non-violently. He said that
he who cannot protect himself or the honour of his nearest and dearest by
non-violently facing death, may and ought to do so by violently dealing
with the oppressor. He who cannot do either of the two is a burden
according to Gandhi. As a worshipper of truth he did not advocate the idea
of peace at all costs or at any price. He did not want the peace found in

[28]   S. Radhakrishnan, *Mahatma Gandhi* (London: Oxford University Press,
       1939), p. 380.
[29]   M.K. Gandhi, *Non-Violence in Peace and War*, p. 85.

the stone or the grave. The question is how did he comprehend truth at the socio-economic-political level.

Concern for Human Needs

Concern for human needs was determinative of truth for Gandhi. He was acutely sensitive to human needs in terms of their anguish and aspirations. He was very much with the people and for the people. They constituted his understanding of truth. With Karl Marx he believed that the dialectic of concept must have a social orientation, must relate to human action. Gandhi realised that absolutism in both religious and political realms is a splendid incentive to heroic action, but a dangerous guide in immediate and concrete situation. So he constantly altered his positions according to the needs of the people. Niebuhr realised the dilemma of Gandhi and said,

> He may, as Mr. Gandhi, make every effort to keep his instrument under the dominion of his spiritual ideal, but he must use it, and it may be necessary at times to sacrifice a degree of moral purity for political effectiveness.[30]

His policy of non-violence emerged through his active and dynamic encounter with people both in South Africa and India. So J.B. Kripalani maintained that Gandhi, working in accordance with the genius of his *people*, their circumstances and needs, discovered his own method of achieving social justice. He was not divorced from the context in which he had to act. He knew the difficulties of the people. Consequently, he confessed that in life it is impossible to eschew violence completely. He knew that the objective standard by which truth can be judged is a human standard expressed in terms of human needs. If Gandhi is properly understood we realise that he puts *people* at the centre of his concern— at the core of his teaching, particularly people who are oppressed and marginalised economically, politically and socially. In his Autobiography he expressed surprise at the passivity of the people in South Africa in the face of racism and discrimination,

> As I proceed further with my enquiry into the atrocities that have been committed on the people, I came across tales of

---

[30] Reinhold Niebuhr, *Moral Man and Immoral Society,* p. 244.

government's tyranny and the arbitrary despotism of its
officers such as I was hardly prepared for, and they filled me
with deep pain. What surprised me then, and still continues to
fill me with surprise, was the fact that the province that had
furnished the largest number of soldiers to the British government during the war, should have taken all these brutal
excesses lying down.[31]

His concern was human needs and his goal was freedom. Therefore,
Gandhi said, "I know *swaraj* is the object of the nation and not non-
violence."[32]

From this perspective, non-violence was relative to Gandhi, and not
an absolute principle and we must realise as Paul Lehmann clarifies, "An
absolute is a standard of conduct which can be and must be applied to all
people in all situations in exactly the same way."[33] This would be an
abstraction from the complexity of the actual situation and people. In the
midst of the existential reality it is not possible to fix upon a single moral
absolute. Gandhi had gone to the extent of stating that if India had to
achieve her freedom by violence, let it be the disciplined violence named
war.

It may be interesting to note Gandhi's own involvement in violence
directly or indirectly. He co-operated with the British during the Boer
war. He took part in the Zulu revolt by organizing an ambulance corps.
He did a similar thing in the First World War.[34] In the midst of the freedom
struggle, "The practical statesman took precedence over the uncompro-
mising prophet," wrote Nehru. He sponsored the 'Quit India' resolution
at Bombay in 1942. Earlier, the "Wardha Resolution" of the Congress
party gave active or tacit support to such resolutions because as he
maintained, "I would rather see India freed by violence than enchained
like a slave to her foreign oppressor."[35] He felt that India should risk
violence a thousand times rather than the emasculation of the race. He

[31] M.K. Gandhi, *An Autobiography*, p. 185.
[32] Romain Rolland, *Mahatma Gandhi* (New York: George Allen & Unwin, Ltd.,
      1924), p. 62.
[33] Paul Lehmann, *Ethics in a Christian Context* (New York: Harper and Row
      Publishers, 1963), p. 125.
[34] C.F. Andrews, *Mahatama Gandhi* (New York: The Macmillan Company
      1930), p. 141-142.
[35] Rolland, *Gandhi*, p. 63.

made such statements in 1920. As a religious man he had an innate aversion to violence, yet as a political and social activist, he realised that it may be needed sometime to liberate India. He could not resolve this existential contradiction till the end of his life. Therefore it is not surprising that not long before his assassination he recorded in his diary,

> Have been awake since 2 a.m. God's grace alone is sustaining me. I can see there is some great deficit in me somewhere which is the cause of all this. All around me is utter darkness. When will God take me out of this darkness into his light.[36]

Now, briefly we need to summarise Gandhi's understanding of the Sermon on the Mount in the light of the above discussion about violence and non-violence.

Gandhi's Non-Absolutist Interpretation

From the discussion so far, we can affirm that Gandhi gave his own interpretation of the Sermon on the Mount. The fundamental hermeneutical principle involved in his interpretation was truth. Truth was perceived in terms of what is conducive to the *well-being of the people* particularly the historical context became the definitive locus of his life and work. But it was not self-determinative. For this, he allowed the text of the Bible particularly the Sermon on the Mount, to enter into a dynamic encounter with the context. Therefore his moral decisions were not pre-determined or pre-conceived. Here he seemed to be pursuing the "hermeneutical circle"—moving from the text to the context and back to the text. From this perspective, he perceived the principles enshrined in the sermon not as directives but as giving a direction. He did adopt the philosophy of non-violence to bring about justice and peace, but he was open and flexible. This is not a negation of the Sermon but a critical and creative appropriation of it in the living situation.

Gandhi did not accept the Sermon in isolation. He viewed it from the whole Biblical witness. He did not take a text out of the context and absolutise it. He understood the Bible in general and the Sermon in particular in their integral wholeness. Secondly, he realised the boundedness of the Bible written in a different time and place. On that basis, the various prohibitions and permissions cannot have an eternal

---

[36] B.R. Nanda, *Mahatama Gandhi* (Boston: The Beacon Press, 1958), p. 469.

character. The various injunctions of the Sermon can at best be indicative and not imperative for Gandhi. He incorporated the precepts of Jesus as guidelines with freedom and responsibility. He realised that Jesus was not a law-giver and the Sermon was not a second Sinai. To understand the various verses of the Sermon as definitive mandates would be to oversimplify them *and* the complexity of the world in which we live.

From the Sermon itself we get the idea of passivity and non-resistance. It does not talk of resistance, either non-violent or violent. It gives the idea of silent resignation to the will of the oppressor. That is not part of Gandhi's constitution. The Sermon does not directly address itself to social and political problems. It seems to be talking about individual enemies and consequently it talks about "turning the cheek", "giving the coat", and "going the second mile." It is true Gandhi himself applied this principle in his public life and was successful to a great extent, but we realise that it cannot be the panacea for all ills, afflicting human society.

The Sermon is a summon to perfection and absolute purity but it cannot be the ethic of fallen human beings in a broken world. God is the central theme of the Sermon. Therefore it is rightly said, "And to offer the esoteric Christian ethic for public use when national passion is rising is to stroke a crocodile or tickle a tiger."[37] So some scholars maintain that the Sermon is not so much a method of how one must act when struck but rather illustrations or signs of the proleptic presence of the Kingdom. It may be samples of Christian behaviour or good behaviour but cannot be a complete ethical system. We know that the Kingdom has broken in Jesus Christ with power, but sin and evil are real and rampant.[38] We have to judge the Sermon in the context of the apocalyptic expectation of the time which Gandhi of course does not suggest.

Gandhi did not make a law of the Sermon. He was not legalistic in his attitude like the Pharisees whom Jesus reprimands. Indeed it would be an idolatory if we were to absolutise the words of Sermon which were written in the past, making it a barrier which would keep God from speaking to us today or tomorrow. Gandhi was a seeker of truth. We must

---

[37] P.T. Forsyth, *The Christian Ethic of War* (London: Longmans, Green and Co., 1916), p. 22. See my booklet *Justice and Peace* will join Hands: Ten Bible Study Outlines (Bangalore: S.C.M., 1986).

[38] Stanley Hauerwas advocates "the peaceable Kingdom" or non-violent Kingdom. That has to be our basic position in this Violent world. See his *The Peaceable Kingdom: A Primer in Christian Ethics* (London: University of Notre Dame Press, 1985), pp. 73-80.

realise that if we give a slavish interpretation of the Sermon we will insult both the sovereign God and the free human being. We are truly free under God when we take upon ourselves all the weight of being free creatures. We cannot tie ourselves too rigidly to abstract principles which will make us prisoners of the past. We cannot impose on our situation rigid structures of abstraction that do not suit them. Principles are tools which have to be used carefully and critically. The general is given in the particular and the verification of the abstract is in the concrete. All principles of the Sermon are contingent, except love. We are not to reject the Sermon but relativise it in terms of human need. That is the spirit of the Bible. In this sense the Sermon is both transcendental and existential. Gandhi realised this double dimension of the Sermon and in his life and work. He was successful in minimising violence against the British but he could not do anything when this pent-up resentment was let loose in the communal riots immediately following Independence. The question still remains how we express *agapaic* love to bring about radical economic, political and social changes?

Gandhi himself was inspired and influenced by this kind of love and he formulated his non-violence on the basis of it. This is creative and redemptive love. To create one may have to destroy. It is love with the objective of creating a better world. We have to realise the limitations of this kind of love in this sinful world and act accordingly. Evil cannot always be overcome. In this realm of our existence evil is persistent, arrogant and strong, while our duty is immediate and urgent. It would be very simple to believe that under all circumstances, in every situation, this kind of love demands peaceful resistance. That would make our task easy. The limitation of love was demonstrated in relation to Nazis and Fascists in the past and now in South Africa and other places where terrorist or extremist violence is rampant. How do we respond to the violence intrinsic to a system like or the Apartheid? So the requirement of love is not easily known in our complex reality. Niebuhr rightly said that Jesus's attitude toward vindictiveness and his injunction to forgive the enemy reveals more clearly than any other element in his ethic, intransigence against forms of self-assertion which have social and moral approval in any natural morality. According to him the ethic of Jesus is in obvious conflict with both the impulses and necessities of ordinary people in typical social situations. So we have to make this love commandment, enshrined in the Sermon, relevant to the relativities of the social struggle, even to hazardous and dubious relativities. Therefore, it is rightly stated,

> Forgiving love has a place in one realm; but in the other realm nothing is known of it. In this realm of Caesar nothing is known but chains, the sword and the law.[39]

Without exaggerating the distinction and promoting dichotomy between the realms, we must concede the limitation of this kind of love. The World's number one women's tennis player, Monica Seles was knifed in 1993 while playing. Thus we cannot condone reckless violence which serves no purpose and is self-defeating.

Conclusion

In this Chapter, I have attempted to demonstrate that Gandhi's hermeneutical principle rendered him a practical idealist. So his pacifism was not absolute. He was immensely inspired by the teachings of the Sermon, but he was open and flexible. This is not to take away from the greatness of the man who dared to preach and practise non-violence against the mighty British empire. The time was ripe and the situation was favourable which rendered his grand experiment successful. In the annals of human history such a success is rare. Stanley Jones paid the greatest homage when he wrote,

> I bow to Mahatma Gandhi, but I kneel at the feet of Christ and give him my full and final allegiance. And yet a little man, who fought a system in the framework of which I stand, has taught me more of the spirit of Christ than perhaps any other man in East and West.[40]

Therefore I have no desire to ignore or undermine the careful analysis and evolution of Gandhian Satyagraha by the former Harvard University Professor, Gene Sharp.[41] But obviously the writer has not viewed the subject sufficiently from a *theological-ethical perspective*. That will make us aware of the complexity of the problem and the human predicament.

---

[39]   Reinhold Niebuhr, *Faith and History*, p. 185.
[40]   E. Stanley Jones, *Mahatma Gandhi*, pp. 11f.
[41]   See Gene Sarp, *The Politics of Non-Violent Action: Power and Struggle Part one: The Methods of Non-violent Action* Part Two; and *The Dynamics of Non-Violent Action* Part Three, (Boston: Centre for International Affairs, 1972).

X

Nuclear Threat to Earth's Future: Anticipating God's Future

In the last chapter I have looked at the issue of violence and non-violence as they affect the problems of our time. In this chapter I will examine the related issue of nuclear threat as it affects international relations.

> Now everything was a nightmare of rubble, yellowish smoke, cinders and ashes. ·The earth itself seemed convulsed in flames. Buses and cars, overturned grotesquely twisted, looked like burned beetles. The wide roads had become narrow trails snaking through huge piles of ruptured concrete and tortured steel. Telephone poles leaned at crazy angles, their wires tangled like spiderwebs on the ground. Thousands of bricks covered the earth in little piles, as if they had never been walls. Torn-up trolly tracks jutted and twisted into the air like snakes...One million, five hundred and twenty thousand people were killed by the weapon fired by Major Butts. Over four million died in the subsequent blasts. The last bombs to fall no longer killed any one. They simply ground the rubble into finer powder.[1]

Such is the scenario drawn up by writers as the aftermath of a nuclear blast. Humanity today is sitting on the top of a volcano. Any time the volcano can erupt, explode and annihilate the whole human race. We are

---

[1] Ronald J. Sider and Richard K. Taylor, *Nuclear Holocaust and Christian Hope: A book for Christian Peacemakers* (New York: Paulist Press) pp. 21.

on the brink of a precipice. Any time we could go down into the fathomless depth and be lost to posterity. The world has turned into a tinder box. Never before in the history of humankind has such a threat of a nuclear holocaust loomed so large as in this century. It is incumbent on our part to analyse the present predicament and realise the ethical imperative. With the discovery of atomic power, humans have opened up a pandora's box with its dangerous and destructive possibilities. It is true that this power has been harnessed for the good of humanity, but its lethal quality is more evident today than ever before. Proliferation of armaments and the consequent escalations of the psychosis of war have assumed epidemic proportions. The nations of the world, particularly the nuclear armament industry have become irrational about it. The survival of the human race is at stake because of the arms race, particularly because of the quantitative and qualitative leap in nuclear armaments. But the greatest tragedy of our time is that people do not seem to reckon seriously the magnitude of the problem and the gravity of the situation specifically in terms of the future we want to affirm for global justice and universal peace. In this unipolar world, the nuclear threat seems to be less but its not true.

In this chapter, I propose to clarify the issue of nuclear warfare as against conventional warfare. To understand the problem I would like to delineate the content, consequences and context of nuclear warfare, identify some of the basic problems involved, understand it in terms of traditional *Just War* criteria, and finally affirm nuclear pacifism from a theological-ethical perspective.

The Nature and Extent of the Nuclear Threat

Today the world military expenditure has reached more than the astronomical figure of $1000 billion (i.e. in dollars, how much in rupees??). This is obviously more than $2.50billion per day which is spent on armaments or about $170 per inhabitant because the global population is more than 5 billion. There are more than 3.5 tons of high explosives for each individual living on this planet and it will take less than twenty minutes to cause the amount of damage done in all the wars fought since the beginning of civilisation. Till recently just between the former USSR and the USA there was a total explosive capacity equivalent to about one million Hiroshima-type bombs. There are more than 50,000 nuclear stockpiles or war-heads in the world with a total explosive yield of twenty billion tons of TNT, 95 per cent of these belong to the U.S.A. and Russia.

In 1992, U.S.A. alone spent about $300 billion on defence, mostly on nuclear weapons.

In 1985, USA spent $322 billion mainly to produce and deploy nuclear armaments. In 1983 the expenditure on armaments was $28 million per hour in the US. Ronald Reagan gave the pentagon $1.5 trillion for rearmament programme over five years, to develop 100 inter-continental MX missiles, the new bombers and the 'stealth' bombers.

The U.S.A. and Russia are engaged in developing accuracy and reliability of strategic nuclear warheads and mobile IBMS. Just one supersonic strategic bomber costs about $87.8 million. They are developing the new technology of multiple independently targeted re-entry vehicles (MIRV). It may be mentioned here that the Soviet SS-10 missile has the capacity of 5000 kiloton (1 kt is equivalent to 1000 tons of dynamite, TNT). The US Titan-11 missile has the capacity of 10,000 kt. compared to this. The power of the warhead that destroyed Hiroshima in 1945 was only 13 kt. The total destructive power possessed by the nations of the world is 11,089,00 kt. This means that humans have developed the dubious distinction of being able to destroy the world many times over. The temperature at the centre of a non-megaton bomb is 150 million degrees Fahrenheit which is more than eight times the heat at the centre of the sun. There are differences in the development of missiles which are enormously expensive: firing submarines, land based missiles, bombs and air-launched and cruise missiles. This is indicative of the fact that the nuclear arsenal has become increasingly differentiated and diversified.

The more recent innovation in this area is the development of Strategic Defense Initiative (SDI) or the Space-based Missile Defence System (SBD) popularly known as 'star wars'. Indeed we have reached a new threshold with the 'successful' experimentation with the Anti-Satellite Weapons System (ASAT). This programme itself will cost $26,000 million and is called, "a futuristic system that would provide the most hopeful possibility of our time." What could be a greater travesty of truth and more perverse instance of human ingenuity!! What does it mean to talk about the 'future' and 'hope' in this context of the militarisation of outer-space? The statistics quoted above are constantly changing for the worse and the Democles' sword is hanging over modern human civilization. India spends a disproportionate amount on defence and particularly for nuclear weapons.

One-third of the energy of a nuclear blast is given off in light and heat from a chemical explosion and is about 3000° C. But of a nuclear blast the heat is 10 million degree centigrade. The following chart indicates the cause, effect and energy of a nuclear explosion.[2]

Cause	Effect	Energy
Heat	incineration, fires, skin burns	33%
Blast	bodies smashed, buildings collapsed	50%
Direct Radiation	Radiation deaths	7%
Radio-active Fall-out	Cancer	10%

This is sufficient to demonstrate the nature and extent of the nuclear threat in our time. Now I will indicate briefly the consequences of nuclear warfare.

Consequences of Nuclear Warfare

I have already indicated something of this in the previous section. Now I will outline some more of the consequences. Firstly, medical care would not be possible after such a war. Roads would be blocked with the debris and the hospitals would be destroyed. In Hiroshima 270 out of 290 doctors were killed and its eighteen hospitals were badly damaged. In a nuclear confrontation, the cities are the direct targets and it is in cities that medicines and medical supplies are concentrated. Those with terrible burns would not be able to receive immediate medical care. There would be broken water mains which would affect the water supply. The sewerage system would break down, resulting in cholera and typhoid.

Secondly, the impact of radiation would be enormous. Twenty per cent of people will die due to exposure to radiation. Ulcers will begin to appear on the skin, hair would start falling, and there will be an internal bleeding, thus breaking down the immune system. Radiation enters the body like X-rays and affects the cell walls and tissues. Indirect radiation or residual radiation continues to affect people for years. The tiniest particles of radio-active dust would be carried to the stratosphere and thus all over the globe, even remote places, depending on wind and rain. It must be remembered that radio-activity is invisible, tasteless and odourless and consequently one would never know what one is breathing and eating.

---

[2]   Sider and Taylor, *Nuclear Holocaust*. p. 46.

Somatic and genetic problems are inevitable in such a situation. It could cause cancer and abortions due to the effect of radiation on chromosomes. It would cause mutations, resulting in deformed babies and increased genetic diseases and this effect could continue for over thirty generations.

Thirdly, basic human needs like food, fuel, clothing, housing and energy would be in short supply. Food production would be affected. Various industries would be destroyed and it would be almost impossible for governments to function with values like freedom, legal rights and democratic political institutions.

Fourthly, the environment would be affected adversely. It would have disastrous and perhaps irreparable impact on the ecosystem on which all life depends. It would seriously disrupt the ozone layer of the atmosphere which protects humanity from the ultra-violet rays. 30 per cent to 70 per cent of the ozone layer would be destroyed. This would either raise or lower the temperature, considerably affecting agriculture, animal population and crops.

Related to this, is the possibility of a 'nuclear winter' resulting from mushrooming clouds of smoke and dust. This could block the sun, causing freezing temperature and mass deaths. In 1984 Carl Sagan, the noted astrophysicist, propagated the theory of 'nuclear winter.' According to him, even a limited nuclear war, consuming just 0.8 per cent of the global arsenal, would mean ecological disaster, not just for the combating countries but for the whole world. There would be a drop in temperature ranging from 10 to 20 degrees Centigrade. S.V.C. Aiyar, an eminent scientist in the field of atmospheric research, recently stated that Indian scientists owe it to posterity to investigate the possible effects of the 'nuclear winter' in the tropical zone where nearly two-thirds of the people of the world live and where there is pervasive poverty. What would be the effect of a nuclear summer?"

The cumulative consequence of all this is that "the planet earth would eventually become inhabited by bands of roving humanoid-mutants barely recognizable as members of our species." Gordon Zahn has graphically portrayed the aftermath of a nuclear war,

> A charred and radio-active planet, peopled with some mon-
> strously-deformed remnant of mankind, has come to represent
> the brightest hope the scientist can offer as the aftermath of
> such a war.[3]

---

[3] Gordon Zahn, *War, Conscience and Dissent* (New York: Hawthorn Books,
(Continued on next page)

Context of Nuclear Preparedness

In view of the pressing global crisis of the poverty of the two-thirds of the world, nuclear armaments are immediately seem to be irrational, even insane. Deprivation and consequent deaths are rampant in the world. An enormous amount of money is being deliberately diverted by nations of the world from economic development to war-mongering. Authentic peace has to be conceived in terms of people's development and liberation. Such wide-spread nuclearisation cannot be conducive to the fulfillment of the basic needs of the teeming millions of Asia, Africa and Latin America who are perpetually submerged in dire poverty. India's defence budget is more than Rs 189 billion which is 4 per cent of the Indian GNP.

$ 1000 billion military spending is more than the entire income of 1500 million people living in poorest countries of the world, according to the Palme Commission. While the NATO powers are busy deploying missile systems, the Trident submarine, cruise missiles and Pershingg IIs in Europe and England, the UNICEF reported that in 1982, 17 million children died of starvation and malnutrition. In statistical terms this means that one child dies every two seconds, or 40,000 children, According to their reckoning, they could have saved one of them with $100, or $ 17 billion for 40,000 children, which is the cost of one Trident Submarine. While thirty children die every minute, $ 1.3 million is spent on armaments per minute in the world. It is calculated that the cost of one jet bomber could pay for one lakh tons of sugar or the money saved on one atomic air-craft carrier could buy 28 lakh tons of wheat. At a meeting of the FAO it was clearly stated,

> The expenditure incurred on a new ICBM could plant 200 million trees, irrigate one million hectares of land, feed 50 million malnourished children, buy one million small biogas plants, build 65,000 health-care centres or pay 340,000 primary school teachers.

In spite of these glaring facts and deep deprivations, the rich and powerful nations are not prepared to change the existing international economic order which is fundamentally based on exploitation, perpetuating a situation in which large sums are diverted for building nuclear armaments. Therefore it is not surprising that the world military budget is more than twenty times the size of development assistance. No country of the North is able to give even 1 per cent of their GNP for development aid. They refuse to perceive the problem of development as a structural or a systemic issue. The result is that the poor nations of the South have not been able to change the policies of such international organisations as the World Bank, IMF, UNCTAD or GATT. Several western countries have decided to boycott current efforts to implement the UN Charter of economic rights which was adopted ten years ago. There are 105 million who are starving in Latin America and half of a million people who died of starvation in 1984 in Africa. Such is the context in which nuclear arms build-up and deployment go on. It was rightly stated, therefore, that "arming today means denying development tomorrow." The USA says that "we will arm today and disarm tomorrow but today's arms can deny millions of their tomorrow." So we have to advocate nuclear disarmament for the sake of development and not just for survival. We are concerned with global justice and universal peace, with health and wholeness of all the people and not for some. Now it is necessary to identify some of the problems associated with nuclear warfare as against conventional warfare.

Problems of Nuclear Warfare

Thermo-nuclear wars would change significantly the character of war. The scale of devastation is very different from conventional warfare. Dr. Hiatt from Harvard has studied the effects of a twenty megaton explosion over the city of Boston. He states:

> The explosion excavates a massive crater half a mile in diameter and several hundred feet deep, but the area of total destruction has a radius of four mile. More than twenty miles from the blast people suffer second degree burns on all exposed skin and additional burns from inflammable clothing and environmental materials. As far as forty miles away people who look at the blast get blinded. As far from the hypocentre as twenty-five miles, the growing firestorm is fuelled by igniting houses, foliage and oil gasoline storage tanks.[4]

The second problem of nuclear warfare is that it is more impersonal

Paul Abrecht and Ninan Koshy, ed., *Before It's Too Late: The Challenge of Nuclear Disarmament* (Geneva: WCC, 1983), p. 47-48.

and dehumanising than conventional warfare. In the wars of the past there used to be direct and immediate encounters or confrontations. In a nuclear war there is no direct or face-to-face conflict. One cannot immediately see or know the human casualities. The damage and destruction are done at a great distance. It is more cold and cruel compared to conventional wars. Thirdly, nuclear warfare is highly mechanised. In this context, we realise the bane of modern science and technology which is dehumanising and destructive. It is supposed to render greater efficiency but *de facto* it cannot ensure hunder per cent safety. There is always the possibility of its malfunction particularly with computers on which much of modern warfare depends. Fourthly, in a nuclear warfare it is not possible to distinguish between the victor and the vanquished because this is not a 'winnable' war. We have to recognise its indiscriminate character. It will affect both the combatants as well as the non-combatants. It is not possible to keep it 'limited'. In a massive retaliatory strike such a distinction is absurd. Modern nuclear warfare will pursue relentlessly the logic of the spiral line and mad momentum intrinsic to it. Escalation is inevitable. Once the threshold of atomic weaponry is crossed it is impossible to control it. Therefore all governments, particularly of the U.S.A. must take note of Reinhold Niebuhr who affirmed, "Every appeal to moral standards thus degenerates into moral justification of the self against the enemy."[5]

The final problem with which we need to reckon with is the deterrence theory which maintains the detente or the precarious peace of our time. According to this theory if each side has enough weapons to annihilate the other, no one would dare to start a war. This is commonly termed as 'mutually assured destruction' (MAD)!! This is supposed to maintain the safety and security of the world—a balance of terror. This theory is fraught with multifarious problems. In an international crisis we know that for the sake of nationalism or patriotism, knowing fully well the irrational or the demonic character of human beings, the national leaders can make a fateful mistake. Human fallibility and fallenness are not the only problems. As has been mentioned earlier, the highly sophisticated technology of nuclear warfare is subject to breakdown. The first-strike capability also reduces the potential of deterrence. Paul Ramsey had advocated this deterrence theory. It seems that his deterrence depends on the threat to kill non-combatants, which he himself argued is murder. So

---

[5]   Reinhold Niebuhr, *An Interpretation of Christian Ethics* (New York: Harper and Brothers Publishers, 1935), p. 125.

the fundamental issue connected with nuclear warfare is the nature and extent of peace ensured by deterrence. Can we human beings be satisfied with this kind of uneasy truce? Such a peace is being encouraged by the leaders of nations who are in active collusion with the industrial-military complex. It is clear that the Pentagon's defence contractors like Lockheed, Rockwell International, Boeing and others play a vital political role with regard to this issue in particular. David Stockman, Reagan's budget director, himself had asserted: "The institutional forces in the military are more concerned about protecting their benefits than they are in protecting the interest of the American people." Obviously, he should have gone further to affirm the security and welfare of all people in the world. Now we need to examine nuclear warfare in terms of criteria stipulated in the Just War theory.

Just War Criteria and Nuclear Warfare

In the Christian community the Just War doctrine emerged in response to two questions. The first question had to do with the circumstances within which participation in war could be considered moral and the second question had to do with the extent and nature of force to be employed in such a warfare. Refinement of the criteria formulated in answer to the first question constituted the j*us ad bellum*, the law which seeks to regulate resort to war. Reflection upon the second question led to the articulation of the *jus in bell*o, the law of war which defines legitimate acts in the conduct of war. The following are the seven criteria which relate to the causes for entering into a warfare and the means to be used in such a battle.[6] *Last Resort*: All other means to be morally just solution of a conflict must be exhausted before resort to arms can be regarded as legitimate. (2) *Just Cause*: War can be just only if employed to defend a stable order or morally preferable cause against threats of destruction or the use of injustice. (3) *Right Attitude*: War must be carried out with the right attitudes. Restoration of justice is the intention and not anger or revenge. (4) *Prior Declaration of War*: War must be explicitly declared by a legitimate authority. This means that individual citizens cannot take up arms. The opponent must have an opportunity to abandon unjust

---

[6] Edward L. Long, *War and Conscience in America* (Philadelphia: Westminster Press, 1968), pp. 22-23. See also "Just War Criteria" by James F. Childress in *War or Peace? The search for New Answers* ed. Thomas A. Shanon (New York: Orbis Books, Maryknoll, 1982), pp. 40-58.

activity and prevent war. (5) *Reasonable Hope of Success*: War may be conducted only by military means that promise a reasonable attainment of the moral and political objectives being sought. This means that one must reasonably be certain that the things for which one is fighting will not be destroyed in the process. (6) *Noncombatant Immunity*: The just war theory has also entailed selective immunity for certain parts of the enemy's population, particularly for non-combatants. The non-combatants or the civilian population cannot be the direct target of such a war. It could be unintended side effect called the principle of double effect. This is permissible within limits. (7) *Proportionality*: Finally the principle of proportionality stipulated that there must be a reasonable expectation that the good results of the war will exceed the horrible evils involved. This criterion applies to both the war itself and the particular strategy adopted in the course of war.

I have already referred above to some criteria, like the issue of noncombatant immunity and the principle of proportionality. This latter principle and the fifth criterion would completely rule out nuclear warfare because it nullifies the very basis to life which is fundamental to human activity. This means that ideological difference or conflict cannot be an excuse to wage a nuclear war. From this perspective, total nuclear war is ruled out. The second option is limited nuclear war in which both sides destroy a few enemy cities. But I have already mentioned that it is very difficult, rather impossible, to keep a nuclear war limited. Noncombatant immunity would rule out any idea of directly aiming for population centres. Because of the immorality of the second option, some people have advocated the idea of a limited attack on military targets only. But as has been said, in a nuclear war, it is not possible to distinguish between the combatants and the non-combatants, between victor and the vanquished. Indeed, a nuclear warfare is a great leveller of humanity ! Its effects are widespread and pervasive. It also cannot be limited because of a possible computer failure, unforeseen effects of nuclear blasts, a desperate attempt to avoid defeat or human irrationality in a situation of nearly total panic and chaos. For this reason Paul Ramsey's justification for limited nuclear attack has been criticised by Walzer. He states:

> He multiplies distinctions like a Ptolemaic astronomer with his epicycles and comes very close at the end to what C.E.M. Anscomb has called 'double-think about double-effect' ... To draw insignificant lines, to maintain the formal categories of double-effect, collateral damage, noncombatant immunity.

and so on, when so little moral content remains is to corrupt the argument for justice as a whole and to render it suspect.[7]

It must be affirmed that even criteria like prior declaration of war and right attitudes cannot be relevant to nuclear war. It may be remembered that it just takes twenty-four minutes for an air-borne missile to travel from Washington D.C. to Moscow. The Just War doctrine was formulated long before the advent of the nuclear age and the threat of nuclear carnage.

At this critical and crucial juncture in history it is imperative to denuclearise military preparedness for the sake of human survival and more important for the sake of global justice. The question still persists: how are we to dismantle the apparatus of human destruction and dislodge those who perpetrate war-mongering? The Catholic Bishops in France have given their guarded approval to nuclear deterrence while the American Catholic Bishops have called for nuclear freeze. Some nations of the world have called for multilateral disarmament or mutually verifiable reduction in arms, particularly nuclear armaments. The real challenge is to seek for unilateral nuclear disarmament, thus taking the initiative and the inherent risk necessary for such a bold step for the sake of the future of humanity.

A Theological-Ethical Perspective

There is a certain sense of inertia and resignation in the face of this nuclear threat. It seems impossible to avert the holocaust. Such a feeling leads to debility, defeat and death. Our will is atrophied and we feel helpless because we think nuclear war is inexorable and inevitable. Therefore for many people the future is pre-determined in the context of this nuclear threat. This is the way the law of *karma* is operative in the world today. This is future determined by the present predicament of humanity. The consequences of the nuclear warfare which I noted earlier, are physical and ecological. But the real tragedy is in terms of the mental and the psychological. This nuclear threat has engendered an ethos which is not conducive towards building a new future. There is a lack of will to move forward and change the future. This issue of the nuclear threat is indicative and illustrative of the problem of anticipating the future. Do

[7]   Michael Walzer, *Just and Unjust Wars: A Moral Argument with Historic Illustrations* (New York: Basic Books, 1977) p. 279.

we have a future on the basis of this stark reality? Can we really anticipate God's future from this perspective? The fundamental question is what is the basis or the rationale for our anticipation or expectation. How can the understanding of the future become normative for the evaluation of the present problem? To view this problem from a futuristic perspective is not to indulge in apocalyptic fatalism. Edward Schillebeeckx rightly maintains that we have to be interested in the remote future and not only our immediate future, although that is important and relevant.[8]

The possibility of transformation and newness are intrinsic to the understanding of the Kingdom of God. This is the definitive Biblical witness (Is. 65:17-25; 66:22; II Peter 3:13; II Cro. 5:17; Rev. 21: 1-8). It is significant to note that this vision of the future which is new is not a formal concept without any substantive quality and character. Peace with justice is constitutive of this concept.

In Psalm 20:7 it is said: "Some trust in their war chariots and others in their horses, but we trust in the power of the Lord our God." In a similar vein we hear: "Because you trusted in your chariots and in the large number of your soldiers, war will come to your people and all your fortresses will be destroyed" (Hosea 10:13). Their vision of the future was in terms of the idea of peace which they termed *shalom* (Is. 2:4, Michah 4:3).[9] For the Hebrew people it did not mean just absence of war or cessation of conflict but fullness of life and well-being of all people. Related to this issue of peace is the question of power. This vision of the future ought to make us question and challenge our existing notions about 'power', 'strength' and 'security'. God's work of atonement and resurrection in Jesus the Christ is indicative of this kind of power. John Macquarrie has stated,

> The basic idea of resurrection is that life is stronger than death, that man never finds himself in a dead end but that always new possibilities open up. This is not blind optimism. It is once again a metaphysical conviction closely related to the ideas of grace and atonement.[10]

---

[8]   Edward Schillebeeckx, "Theology and Nuclear Weapons", in Abrecht and Koshy, *Before It's Too Late*, p. 83.

[9]   See Ronald Stone and Dana Wilbanks ed. *The Peace-Making Struggle: Militarism and Resistance* (New York: University Press of America, 1985), Specially on "Shalom and Eirene", pp. 123-133.

[10] John Macquarrie, *The Concept of Peace* (New York: Harper and Row, Publishers, 1973), p. 73.

From this perspective we need to be peace-makers (Matt. 5:9) in the context of the nuclear threat.

In the previous chapter I have criticised the Gandhian concept of satyagraha. This is precisely because our hope for this kind of future is not naive, shallow or cynical. As the Bible summons us to peace with justice, I mentioned that sometimes it may be necessary to commit ourselves to change through violence. But in the context of the nuclear threat, I would affirm nuclear pacifism because it destroys all life, human and whole creation, which we want to support, sustain and promote. These two forms of violence are very different. Commitment to violence is warranted in certain situations but this cannot be the basis for indulging in nuclear warfare. This existential problem has been portrayed by Potter when he states:

> Moral power belongs to those who affirm both the obligation to contend for justice and the ideal not to harm...The two duties seem to draw in opposite directions. There is a constant temptation to relieve the tension by scanting one claim or the other and thus by simplifying the moral situation... Their concern for moral purity can bear the scent of sublimated selfishness, and their righteousness the taint of self-righteousness.[11]

Related to the issue of peace, the Kingdom of God entails the exercise of a different kind of power than what is displayed by nuclear preparedness. According to the Biblical witness, God triumphs through powerlessness. Only a vulnerable God is viable. The cross of Christ stands as a mute testimony to God's character and his purpose for humanity. It has a double dimension. On one hand, it stands for God's solidarity with human agony. While on the other hand, the Cross embodies God's deep desire to overcome human suffering. It is indicative of the fact that suffering is necessary to overcome suffering in its multifarious forms in the world. Such is the paradoxical character of the cross. Suffering is

---

[11] Ralph B. Potter, *War and Moral Discourse* (Virginia: John Knox Press, 1973), p. 53. Read the discussion "The Just War and Nuclear Deterrance" by Paul Ramsey in Arthur F. Holmes ed. *War and Christian Ethics* (Grond Rapids: Bakes Book House, 1975), ch. VII, No. 2, pp. 341-381 and Thomas A. Shannon, *War or Peace? The search for New Answers* (New York: Orbis Books, Meryknoll, 1982) on 'Pacifism' Part II and III.

integrally related to salvation. This idea is well expressed by Koyama when he states:

> The truth about Jesus Christ is that he affirmed his lordship by giving it up. He was so intensely involved with the people that the thought of his own salvation never occurred to him...Christians belive in such a Lord. Their life must point to such a strange lordship.

We have to anticipate the future by participating in the promise of God through struggles, suffering and sacrifice.[12] This is intrinsic to the salvific process. Asian theologians like C.S. Song and Fr. Tissa Balsuriya have accented on this aspect of Christ's work. Earlier Kazoh Kitamori conceived of God's pain-love as his very essence. We can achieve authentic peace not through muscle power or nuclear power but through the power of the Cross. The Book of Revelation affirms: "These are of one mind and give over their power and authority to the beast; they will make war on the Lamb, will conquer them, for he is the Lord of lords and King of Kings" (Rev. 17:13). Such is the vision of the future. In the context of the nuclear threat we have to affirm this kind of power. Nuclear strength does not bring security. On the contrary, there is a greater sense of insecurity in the modern world because it is based on a false perception of power and strength.

This position does not render null and void the position I affirmed in the previous chapter. There is a definitive place for redemptive suffering for Christians. It has a creative and liberating role. In the light of the above affirmation we cannot indulge in violence recklessly and irrationally. We must be able to draw the line between redemptive suffering and suffering that seems to be meaningless. For this reason it is possible to advocate violence in some situations very selectively while in the context of the nuclear threat we have to advocate nuclear pacifism. Such is the paradox of Christian life. We have to exercise our judgement with responsible freedom, knowing fully well that we constantly stand under the grace and judgement of God.

This power of the future makes us sensitive to our own powers and

---

12   *Read Seeking God's Peace in a Nuclear age: A Call to Disciples of Christ* (St. Louis: CBP Press, 1985). Read the theological debate about the nuclear issue in Robin Gill, *Christian Ethics in Secular Worlds* (Edinburgh (T & T Clerk, 1991), Ch. 7, pp. 115-132.

possibilities.　Instead of passively waiting for the doomsday, it is important to realise that there are people in large numbers who have opposed nuclear warfare. Massive protests in London and West Germany bear eloquent testimony to the invincible spirit of those humans who visualise a new future. It is for us to identify and support such signs of the absolute future in the present. It is with courage and hope we need to stem the tide and avert the holocaust, thereby moving meaningfully towards the future of God. So we can anticipate the future not on the basis of the present actuality but on the basis of God's reality. In the final analysis it is an anticipation and of participation in the promise of God. In this context, even after two hundred years, William Carey's theological formulation is very much relevant,

EXPECT GREAT THINGS **FROM** GOD
ATTEMPT GREAT THINGS **FOR** GOD

Then we will realise that nuclear warfare is not a matter of inevitability but that the possibility of change is real. Are we prepared to accept the challenge posed by Ronald Bainton more than thirty years ago?

> Shall the scrupulous then become unscrupulous in order to survive? Are we to renounce honor, shame, mercy, and compassion in order to live? The ancient 'pagans' would not have said so... Shall we allow the 'pagan' (Aristotle) to take over the virtues which we have been wont to all Christians, while we invoke Christ to justify nuclear annihilation?[13]

---

[13]　Ronald H. Bainton, *Christian Attitudes Toward War and Peace: A Historical Survey and Critical Re-evaluation* (New York: Abingdon Presess, 1960), P. 268.

XI

A Critique of Modern Development

In the previous chapters we have looked at the political life which could lead to violence sometime within the country or war between countries. In this chapter, we will see that the issue of violence and war is more political than ideological. They could have economic base in particular with their own ideological orientation.

We live at a time when there is wide-spread deprivation and active marginalisation of the vast majority of the people of the world. Economically they are exploited, socially they are discriminated against and politically they are rendered powerless. Such is the predicament of the two-third people of the world. At a global level, there is the North-South divide which has been very well portrayed by many economies and people like Willy Brandt and Olof Palme.[1] It is a broken world or, as Barbara Ward had designated as, a 'lopsided world'. She wrote in 1968 that some 20% of the world's population controls 80% of the world's wealth. Today, after twenty-five years the situation has not improved. The vast majority of the people of Asia, Africa and Latin America live in absolute poverty which has been defined by Robert MacNamara as,

> a condition of life so degraded by disease, illiteracy, malnutrition and svualor as to deny its victims basic human necessities: a condition of life so limited as to prevent realization of the potential of the genes with which one is born; a condition of

[1] *North-South: A Programme for Survival* (The Report of the independent Commission on International Development Issues under the Chairmanship of Willy Brandt, London: Pan Books Ltd., 1980). See also *Common Crisis. North-South: Co-operation for World Recovery*, (The Brandt Commission Report, London: Pan Books Ltd., 1983).

life so degrading as to insult human dignity; and yet a condition
of life so common as to be the lot of 40% of the people of the
developing countries.[2]

This means that we have to distinguish between absolute poverty and
relative poverty. We cannot confuse the issue and generalise the problem.
One billion people are in absolute poverty and another one billion are
hovering between existence and extinction in the world. At the same time
there are 71 billionaires in the United States alone.

Poverty at the Global Level

The world population at present is approaching Six billion. More than one
billion out of this population are under-nourished, 1.4 billion are without
safe drinking water and 1.4 billion are without adequate medical care.
According to the UNICEF, about 40,000 children die every day all over
the world because of extreme poverty. It is very much a divided world—
divided into first, second, third and even fourth world in terms of per
capita income and GNP. Calorie in-take is about 200 per person per day
in the South as against 3,300 calories per person per day in the North. the
real income in the US is more than fourteen times that of an Indian and
seventeen times that of a Kenyan. The per capita income is about 710
dollars in the South as contrasted with $ 12.51 in the North. In terms of
Income distribution in India it rose from 65 dollars in 1953 to $ 110 in
1973.[*] One-fourth of the world's population enjoy 83% of the world's
income, 80% of the economic growth and consumes 87% of the world's
produced wealth. Among the largest hundred economic units in the
world, only fifty nino are countries and forty-one and MNCs or TNCs.
Exxon and GM are ahead of some countries in terms of net sales or GNP.
By 1972 the gross annual sales of the twelve largest MNCs was 144 billion
dollars which is more than the total annual national income of the world's
35 poorest countries with a population of one billion. There are about
10,000 MNCs in the world. Among the 4534 are in Europe and 2579 in
USA. In 1973 New York city with a population of eight million had an
annual budget almost the size of India which had a population of 600
million people. Pakistan's per capita GNP remains at 380 dollars, while
that of Bangladesh is a mere 160 dollars. That is the condition of the

[2]   R.S. MacNamara, *Address to the Board of Governors* (Kenya, 1973), p. 7.
[*]   In the USA it rose from 2,100 dollars in 1953 to $ 5,015 in 1973

'global village' or the 'spaceship earth'. The 'invinsible hand' of Adam Smith is very visible. It is indeed the hand or handle of the rich. Galbraith has rightly said, "Left to themselves, economic forces do not work out for the best, except for the powerful." an income of less than half of the European Community average of £150 ($232) per week, is considered poor in Europe. The GNP of the US is more than $ 5,238 billion.

Poverty Within India

India, which is a pyramid on its point geographically, is a pyramid on its base economically. It is the tenth most industrialised country in the world but belongs to the fourth in terms of per capita income and GNP. According to *The World Bank Atlas, 1992*, the Indian per capita income is $ 350, a marginal increase of 10 dollars in the last three years. While our country is interested in super-computers, Agni missile, introduction of management techniques, and a quantum jump into the twenty-first century, safe drinking water is not available for most of the villages in India. While Indian astronauts have gone into space and India is a member of the exclusive, elitist nuclear club, about 36% of India's villages remain without a road link and 70% villages do not have all-weather access roads. There are about forty million who are educated but unemployed. The top 10% of agricultural households own 55% of agricultural lands. 10% of rich farmers have all the marketable surplus and corner the bulk of the concessions. 50 to 60 percent of the 890 million Indian population live below the poverty line in terms of income and per person per day calorie intake. For the Seventh Plan (1985-90), the updated poverty line was Rs. 6,400 per annum in rural areas and Rs. 7,300 in urban areas. In this context, it is significant to note that the minimum wages fixed by the State governments and the centre for the unorganised labour vary between Rs. 3,600 and Rs. 4,200 per annum.

This is indicative of the plight of the poor people in this country. In 1985 it was reported that while we have 30 million tonnes of foodgrain in our stocks, 300 million people went hungry every day. Starvation deaths have been reported from Bihar and Orissa while the food production has increased from 55 million tonnes in 1951 to 172 million tonnes in 1991-92.

The monopoly houses or the big businesses are flourishing in this country in collusion with the Centre and in some cases in collusion with some MNCs. 75 business houses led by the Tatas and Birlas control 1,536 companies and 46% of the assets of the private corporate sector excluding banking which amounts to Rs. 5,552 crores. The state sector, including financial institutions like the LIC, the Industrial Finance Corporation have been used to support and strengthen monopoly houses. They have wrecked the interests of the non-monopolies by producing on a large scale and by undercutting prices and thus controlling the market. Once the market is captured, the monopolies back up the prices and so the consumer has to pay more than the cost of production for his needs. Unable to expand production, barred from adapting manufacture to local conditions or encouraging local ancillary industries, they become hopelessly dependent on foreign collaborators who manage to exploit the situation to their advantage. As a result there is a concentration of economic power and wealth and we have the 'top ten percent' economy according to C.T. Kurien.[3] He says, "Poverty, indeed is the carcass left from wealth acquisition."

From this brief survey, it has become abundantly clear that we are not just concerned with poverty but *mass poverty*, or more rightly with the yawning chasm between the rich and the poor at the national and international levels. This is an active process and not a static condition. The rich are becoming richer and the poor are becoming poorer. It is increasingly realised that it is not a scourge of God but the scandal of humanity, not some fate for there seems to be a conspiracy. What is really disturbing and makes us restless is not the existence of poverty but rather the *co-existence* of the very rich and the very poor in the same world and at the same time. Deprivation and impoverishment of the many and the affluence of the few simultaneously cause frustration and anger in the Third and Fourth World Countries. It has been rightly stated, "Hunger used to be the silent enemy of man. Starvation used to be the silent way of death, not any more. Instead of silence, today it can mean a resounding roar of violence." While India is becoming 'market-friendly', the UN Human Development Report 1993, warns against unchecked privatisation and liberalisation.

The Nature of the Problems of Development

The question is what has caused this pervasive poverty and wide-spread deprivation? Such a situation has developed over a long period of time.

[3] C.T. Kurien, *Poverty, Planning and Social Transformation*. (Bangalore: Allied Publishers Private Ltd., 1978) pp. 70-77. Similar critique has been made by Rajni Kothari, *Rethinking Development: In Search of Humane Alternatives* (New York: New Horizons Press, 1989), Ch. 8-11.

Certain historical forces[4] established a pattern of relationship characterised by elitism, hierarchy and submission. Such a pattern has been maintained and strengthened through the present conceptualisation of development. This is best understood in terms of certain images or symbols used by economists. This kind of development could be compared with a *pyramid* which has perpetuated the pattern of relationship developed under colonialism and now under neo-colonialism—a pattern of dominance and dependence. This pyramidal structure is quite evident at the global and national levels. Some scholars compare this type of development to a *ladder* which presupposes the idea of 'catching up'. And this is considered to be a virtue in itself. Those who are on the lower rungs of the ladder are expected to catch up with those who are on the higher rungs of the ladder. In this context, modernisation automatically or mechanically means Westernisation. Dom Helder Camara has captured the mood of such people when he states, "When I give food to the poor they call me a saint, when I ask *why* the poor have no food, they call me a communist."

For some scholars, development is best achieved in the world through a careful process of selection by the rich countries of the world. This process has been called *Triage* or Life boat. Triage comes from the French verb *trier*, meaning to sort. It was considered to be the most efficient way to use the scarce medical resources available during World War I. That principle took care of only those who could survive if given treatment immediately. A Food Triage was first proposed in 1967 in a book entitled *Famine 1975*, written by William and Paul Paddock. In 1968, Paul Ehrlich approvingly referred to the triage principle in his book, *The Population Bomb*. In the same year an article appeared in a Science Journal entitled, "The Tragedy of the Commons" written by the University of California ecologist-biologist, Garrett Hardin. Jay Forrester of MIT, Cambridge, espoused his gospel of moral complexity in 1971 and categorically stated, "The church should begin to examine the limits and consequences of humanitarianism." Dale Runge, a doctoral student of Dr. Forrester, wrote in a similar vein.

Garrett Hardin, went on to refine this idea of selection in terms of a *Life-Boat* which established a case against helping the poor. He claimed: "We're all descendants of thieves, resources are inequitably distributed, but we must begin the journey tomorrow from where we are today."[5] He

---

4   See Julio de Santa Ann ed. *Separation without Hope: The Church and the Poor during the Industrial Revolution and Colonial Expansion* (New York: Maryknoll, Orbis Books, 1978).

was saying all this at a time when the USA was giving 200 million tonnes of grain as food to their animals and was using three million tonnes of fertilisers per year for lawns, gardens and golf courses!! Philip Handler, the President of the US National Academy of Sciences at that time suggested, "Cruel as it may sound, if the developed and affluent nations do not intend the colossal, all-out effort commensurate with this task, then it may be wiser to 'let nature take its course'," This became a controversial issue in the 70s and some scholars in the US itself opposed this vehemently. Richard Neuhaus had to say, "A world that would choose Garrett Hardin's options is a world in which I for one would not care to survive." Daniel Callahan demolished the various assumptions undergirding the idea of triage and Life-boat. He had stated that the developed nations, led by the US, continue to use a disproportionate percentage of the world's resources.[6] This idea is indeed quite arbitrary and biased. The rich nations of the world are to decide on their own terms and with their own criteria who are so hopelessly poor that they are beyond liberation. Such is the attitude, if not the actions, of some of the rich countries of the world. The fact is that the rich nations are not on a life-boat but on a luxury liner and they will not permit others to get into it.[7] Therefore it is not surprising when the USA imposes "Super 301".

For some scholars development is basically linear in nature and could be compared with an even bigger *piece of pie*. Obviously this metaphor overlooks the necessity of just distribution and is obsessed with an ever-increasing production. This symbol does not respect earth's limits and

[5]   Garrett Hardin, "Life-Boat Ethics: The Case Against Helping the poor," in *Psychology Today*, Sept. 1974, p. 126. See also the discussion about Life-boat ethics in the article entitled, "Famine and Global Policy: An interview with Joseph Fletcher" in the *Christian Century*, Sept. 3-10, 1975. It is not surprising that Daniel Moynihan, former US Ambassador of India, said that "We are going to have to face up to the fact that we're a different people than we thought we were." *New York Times* Magazine, 1975.

[6]   D. Callahan, "Doing Well by Doing Good: Garrett Hardin's Life-boat Ethic" in the *Hasting Centre Report*, Vol. 4, no. 6, Dec. 1974. Alan Berg has given similar kinds of criticism in his article, "The Trouble with Triage", in the *New York Times*.

[7]   James B. McGinnis, *Bread and Justice: Toward a New International Economic Order* (New York: Paulist Press 1979), pp. 299-303. See also Arthur Simon, *Bread for the World* (Ny: Paulist Press, 1975), pp. 36. It may be useful in this context to look at Ronald Sider, *Rich Christians in an Age of Hunger* (London: Hodder and Stoughton, 1977), pp. 118-46.

resources. It presupposes uniformity of aspirations and considers the world as a single economic unit. We will need a different set of bakers and also of ingredients that make up the pie. Otherwise the pie will not be distributed any differently. This is the kind of thinking and attitude that has created a consumer society which is compulsive and conspicuous in character. Such a system of development aggravates the acquisitive and aggressive instincts of people. Such a structure is not conducive to control and reorganize of the fallen and fallible, selfish and arrogant nature of the humans.

Modern type of development is based on modern technology which is capital-intensive and consequently gravitates towards the modern organized/urban sector to the near exclusion of the large traditional/rural/ agricultural sector. Therefore, modern type of development has not achieved (1) eradication of unemployment or under-employment in a country like India; (2) reduction of socio-economic inequalities; (3) curbs on concentration of economic power; (4) promotion of a process of self-reliant development; (5) establishment of a socialist pattern of society mentioned by our founding parents in the Indian Constitution. This is the crux of the problem. For the nations of the developing world like India, such a development has meant imitative technology which is the carrier of consumerism and bearer of values foreign to the people. As a result there is more production of luxury items, promotion of 'five-star' culture and less of essential commodities for the common people. C.T. Kurien has therefore rightly asserted that from the time of the British, in the name of development our leaders are encouraging a "want-based economy" rather than a "need-based economy". There is a definitive misdirection of resources which subverts the process of rational allocation. So Kurien has conceptualised poverty as, "the socio-economic phenomenon whereby the resources available to a society are used to satisfy the wants of the few while the many do not have even their basic needs met."[8] The new economic policy of Dr. Manmohan Singh illustrates the problems indicated above. There is a new colonialisation of the financial sector. IMF-World Bank is infringing on the Sovereignty of India. Dunkel's proposals about the agricultural sector is another clear indicator. Privatisation—liberalisation of the economy means that the MNCs, Foreign banks, NRI and such others can come freely and take over the Indian Economy. The Sultan of Brunei alone has net assets of £18.5 billion or $25 billion.

---

[8]   C.T. Kurien, *op. cit.* p. 8

Consequences of Modern Type of Development

I have already suggested some of the problems related to modern type of development. For our purpose, I would like to summarise them under three categories. Firstly, we have to take cognizance of the *psycho-social* costs of modern development. Life has become so fragmented and broken, impersonal and dehumanised. Rugged individualism is on the increase losing our sense of wholeness. We seem to subscribe to what William James called the 'cash value' of people and not recognise their intrinsic worth. He had said, "By their fruits they shall know them, not by their roots."[9] Such an empiricist criterion creates a radical disjunction between the roots and fruits of a people and thus denies them their inherent dignity. Marriage, family and communities have been disrupted and even destroyed in some situations in the name of development. The very perception of the people changes in this context. Communitarian values are at stake as people are induced to believe that community is not written into the very constitution of the human. The traditional fisherfolks' struggle against the modern, mechanised trawler-fishing testifies to this problem. Individualistic competition breaks up community and thus they lose their sense of cohesion.

Secondly, I have already mentioned about the *economic costs* of such a development in terms of unemployment and under-employment. There is a unit-cost of production at the cost of society. It has not mobilised the productive potential of the vast population of India. It is not able to absorb India's vast labour force and we have to reckon with this problem. 20 million are fully unemployed and 200 million are underemployed in India. For the sake of efficiency and speed, modern development is prepared to sacrifice effectiveness and relationality. Imitative technology has resulted in import liberalisation. Consequently the total external debt of the developing countries crossed the one trillion dollar mark in 1986. India's external debt itself is about $ 75 billion dollars, which is not as bad as Brazil ($ 120 billion) and Mexico ($ 125 billion). Indian imports are up by 21.9% while exports are down 17.5%. Due to this trade deficit there is a balance of payment to the tune of Rs. 6000 crores per year for the past five years. This kind of modern development is resulting in the flight of capital from Asia to the tune of 75 billion dollars according to a study by the International Monetary Fund. $ 1.5 trillion is the Third

---

[9]   W.James, *Varieties of Religious Experience: A Study in Human Nature* (NY: New American Library, 1958) p. 34.

World debt and the consequent debt servicing is enormous-88% of the foreign aid.

Thirdly, *ecological-environmental damage* caused by this kind of development is beyond repair. It is felt both in the developed and developing courtries. The Black Forest in West Germany and Silent Valley in Kerala are a witness to this problem. Therefore, people in the West talk about 'natural food' as against artificial food which is available in abundance. Depletion of the renewable and non-renewable resources is taking place at an accelerating speed in the name of progress. The future is arbitrarily and recklessly sacrificed for the present. Ecological imbalance and environmental collapse are endangering marine, animal and human life. Modern development has resulted in rapid soil erosion, deforestation and desertification. I have developed this further in Chapter XII.

Related to this is the problem posed by the all powerful **military-industrial complex**, nurtured and encouraged by this kind of development. Militarisation of the whole world and even of outer space is their avowed objective. Rampaat nuclear proliferation is resulting in direct radiation and radio-active fall-out causing all kinds of problems, both physical and psychological. Bhopal gas tragedy in India and Chernobyl nuclear plant disaster in the 'USSR' caused near panic among European countries. There is the possibility of a 'nuclear winter' or even of a 'nuclear summer' resulting from mushrooming of smoke and dust. This could block the rays of the sun reaching the earth, reducing the temperature considerably. India's defence expenditure has grown from Rs. 3,800 crores in 1980-81 to Rs. 16,000 crores in 1990-91—four fold.

Modern type of development is based on an enormous waste and unnecessary speed because it is interested in efficiency at the cost of effectiveness. An affluent society produces its own effluents which it is not able to control. USA has 7% of the population of the world but has used up in the decade of the 60s more resources than the entire humankind in all previous history. The "American Way of Life" cannot be sustained in America itself and there cannot be another America. The fact is that one American is drawing on resources that could sustain fifteen Indians, according to Schumacher. Seeing the problems and consequences mentioned above, we have to ask questions not with regard to development *per se* but the nature and extent of development which will enable us to focus upon deeper human values and to promote the consciousness that what is at stake in economic questions is the well-being and community relationships of the whole human family, each of whose members is a person of incalculable worth. That is the challenge before us and the demand of Gospel of Jesus Christ.

Two Principles of Authentic Development

I have mentioned above that the present development process raises value questions which are fundamental in nature. This kind of development has resulted in various kinds of reductionism. The goods of life amount to the good life, having has come to be identified with our being, and the quantity of life seems to exhaust the quality of human life. This is the predicament of our development. We are not to indulge in falsification of reality in the name of development. In our thinking and doing development, we should neither indulge in false dualism between having and being, quality and quantity and the goods of life and the good life, nor should we *collapse* them together and thus lose a sense of transcendence. We have to be concerned both with the standard of living as well as the standard of life as Mahatma Gandhi had said many years ago. For this reason I would like to concentrate on two fundamental principles which can provide the matrix for development.

The first principle that we have to affirm is self-reliance. Mahatma Gandhi called it *swadeshi*. It is foundational for development. He defined it as "that spirit in us which restricts us to use and service of our immediate surroundings to the exclusion of the mote remote."[10] More recently, Richard Dickenson has defined it as to opt for those forms of production which permit local grassroots initiative and innovation, yielding results compatible with local tastes, conditions, and culture."[11] Another scholar has defined it as, "a model of development that emphasises meeting the basic human needs of the masses of people in a country through strategies geared to the particular human and natural resources, value and traditions of the country through strategies maximising the collective efforts of

---

[10] M.K. Gandhi, *Economics of Khadi* (Ahmedabad: Navjivan, 1961), p. 3. On another occasion Gandhi said, "The broad definition of *swadeshi* is the use of all home made things to the exclusion of foreign things, in so far as such use is necessary for the protection of home-industry, more especially those industries without which India will become pauperized" (*Young India*, 17 June, 1926)

[11] R. Dickenson, *Poor, Yet Making many Rich: The poor as Agents of Creative Justice* (Geneva WCC, 1983) p. 33.

people within each country and among third-world countries."[12] The MNCS control (1) finance capital; (2) technology; (3) ideology and marketing; (4) the trading pattern and thus rob the people of independence and integrity. Such economic activities militate against the principle of self-reliance which is not the same as self-sufficiency. A spirit of self-reliance will give the people self-respect and dignity. The *khadi* programme and the *charka* came to represent this principle during the freedom struggle. Increasingly the significance of this principle is being realised. Even Rajiv Gandhi called upon Telecommunication engineers and experts to evolve a technology suited to Indian conditions instead of continuing to depend on technology borrowed from foreign countries. He said that we should break away and shift to more aggressive, imaginative and indigenous thinking and solutions (*Indian Express*, 4th February, 1987). It is this principle that can make our *swaraj* (self-rule) real and concrete and liberate us from the slavery described by Gopal Krishna Gokhale in the early part of this century:

> A kind of dwarfing and stunting of the race is going on under the present system of government. We must live all the days of our life in an atmosphere of inferiority and the tallest amongst us must bend in order that the exigencies of the system may be satisfied till at last our lot as hewers of wood and drawers of water in our own country is stereotyped.

Swaraj will have real meaning if it is conceived in terms of *swadeshi*. This is not negate the interdependent world in which we are living. This essentially means that we are not to be unduly dependent on foreign personnel and obsessed with foreign goods. The modern form of slavery is the "debt trap" or the "black hole" - a new form of colonialism.

Fundamentally, the principle of self-reliance emphasises that development must be need-based and non-exploitative in character, helping people to use simple skills and locally-grown raw materials. Self-reliance will prevent the evil of parasitism in which the wealthy are dependant on the working class, cities on the villages and industrial nations on the agricultural nations. We must remember that India has 6,00,000 villages.

The second principle is the development of the whole person and all

---

[12]   J.B. McGinnis, *Bread and Justice*, p. 261. See also J. Philip Wogaman, *The Great Economic Debate: An Ethical Analysis* (Philadelphia: The Westminster Press, 1979), Ch. 3.

the people. Gandhi called this *sarvodaya* which literally means uplift of all or the welfare of all.[13] This kind of development can take place on the basis of the spirit of *swadeshi*. It encourages self-help schemes at the grassroots level and thereby becomes an indigenous movement for development. This movement has not been successful in India in spite of or may be because of people like Jaya Prakash Narayan and Acharya Vinoba Bhave. But it has taken roots in Sri Lanka under the dynamic leadership of Dr. A.T. Ariyaratna. Almost 30 years ago he founded the movement in a remote village, but today there are 6000 villages which have community schemes based on harnessing of human potential and natural resources immediately available. Increasingly it is drawing its philosophical inspiration from Buddhism.[14] It is basically an integral approach to development, empowering the people themselves to think and act on their own. This experiment could be taken as a paradigm.

We must realise that *swadeshi* and *sarvodaya* are basically principles that cannot be fully realised. Such a spirit should become normative for our development. It makes explicit that modernisation is not a self-evident process. Through the two principles that I have mentioned we need to establish a creative and critical dialectic between tradition and modernity, between continuity and discontinuity. We may have to affirm that a selective form of traditionalisation is congenial for authentic, indigenous development. Decentralisation and diversification must become our watch-words. Gandhi had written sixty years ago, "I suggest that if India is to evolve along non-violent lines, it will have to decentralise many things."[15] Later he asserted, "distribution can be equalised when production is localised; when distribution is simultaneous with production" (*Harijan*, 2 Nov. 1934). Gandhi was able to take this position because he did not separate economics from ethics. He had categorically stated in 1921, "I must confess that I do not draw a sharp distinction

---

[13] M.K. Gandhi, *Sarvodaya: The Welfare of All* (Ahmedabad: Navjivan, 1954), pp 3.5. See also Suresh Ram, *Vinoba and His Mission* (Kashi Akhil Bharat Serva Seva Sangh, 1962), pp. 470-482. The same principle has been advocated within the American context by J. Philip Wogaman in his book, *Economic and Ethics: A Christian Enquiry* (London: SCM Press Ltd. 1986)

[14] Detlef Kantowsky, *Sarvodaya: The Other Development* (New Delhi: Vikas, 1980).

[15] M.K. Gandhi, *Sarvodaya*, p. 35. It may be useful to note his discussion on industrialism and machinery in this context (pp. 39-45). See also Shriman Narayan, *Relevance of Gandhian Economics* (Ahmedabad: Navajivan Publishing House, 1970).

between economics and ethics. Economic that hurts the moral well-being of an individual or a nation is immoral and therefore sinful. Thus economic that permits one country to prey upon another is immoral" (*Young India*, 13 Oct. 1921). It is in this spirit that we have to understand these principles.

Modern Scholars who Endorse these Principles

I would like to make a rapid survey of some selected scholars who encourage the above two principles directly or indirectly. Denis Goulet has made the significant distinction between the goods of life and the good life and between the quantitative and qualitative aspects of development. He even goes to the extent of designating much of modern development as anti-development for the reasons expressed above. He does not limit development to per capita income and GNP.[16] In another book,[17] he recalls a French economist, Louis Joseph Lebret, who had made the vital distinction between "to have more" and "to be more". According to Lebret, all human beings in every society are entitled to enjoy the structural and institutional conditions which foster universal human ascent. Robert Heilbroner, another economist, suggests that because of the kind of problems that we are confronted with in modern development, that we need to inculcate the spirit of Atlas as it is not enough to have the Promethean spirit, his nervous energy and his intellectual daring. He has said,

> This is the stunning discovery that economic growth carries
> previously unsuspected side-effects whose cumulative impact
> may be more deleterious than the undoubted benefits that
> growth also brings.[18]

For the various problems and consequences mentioned above Heilbroner says that industrial civilisation is losing its self-evident

---

[16] D. Goulet, *The Cruel Choice: A New Concept in Theory of Development* (NY: Atheneum, 1971), pp. 119, 215-25.

[17] D. Goulet, *A New Moral Order: Development Ethics and Liberation Theology* (NY: Orbis Books, Maryknoll, 1974), p. 43.

[18] R. Heilbroner, *An Inquiry into the Human Prospect* (Ny: W.W. Norton, 1974), p. 19. See also his *The Nature and Logic of Capitalism* (New York: W.W. Norton & Co., 1985) and *Beyond Boom and Crash* (New York: W.W. Norton & Co. 1978)

justification. E.F. Schumacher has brought out clearly the concerns of these two principles in terms of what he calls 'appropriate' or 'intermediate' technology. According to him, the problem can be explained in economic terms by reference to the distinction between capital and current income. No business would consider itself if it had to balance its books by consuming its capital, and that is exactly what industry as a whole is doing by rapidly consuming the non-renewable resources which took nature billions of years to create. For this reason, he is stimulated by Buddhism and talks about optimal consumption rather than maximum consumption. He brings out the non-economic factor in economic consideration when he asserts,

> What is at stake is not economics but culture, not the standard of living but the quality of life. Economics and standard of living can just as well be looked after by a capitalist system, moderated a bit by planning and redistributive taxation. But culture and generally, the quality of life, can now only be debased by such a system.[19]

His emphasis on people and making them self-reliant is of enormous significance. Another well-known person, Julius Nyerere, the former President of Tanzania, has clearly written about people-oriented development. For him roads and buildings are not development *per se* but only tools of development because the issue will be who made the roads or buildings and who actually uses them. He explains his type of socialism in terms of *ujamma*, a Swahili word signifying 'family-food'. He wants his country to grow out of her own roots but in a particular direction and towards a particular kind of objective.[20]

Samuel Parmar, an Indian economist who was in the WCC, in his many articles articulated this concern for self-reliance and 'commonwealth'. He has said that social justice and self-reliance should be the precondition of growth rather than the consequences of growth, social justice and self-reliance. For him, "Self-reliance means a new understanding of development based upon the socio-economic realities of a developing country..." He mentioned about the more insidious form of domination in terms of consumerism, giantism, rapid industrialisation,

---

[19] E.F. Schumacher, *Small is Beautiful: Economics as if People Mattered* (London: Harper & Row, 1983), p. 217.

[20] Julius Nyerere, *Ujamma: Essays in Socialism* (Dar es Salaam: OUP, 1968).

and advanced technology. As poverty is not simply a question of resources but of relationships, he said that the poor must participate more effectively in the process of development. And this would require tears and struggle. For him people are more important than material resources and therefore the notion of human development must place them at the very centre of the economic process.[21] Finally, M.M. Thomas affirms,

> True development is development of people, the release of people from their enslaved conditions so that they can have the rightful dignity of participating in the process of making decisions which affect their life and labour.

Therefore he rejects the Taj Mahal philosophy of development which is based on brutalising exploitation and forced labour.[22]

I have done this rapid survey of modern scholars and statesmen to indicate their focus on people. People are not to be mere beneficiaries of recipients of development but active agents or participants of this process. This means that human development has to be approached from below and not from the top, which is normally hierarchical, pyramidal and elitist in character. People are to be considered not as objects of development but rather its subjects, the ones who know and act as Paulo Freire states.[23] This means that people are the subjects and goals of development. This perspective could be stated as development *of* the people, meaning that they must become the source and origin of development; development *by* the people meaning that they must be its means and methods: development *for* the people is indicative of its purpose and objective. Essentially development must originate from the needs and aspirations of the people in their particularity. Professor Galbraith has also drawn our attention to "our failure to invest in people" and writes, "The test will be less the effectiveness of our material investment than the effectiveness of our investment in men."[24] In concluding this section, it may be good to recall what Kusum Nair had written in 1961. She had said that there cannot be

---

21 S. Parmar, "The Politics of Development", in *One World* (WCC July/August, 1976), pp. 7-9. See also *E.A.C.C. Report*, July, 1970. See also a study document from the WCC *Christian Faith and the World Economy Today* (Geneva: WCC Publications, 1992)

22 M.M Thomas, *Response to Tyranny* (New Delhi: Forum for Christian concern for people's struggle 1979), p. 88.

23 P. Freire, Pedogogy of the Oppressed, pp. 16-18.

any economics in isolation from sociology and social psychology. Introduction of new techniques from outside will help only to a limited extent. It will be a kind of 'induced prosperity'. She explicitly asserts,

> Development will not become a self-generating process with its own momentum unless the value system of the community, and the social structure containing it, are first altered and adjusted to be in harmony with the socio-economic objective of planning.[25]

Conclusion

I think I can sum up what I have been saying with regard to the nature and extent of development in terms of three stories: One from the sacred text of our Indian religious tradition and two from Western literature. This is indicative of our convergence and common humanity. McGinnis interprets the story, *One Flew Over the Cuckoo's Nest*, Ratched, a nurse represents the modern type of development in the story. Normalcy/sanity/development is defined by Ratched. Certain kinds of pills, listening to the right kind of music and participating in therapy sessions are determined by Ratched and of course comes to express her 'benevolent' and 'generous' acts. She determines and controls the behavior pattern of the patients. In this context, the patient, R.P. McMurphy, perceived Ratched as manipulating the people to become docile and dependent. This is done in a subtle and sophisticated way. The therapy sessions seem democratic but in fact Ratched sets the agenda, exploits the patients' emotions and uses 'divide and rule' tactics. This is the kind of development going on in the world today and does not lead to authentic human liberation and justice. Leo Tolstoy had put it, "I sit on a man's back, choking him and making him carry me, and yet assure myself and others that I am very sorry for him and wish to ease his lot by any means possible, except getting off his back."

In *Alice in the Wonderland*, there is an interesting dialogue which summarises to a great extent what I have attempted to state. "I wish you wouldn't squeeze me so", said the Dormouse, who was sitting next to her.

---

[24] K. Galbraith, The Affluent Society, pp. 277.
[25] Kusum Nair, *Blossoms in the Dust: The Human element in Indian Development* (Chicago: The University of Chicago Press, 1961), pp. 189-197. See also Donald A. Hay, *Economics Today: A Christian Critique* (Leicester: Apollo, 1989)

"I can hardly breathe"."I can't help it", Said Alice very meekly, "I am growing". "You have no right to grow here", said the Dormouse. "Don't talk nonsense", said Alice more boldly: "You know that you are growing too." "Yes but I grow at a reasonable pace", said the Dormouse, "not in that ridiculous fashion."

Finally, as we are trying to understand the normative bases for development, I would like to recall the fine distinction made in the Upanishads between *preya* and *sreya*, which I have mentioned in chapter two. For the Pundits in ancient India, I have said that *preya* represented all that is pleasing and ephermal. *Sreya* was understood by the—as that which is of abiding value. Indeed they were able to make a fundamental distinction between *satisfaction* and *gratification*. As we are caught in the vortex of modern technological development, it is for us to appropriate and approximate to the principles I have mentioned above on the basis of this definitive difference. This in turn will make a difference to the nature and quality of development, leading all people towards liberation and justice.

XII

Stewardship of Material Possessions in the Context of the Environment: A Biblical-Ethical Perspective

I. Stewardship of Material Possessions

The main focus of this section will be to learn from the Bible about the understanding and use of material possessions. This will be related consciously to our stewardship responsibilities in the world. We need to know how we possess the material things of life and how we utilise them for the common good. We know very well that material possessions can be both a boon and a bane in the life of the Church — in the life of the community. On the one hand the Church needs to be solvent to function effectively and relevantly. For greater efficiency and creativity, we need more than the minimum so that the work of the church becomes more diversified and meaningful. But on the other hand, undue preoccupations or obsession with material things can rob the Church of her vigour and vitality — her life and meaning. She begins to lose her soul — her spirit. She begins to deteriorate and disintegrate, if not externally and immediately but surely internally and in the long-run. It may be able to maintain her fascade but there is nothing deep and substantial to support and sustain her 'spiritual' life understood in a holistic and wholesome manner.

Secondly, there is also a wider and broader contextual consideration about material possessions. We must take cognizance of the fact that as a community we are located in a poor country like India. In that context we need to reflect on the stewardship of material possessions. One thing it does mean definitively that we have to be *extra* careful how we acquire, maintain and promote material possessions. It may be mentioned that the

Christian Church is the biggest voluntary agency in India, receiving the highest amount of foreign assistance. Now the question is how much of this amount is used to maintain the establishment, and how much for bringing about radical socio—economic transformations? Having made these preliminary remarks, now I would like to turn to the Bible for guidance and direction.

Biblical Perspective

The Bible is quite ambiguous and ambivalent about the understanding and use of material possessions. At the outset in the Book of Genesis it affirms the essential goodness of the created order (1:31). Jesus himself is quite aware of the need of material things in life. Therefore, on the one hand he asserts, "Man shall not live by bread *alone*" (Lu. 4 4), while on the other hand, he has taught us to pray daily, "Give us today our *daily bread*" (Matt. 6:11). Material goods are essential for sustenance and increase. We need food, clothing, shelter, education and employment to live as human beings. But there is always a word of caution:

> Keep your life free from *love of money*, and be content with what you have; for he has said, "I will never fail you nor forsake you". Hence we can confidently say, "The Lord is my helper, I will not be afraid. what can man do to me?" (Heb. 13:5-6).

Paul has uttered a piece of warning in his own way,

> There is a great gain in godliness with contentment, for we brought nothing into the world, and we cannot take anything out of the world, but if we have food and clothing with these we shall be content. But those who desirè to be rich fall into temptation, into a snare, into many senseless and hurtful desires that plunge people into ruin and destruction. For the *love of money* is the root of all evils, it is through this craving that some have wandered away from the faith and pierced their hearts with many pangs (I Tim. 6:6-10).

Jesus himself said, "It is easier for a camel to go through the eye of a needle than for a rich man to enter the Kingdom of God" (Mk. 10:25) Therefore on the one hand the Bible is clear about the many blessings of material possessions but on the other hand it categorically affirms that in the ultimate sense we must realise that they all belong to God (Is. 66:2, Lev. 25:23, Ps. 24:1, 95:5). Consequently we need to be very careful about the use and abuse or misuse of material possessions. It is a gift of God to be held in trust by people and used for human welfare (Lev. 19:9 ff, Job 31:16-33, Is. 58:7-8). Jesus expresses this positive attitude (Matt. 6:32, Mk. 6:37). On the whole there is a joyful, grateful acceptance of material possessions which come as a blessing from God to be used for the common good.

At this juncture, it would be interesting and useful to recall one of the ancient writings. Clement of Alexandria (150 A.D.—220 A.D.) wrote a treatise on *The Rich Man's Salvation.* He had understood Jesus' injunction to "sell your possessions" as not abandoning one's property but to banish from one's soul the notion about wealth, his excitement and morbid feeling about it.[1]

Riches which benefit people should not be thrown away but the fundamental question is "Are you able to make a right use of it?" Precisely, in attempting to answer the question it is important to exercise restrain and limitation in acquiring and using material possessions. Therefore, the Bible goes on warning about pre-occupations with matter which becomes materialism. The story of the Rich Fool (Lu. 12:16-21), the man who had great wealth (MK. 10:23-24), Rich man and Lazarus (Lu. 16:19-31), and the injunctions of James (5:1-6) are a summon to understand material possessions within the divine-human matrix or in matter-spirit dialectic. They cannot take the place of God (Matt. 6:24b see also 19-21). We must not allow them to come in the way of our true happiness and human welfare. Much of modern life has become commercialised. People and things are meticulously measured and weighed in terms of monetary gain. We must remember that surely people have to live by material possessions but they also have to live by values and meanings and for values and meanings of the Kingdom of god. Material things cannot buy God's favour in the final judgement (Job 34:19-20, Zeph). Therefore mercenaries cannot make good ministers or ministers must not be mercenaries. We must not allow quantity of material goods determining the quality of our community life. They are an effective means to a higher end. No money can buy the new life or the gifts of the spirit as offered in Jesus (Acts 8:18-24; 1 Pe. 1:18-19). So on

---

[1]   Quoted in Waldo Beach and H. Richard Niebuhr, *Christian Ethics: Sources of the Living Traditions.* Second Edition (New York: The Ronald Press Company, 1973), pp. 94-98.

the whole, Bible recognises the value of material goods, capable of serving positive ends but it equally recognises their dangers, inducing people, organisations and communities to greed, avarice and even crimes of various sorts. We must develop a proper *perspective, priority* and *proportion* with regard to material goods. The good life should not be confused or reduced to the goods of life. This leads me to the final point.

If we recognise material possessions as a gift from God, we are at best its administrator. In the community we are not handling our own money or property. We have to hold them in trust as faithful and honest deputies. Therefore as mentioned before we need to be extra careful and not indulge in erratic and *ad hoc* behaviour about such money and property. By speaking about "unrighteous mammon" (Lu. 16:17). Jesus suggests that as we use our material possessions in the community we are in constant contact with forces of good and evil and therefore need to be cautious. Steward, *oikonomos*, or God's administrator, implies the obligation to perform the services for which we are made capable by means of our resources and abilities. Stewardship in this context means that we have to exercise a high degree of responsibility. The concept of responsibility is not self-evident. It means basically four things namely 1) response or responsiveness or sensitivity, 2) interpretation of what is going on around, 3) accountability, 4) social solidarity. These four elements together constitute the concept of responsibility which is the other word for stewardship. What does these mean specifically in terms of the life and work of the society? **Firstly,** to be responsible about material possessions means that together or corporately we need to be responsive to or sensitive about the real needs facing the community and thereby respond in a conscious and critical way to the real situation or the "lived experience." Very often we are dealing with artificial needs and concerns in the world. Our time, energy and resources are expended on non-issues which are forced into issues. **Secondly,** to be responsible stewards, it entails careful interpretation of the situation in the society which of course is integrally related to the first element. This requires hermeneutical tools and exegetical skills, both Biblical and Sociological. We need to be educated and equipped for interpretation. Majority people in the society or the Church as a whole view their context with lot of presuppositions, pretensions, assumptions and biases. As such they remain ignorant about their own situation. They think they know when in fact they do not know. Selfishness, stubbornness and sin prevent people from interpreting authentically the reality around them. **Thirdly,** to be responsible stewards mean to be accountable in the literal sense of the word as well as in its larger sense. The Church or the society is accountable to God and the people for every paisa, a piece of property, which are at its disposal. It is accountable to the people *from* whom the wealth is acquired and *to* the people *for* whom it is spent. Keeping and giving an authentic account is an indispensable ingredient of stewardship. The story of Ananias and Sapphira is a reminder of this (Acts 5:1-11). We know that in India more than 500 crores have been received by the churches in India. According to the report 67% are spent for the administration, for the establishment. Is this stewardship or accountability? We have to ask hard questions particularly when it is about material possessions at the disposal of the society. We have to be guarded about their acquisition, administration and thereby be accountable. Jesus' behaviour in the temple in Jerusalem (Mt. 21:12, Mk. 11, 15-19, Lu. 19, 45-48; Jn. 2:13-22) is a stern warning. **Fourthly,** we still conceive of our spirituality in an individualistic (non-relational), atomistic, and isolated manner and not being able to compre-hend the social solidarity or the communitarian character. Consequently, our notion of Stewardship is limited and narrow. We must learn as a nation, as a Church to identify without losing our identity as followers. But we should not be exclusive, aggressive, and selfish in the process. The community does not exist for itself or in itself. It lives for others, for the renewal of the *whole creation*.

Essentially, I am saying that our attitude and actions with regard to material possessions are not extraneous or peripheral to our understand-ing and acknowledgement of Jesus the Christ. On the contrary, our stewardship or accountability about our material goods is intrinsically and organically related to the Gospel. It is a test of our spiritual life. It is a joyful, grateful response to what God has done and is doing in the world for the liberation of humanity. God in Jesus became material in the flesh-with its concomitant needs of food, clothing, shelter and work. Our fidelity to God is expressed through our accountability about material goods. Peter affirms, "Each one, as a good manager (administrator, steward) of God's different gifts, must use for the good of others the special gift that he/she has received from God" (I Pe. 4;10).

Finally, we must remember that the Church is not fundamentally an economic community—its task is not to make money for profit but its task is to be *prophetic*. Obviously, as an organisation it must employ people at various levels and assist people and promote just cause. In view of the intrinsic power of material goods, very often the church in attempting to do the above things, has become mercenary-minded and in the process its essential task is forgotten. It must not lose sight of the vision of the

Kingdom of God. At the end it is good to remind ourselves of the Parable of the dishonest, shrewd steward (Lu. 16:1-13) and the two verses following (14-15):

> The Pharisees who **dearly loved** their money, naturally scoffed at all this. Then He (Jesus) said to them, "You wear a noble, pious expression in public, but God knows your evil hearts. Your pretense brings you honour from the people, but it is an abomination in the sight of God," (Living Bible; See other translations).

II. Stewardship of the Earth

We cannot consider the idea of stewardship of material possession in isolation. It has to be conceived in the larger, broader context of the whole, wide world-**MOTHER EARTH**:

> The Indian Summer is hotter. More Himalayan ice melts into the Ganga and the Brahmaputra swelling them tremendously. The Bay of Bengal and the other seas have risen by a metre, and the excess waters have flown into the fertile fields of Bengal and Uttar Pradesh. The Sunderbans have been submerged. Thousands are drowned and many more in the rest of the country face death by starvation.
> More than a tenth of the Bangladesh population need to be evacuated. Several of the Maldives islands have been submerged. Nearly six lakh Americans run the risk of dying of brain cancers caused by exposure to ultraviolet sun rays.

Such is the scenario of environmental-ecological degradation. Never before humanity has been confronted with such a judgement. In the last twenty years, from Stockholm, 1972 to Rio de Janiero, 1992, there is an increasing recognition and awareness that there are countries of the world that have deliberately developed at the expense of the earth, air and water. It has affected adversely the nature and quality of the whole inhabited earth which means both *Oikoumene* and *Oikos*. The delicate, fragile balance in the eco-system has been disrupted as a result of the environmental collapse, depletion of the non-renewable resources, and the degeneration of the earth, air and water. This has attained an alarming proportion.

In 1972, the warning was sounded in a book entitled *Limits to Growth* but selfish people of the earth did not pay heed to the warning. After twenty years another book has been written.[2] In the latter book the authors have basically reiterated and reinforced the former book but with a new awareness. Even after twenty years, in the midst of "Satellite television and cellular phones", we have millions of villages without safe and adequate drinking water, health and educational systems. The planet is being stretched to its limits. They reaffirm "We have to do more with less." Indirectly they blame the modern, western type of development which has resulted in this kind of disaster. Finally the authors point out that the planet develops *without growing*. The global economy is a sub-system of the finite earth. It is high time to give up our unsustainable obsession with a continuously expanding 'frontier' economy as the solution of poverty, unemployment and social mobility, "For although there are limits to growth of global economy, there are no limits to the development of human society."

In these years, the Worldwatch Institute with its President, Lester Brown has been issuing similar warnings and have suggested definite steps to save the earth. According to the Institute the world has forty years to save itself, upto 2030. In 1992 they stated that 300,000 soviet citizens were treated for radiation sickness, respiratory diseases were widely prevalent in the Los Angeles basin, and 200,000 skin cancer fatalities in the U.S. because of ozone depletion.

Ozone layer is thinning over the Antarctic and the Northern Hemisphere. This is carcinogenic ultra-violet sun rays protecting the earth. It is feared that 10% of the layer would be removed by 2000 A.D. in the temperate zone and the skin cancer would go up by 26%. The Ozone layer is being eaten away directly or indirectly by the carbon-dioxide exhaled by us, our factories and motor vehicles, the Chlorofluorocarbons (CFCs) from our refrigerators (90%) and air-conditioners and the methane from our paddy fields. Montreal protocol, 1987, had sought to limit the use of CFCs. Just in a section in Calcutta 28,550 petrol and 9,605 diesel vehicles ply between 8 a.m. and 8 p.m. emitting about 13.2 tonnes of gaseous substances every day. They include 82% carbon monoxide; 14.7% hydro-carbons; 3.2% nitrogen oxide; 0.05 % ammonia and 0.11% aldehydes. 60% of the CO_2 between 1850-1985 has been released by the industrialized nations.

2 Donella H. Meadows, Dennis L. Meadows and Jorgen Randers, *Beyond the limits: Global Collapse or a Sustainable Future* (London: Earthscan Publications, 1992).

Related to this issue is the global warming or green house effect. Worldwide temperature will rise by 2° within 35 years and by 6° by the end of the next century, raising the sea level and submerging islands. It has happened because of burning fossil fuels, cars and smoke stacks produce gases that turn to acid in the atomsphere; drift for miles and then fall as acid rain damaging lakes, killing fish, and destroying forests. U.S. alone produce 25% of the green house effect. Forests are vanishing at a rate of some 17 million hectares per year. Amazon Rain Forests are being destroyed at 50 million acres per year.

Another important area of concern is biological diversity or bio-diversity in wetlands, arid deserts and forest. Variety and variability of plants and animal species are degenerating rapidly. In Australia alone 28% of its 102 native animals are extinct. The total number of species is estimated to be between 5 and 50 million of which only 1.14 million have been identified. India and such countries in Asia, Africa and Latin America are rich in bio-diversity. Our flora and fauna have to be protected from plunderers. Wetlands are transitional areas between aquatic and terrestrial ecosystems. They include marshes, swamps, flood plains, peatlands, and shallow ponds. They are the breeding nursery grounds for water fowl and acts as filter for sediments and pollutants.

Just when the world thought that is has raised the ecological con-sciousness of humanity, a Siberian blast took place on 6th April, 1993. At Tamsk-7, an underground tank of radioactive waste exploded when an acid was added as a cleanser. A radioactive cloud moved across the vast Siberian forest endangering its villages. It is stated that the nature of the damage caused by it is nothing compared to Chernobyl chemical explosion in 1986. It displaced 25,000 people, killing hundreds through cancer and related illness. It sent a radioactive cloud over Europe. Such is the nature of nuclear power plants!

To this crisis has been added nuclear proliferation, causing direct radiation and radioactive fall out. The possibility of a "nuclear winter" or even of a "nuclear summer" is real. According to an astro-physicist, Carl Sagan, even a limited nuclear war, consuming just 0.8% of the global arsenal, could destroy 30% to 70% of the ozone layer.

Environment Crisis in India

At one time we were concerned about only the Silent Valley in Kerala. But today we are concerned and duly alarmed about the deterioration from the Himalayan range to the Indian Ocean, from the Bay of Bengal to the Arabian sea. Our forests, water and air are polluted beyond repair in spite of the role of Maneka Gandhi, the Green Crusader, the first Green politician of India, Chipko leader, Sunderlal Bahuguna, Baba Amte and Medha Patkar. Bahuguna has opposed the Tehri Dam in U.P. and Amte, Patkar and others have opposed the Sardar Sarovar dam in Gujarat and Narmada Sarovar Dam in M.P. The latter will destroy 50,000 hectares of forest, about 500 villages and displace one million people (mostly tribals) robbing them of their living and life style. The few rural rich will benefit at the cost of the millions.

The Independent Panel headed by a former U.S. Congressman, Mr. Morse found the project flawed, 85,000 hectares of forest will be flooded, trees, herbs, plants, many species of vegetables, wild life and insects will be destroyed. But some other internal-external forces are compelling the government to go ahead.

The Thar desert in the north is advancing as the 692 km. Aravalli Range is been denuded. It has shrunk from 40,000 sq. km. in 1947 to 6,000 sq. kms.. in 1987. Consequently, the rain fall has been affected and the crop yields have considerably slumped. Deforestation in India is at 2.7% annually. 11% of earth's soil has been degraded due to chemicals, erosion and overuse (over grazing).

Dr. Vandana Shiva, an environmental scientist, has mentioned that we cannot continue with capital-intensive, externally-controlled model of economic development if we are to implement the Earth Charter and Agenda 21 passed at Rio, 1992. Ozone hole is the creation of the North. Instead of pollution and wastes being treated at source, the North wants to export these hazardous toxic wastes. The Union Carbide plant in Bhopal is an example. Therefore the poor nations of the world should not accept *in toto* the Western Agenda about ecology-environment. Africa, Asia and Latin America have to determine their own local priorities. The Cuban President, Fidel Castro had therefore declared at Rio, "An important biological species is in danger of extinction—Man (Women)... The greatest damage to the global ecosystems have been caused by emulating the consumption-based development models of the industrialised countries." We must realise that in the final analysis wide-spread, pervasive poverty is the greatest pollution. At least one billion people of the world live in acute poverty. Our population is not just the cause of poverty but its consequences. As a result, India's population rose from 360 million in 1951 to 850 million in 1991 and now approaching 900 million. A whole new India has been added in forty years. India is certainly caught in a demographic trap with 16% of the population of the world and growing at 2.1%. 45,000 children are born every day in India. One baby is born every two seconds and 34 babies per minute in India. World-wide it is growing at 92 million annually. In this context, ecological-environmental quality could improve if the rich nations of the world promote and strengthen a right type of economic development.

A Biblical-Theological Perspective

According to the Old Testament, *GOD* is the creator of plants, animals, fish in the water and the birds of the air. God created *all* the living creatures. He took a long time to do this-five long days. According to the Biblical calculation, each day did not mean just twenty four hours but at least one thousand years. Thus the earth was carefully arranged and organised. It was neither too big nor too small; neither too far nor too close to the sun and neither too hot nor too cold. It was made just right and each time it is mentioned, "God saw that it was *good*" (Gen. 1:12 and 18). Indeed, God is the source and origin of this beautiful creation.

There is a logic in creation, a causal relationship and a built-in interdependent structure which nurtures and nourishes, supports and sustains life in its totality. Human beings and human life are located within this larger context. After creating for five long days, light and separating watery lands from dry lands and other creatures, only on the sixth day, God creates the humans and it is mentioned, "God saw *all* that he had made and it was *very good*" (1:31).

It is true that the second chapter of the Book of Genesis leaves out all the vivid detail of chapter one but fundamentally it is a reiteration with certain significant additions about the creation and fall of the humans. For our purpose it is necessary to note that both the creation episodes emphasize the *ochlos* in relation to or in the context of the *oikos*.[3] But it is the first story (Gen. 1) written around 450 B.C. which is theocentric in character accenting on the intrinsic worth, dignity and value of the non-human creation. It belongs to the Priestly tradition, Genesis chapter two contains the Yahwahist tradition written around 800 B.C., emphasizing the anthropocentric perspective. In their selection work the editors could have chosen only one of the creation stories. But they chose the democratic way and included both the J. and P. traditions. It is significant

---

[3]   Read "Nature in the Bible" in Lawrence Osborn, *Guardian of Creation: Nature in Theology and the Christian Life* (London: Appllos, 1993) Ch. 5, pp. 81-100

that they did not work chronologically but with the theocentric perspective.

Both the traditions mention about *God* handing over to the humans the responsibility for sustaining and promoting this creation (1:26-28; 2:15-17). Thus human beings have been made co-creators or partners with God. But instead of being stewards or trustees, they exploited and dominated the earth. The words *radhash* (Dominion) *kabash* (subdue by putting one's legs on the back as on a slave) in Hebrew convey this very well. This is an indication of human sinfulness which dominates and destroys this beautiful creation. Instead of glorifying God through creation, humans managed to make a 'mess' of it although he/she was made in-charge of it. Such is the human predicament. But God does not give up.

God gives another chance to humanity. Thus the systems of the sabbath and Jubilee year are introduced and instituted (mentioned in Lev. 25 and Deut. 15) to renew and reclaim the whole of creation so that it does not slip into nothingness (ex-nihilo). Human greed and selfishness have distorted the purpose and direction of creation. God claims it and wants to recreate it through his promise of a "new heaven and a new earth" (Isaiah 65:17-25). Therefore it is not possible to conceive of the humans apart from or to the exclusion of the totality of reality (Is. 11:6-9). So the psalmist sings of the "new song" (33:3; 96:1; 98:1; 144:9; 149:1). Consequently the vision is understood in the following words:

> The wilderness becomes a fruitful field, and the fruitful field is deemed a forest. Then justice dwells in the wilderness, and righteousness abide in the fruitful fields. Happy are you who sow besides all waters who let the feet or the ox and the ass range free (Is. 32:15-16, 20; See also Zech, 8:12; Eze. 37:25).

Therefore from the Old Testament perspective human liberation is viewed within the larger recreation of the whole earth.

In the New Testament we know that Jesus' beloved disciple, Peter denied him three times and another disciple betrayed him and handed him over to his enemies. Thus it is not surprising that immediately after his crucifixion, his disciples fled, thinking him to be an imposter and a grand failure. Even after his resurrection Thomas doubted him. This experience brought the frightened lot together. Then they became aware of the universal and cosmic significance of the life and work of Jesus. Therefore they designated him as the *CHRIST*. The apostolic tradition proclaimed that nature has the potential within it which needs to be recovered and redeemed. Christ's work of redemption includes this possibility. According to the Pauline proclamation it is being renewed and reconstituted. Thus the prophetic promise materialises in the salvific work of Jesus. Paul purposively participates in the prophetic promise and categorically affirms,

> For the *creation* waits with eager longing for the revealing of the sons of God... because the creation itself will be set free from its bondage to decay and obtain the glorious liberty of the children of God. We know that the whole creation has been groaning in travail together until now and not only the creation, but we ourselves (Romans 8:19, 21-23a).

Thus the priority and perspective of Paul becomes perspicuously clear. Decisively and definitely he situates the *ochlos* in the midst of or in relation to the liberation of whole of creation. In the very purpose of God, it is meant to be cosmos and not a chaos—a universe and not a multiverse. Thus there is an underlying unity or harmony in creation itself. That is being restored or recovered. The human liberation is reconciliation with God, fellow human beings and the whole of creation. In the process of recreation and reconciliation we apprehend our fundamental unity or oneness with the *WHOLE*, with the *ALL*. Therefore the Pauline perspective in the epistle to the people of Corinth becomes categorically clear when he asserts, "If any one is in Christ, he is a new **creation**, the old has passed away, behold, the new has come" (II Cor. 5:17). King James version translates it as "if any men be in Christ, he is a new creature..." That is how it is translated in some of the versions like the Living Bible. Todays English Version and the Phillips Modern English. But along with the Revise Standard version, New International version, Jerusalem Bible and the New English Bible emphasise this **cosmic** dimension of salvation. The New English Bible affirms, "When anyone is united to Christ, there is a new world; the old order is gone, and a new order has already begun." This Pauline perspective is repeated and endorsed in his letter to the Colossians-God has created all things, in him everything coheres and through him everything becomes reconciled through the blood of the Cross (Col. 1:15-20). Thus it is not possible to miss this message of salvation. It is for us to appreciate and appropriate this wider, bigger solidarity. We cannot or must not individualise or privatise the Gospel.

The apostolic tradition particularly, the Pauline perspective, has its origin or source in the life and work of Jesus as it is recorded in the various gospels. It is obvious that the gospel writers did not conceive of the salvific work of Jesus in isolation-in the air or in a vacuum. It is well embedded in history, among the people and in the midst of the whole of creation. This is indicated in Jesus' relationships and references. He was in complete harmony with the natural world of animals and vegetation. He talked easily about the birds of the air, lilies of the field and the foxes in their holes. (Matt. 6:26-30). Jesus reaffirms in speech and actions the Lordship or sovereignty of God over history and creation. "God so loved the world" is the basic theological affirmation which is reaffirmed in the person and work of Jesus. We cannot abandon the cosmic dimension. Christology is related to anthropology in the context of cosmology. Therefore God becomes human in Jesus and the nativity story is told in detail with animals, shepherds, stable and a manger. The host of angels announces the good news, "Glory to God in the highest heaven, and peace on *earth* for all those pleasing him" (Lu. 2:14). Jesus has come so that all and everything are at peace, living and promoting fulness of life understood as **shalom** in the Hebrew thinking. Therefore it is positively wrong to indulge in reductionism about the Gospel of Jesus making it individualistic, non-relational and non-natural. Indeed that distorts and subverts God's revelation in Jesus. We have made God small and concomitantly his disclosure in the world, in the *oikoumene*, in the *oikos*.

The Bible on the whole testifies to God's affirmative relationship to the whole of creation and asserts its essential and intrinsic goodness and significance. Thus *oikos* comes within the purview of God's salvific purpose and goal in a systematic and sustained way. According to the Biblical witness human liberation is viewed from this cosmic perspective—"the new heaven and new earth". This is made possible through the initial dynamic activity of God which is ongoing in character. God is not an absentee landlord or a watchmaker who leaves his creation. There is constant interventions or impingements which make recreation possible. Such is the nature of God as declared in the Bible. We need to be caught up in or be grasped by this unified and a recreated vision of reality. Disjunction creates its own distortion. It has been rightly said, "the loss of the relation to nature goes hand in hand with the loss of one's own self"[4]

Rollo May, *Man's Search for Himself* (New York: Norton, 1953), p. 53.

Conclusion

From this perspective, we can fully understand and endorse the historical shift made by the World Council of Churches since its inception in 1948. It commenced with the concept of "the Responsible Society" defined in various ways by the stalwarts. By the 60s W.C.C. was expounding the cause of "the responsible *world* society" expressing a wider solidarity and unity. But things were obviously getting more difficult in the areas of development and ecology and therefore it changed its language or strengthened its vocabulary by crusading for "Just, Participatory, *Sustainable* Society." In the process, it was redefining or refining the meaning of *SOCIETY*-enlarging it. This was not enough and consequently it began to talk about, "Justice, Peace and Integrity of *CREATION*." Obviously, this was a great improvement in the language and understanding of the W.C.C.—expanding the scope and character of justice and peace which must include the whole of creation. Thus it was able to locate the *ochlos* in the context of the *oikos*. It is meaningful and relevant. But this call of the W.C.C. seemed to have failed and the rich nations of the world persist in their willful ways, aggravating the hiatus between the rich and the poor, the humans and nature. They had become irresponsible. It is in this context it was significant that the W.C.C. was compelled to summon the Holy Spirit to deliver humanity from the confusion that they have created—"Come Holy Spirit, Renew Your *Creation*." Ultimately, the Holy Spirit could help us but we have to exercise our God-given responsibility. Let us be awakened and respond positively to God's promise. "Behold, I make *all* things new" (Rev. 21:5) It would be good to remember,

> The ecological conscience views the natural world as a series or inter-related system which are in a state of dynamic equilibrium, and within which man (Woman) must play his (her) part as a responsible spectator and participant. In the balance of ecology, the responsibility and irresponsibility of an act is defined by its ability either to preserve or destroy the integrity of the biotic community.[5]

William Wordsworth had written in the eighteenth century,

---

5   S. Cromwell Crawford, *Evolution of Hindu Ethical Ideals* (Calcutta:FA K.L. Mukhopadhyay, 1974), p. 231.

The world is too much with us; late and soon,
Getting and spending, we lay waste our powers;
Little we see in Nature that is ours;
We have given our hearts away, a sordid boon!
This sea that bares her bosom to the moon,
The winds that will be howling at all hours
And are up-gathered now like sleeping flowers.
For this, for everything, we are out of tune.
It moves not.-Great God! I'd rather be a
Pagan suckled in a creed outworn,-
So might I, standing on this pleasant lea,
Have glimpses that would make me less forlorn;...[6]

Much earlier the *Ved Gathas* proclaimed in India,

On earth grows food, on her the ploughman toils;
She carries likewise all that breathes and stirs,
The home of cattle, horses and birds.
May earth vouchsafe us her good fortune and her glory;
Bearer of all things, hord of treasures rare,
Sustaining mother, Earth the golden-breasted,
May she grant us wealth.
Impart to us those vitalising forces
that come, O Earth, from deep within your body.
The Earth is mother, I am child of earth.
Whatever I dig up of you, O Earth,
May you of that have quick replenishment.
O Purifying One, may my thrust
never reach right to your vital parts, your heart.

A recent theological-ethical statement is by Robin Gill in the Chapter entitled, "Faith in the Countryside", in his book, *Christian Ethics in Secular Worlds* (Edinburgh: T & T Clark, 1991), pp. 45-60.

XIII

Liberation of the People:
A Biblical-Theological Perspective

In chapter eleven I have looked at the priority of the people. In this chapter I will pursue the topic further from a Biblical-theological perspective.

People are taken for granted or assumed. Powerful people take advantage of the majority, weak people's goodness of weakness. Their ideas and ideals, ambitions and achievements are not taken note of. People remain voiceless and the powerful indulge in arrogance in the midst of their ignorance. Such is the plight of the people! But there is a new awakening-a new consciousness. People are becoming participants in the processes of development. *Panchayati raj* and *Nagarpalika* systems are urgent needs of our time. There is a definitive shift from *Rajniti* to *Lokniti* (rule of the people). The cries are not being heard authentically and consequently the life goes on as usual. That is the dilemma. But the Bible affirms God who makes and responds to the cry of the people.

a) Old Testament Traditions

God's righteousness (dikaiosune) is known in the deliberate way he makes people and relates to them in a sustained way. He makes them in his own image, *imago-dei*. This image is broken because human beings are selfish and stubborn. In the Bible God knows them as stiff-necked people (Ex. 32:9; 33:3 and 5; 34:9; 2 Ch. 30:8; Acts 7:51). Yet God does not give up. He takes the initiative and condscends to convenant with stiff-necked people so that they can recover their Original image and God could reclaim them. Such is the love of God—*hesed* in the Old Testament and *agape* in the New Testament! It is a persisting and an enduring love which is sacrificial and liberating in character. God remains faithful in-spite of the infidelity of the people. This constancy is very well portrayed in the Book of Hosea particularly when it says,

> I will not execute my fierce anger,
> I will not again destroy Ephraim;
> for I am God and not man,
> the Holy One in your midst,
> and I will not come to destroy (11:9)

Thus through various ways God owns them through creation, recre-ation, covenants, through promise and fulfillment, through seeking and saving, God claims and reclaims the people and utters, "you are a people holy to the Lord your God" (Deut. 14: 2a; 26:19; 28:9). Through this active and dynamic relationship God is able to affirm, "I will be your God, and you shall be my people" (Jer. 7:23; 11:4b; 24:7; 30:22; 31:22 Eze. 14:11; 36:28b; 37:27). Thus this mutual relationship becomes the *raison d'etre*. God cannot exist apart from or to the exclusion of the people particularly, the *ochlos*. God deliberately and purposively chooses to do this. But it is equally true, people cannot and should not think of their life apart from God because of what he has done and is doing. This is the divine subsistence for the humans. Therefore the psalmist sings,

> Know that the Lord is God!
> It is he that made us, and we are his;
> We are his people, and the sheep of his pasture.
> For the Lord is good;
> his steadfast love endures for ever,
> and his faithfulness to all generations (100:3 and 5)

The multifarious traditions of the Old Testament testify to a God (Yahweh) who listens to people. He is not insensitive and deaf. He is not the Unmoved mover, deity of Olympus or one of the gods of Epicurus. In several verses scattered throughout the Old Testament, we hear of a God who hears the 'cry', the 'groaning' and the 'murmuring' of the powerless people of Israel (Ex, 2:11-25; 3:7-9; 5:1, 22; 6:5-27). This is pronounced in the Exodus tradition of the Old Testament which is quite potent and pervasive. Hans-Reudid Weber maintains,

> Seldom has an event in history had such a strong and enduring

echo as this liberation of some Israelite clans who were subjected to forced labour in Egypt....(it) has echoed through successive periods of biblical history, how it was told, remembered through liturgical celebration, re-interpreted and re-enacted.[1]

This saga of deliverance of the slaves has been summed up in liturgical affirmations of faith and catechetical teachings (Jos. 24:2b-13: Deut. 6:20-24 and 26:5-10). It was celebrated and chanted in psalms like 105. These slaves were few patriarchal clans considered later to be *habiru*, the semi-nomadic or ethnically-mixed socio-political 'outsiders'. They were the marginalised from the mainstream of life. During the period of the Babylonian exile of the Hebrew people, they looked forward to a new exodus.

They visualised the future intervention of God when Yahweh would respond redemptively to the cry of the people,

Behold, the days are coming, says the Lord, when I will make a new covenant... not like the covenant which I made with their fathers when I took them by the hand to bring them out of the land of Egypt... I will write it upon their hearts; I will be their God, and they shall be my people (Jeremiah 31:31-34).

Related to the exodus tradition, is the *anawim* tradition which crystallises the sensitive, responsive God. God heard the cry of the poor, *rash, ebyon, dal* or *anawim*. According to the scholars, the last Hebrew word specifically means "to be bent over" or "to be crushed". The prophets of the 8th century B.C. in particular, understood God as the defender of the poor and the oppressed. The rights of the poor are safeguarded by God. This is the preferential divine option for those who are poor, small and vulnerable (Deut. 10:17f). In the Old Testament poverty is understood in terms of body, mind and spirit. They did not conceive of the human in a dichotomous way but as a psycho-somatic unity. Thus *anawim* cannot be spiritualised. It is material, physical poverty and God is on the side of the poor slaves and against Pharaoh. Thus Hans-Reudi Weber states,

---

[1]   Hans-Reudid Weber, *Power: Focus for a Biblical Theology* (Geneva: WCC Publications, 1989), p. 30. See also Karen Lebaeqz, *Professional Ethics: Power and Paradox* (Nashville: Abingdon Press, 1985), Ch. 8, pp. 124-136.

The anawim are totally theocentric, but they live in a relationship with God which is full of tensions. The presence of the
God whom they trust is often hidden.... In such situations the
anawim can only cry out, struggle with God in prayer, confront
the absentee and the enemy God of their present experience
with the God who had made the promise of enduring convenant
love.[2]

I have highlighted the exodus and anawim traditions which are
mentioned several times in the Pentateuchal, Historical, Poetical and
Prophetic literature of the Old Testament. It is not an aberration or an
exception but the fundamental character and thrust. The total thrust
crystallises and clarifies the issue of poverty on the one hand and justice
on the other. Yahweh had heard the cry of the people who where in
bondage. His response did not end there. He affirmed that the slaves must
be liberated and that is how the ancient Hebrew people perceived of their
history. LET MY PEOPLE GO became the cry of God as a response to
the cry of the people. This meant complete liberation and justice for the
people. Nothing less than this satisfies God who is just and righteous.
Therefore he cannot be amoral or neutral. He has to take sides with the
poor and the down-trodden. God has persisted with his cry in the midst
of grumbling and murmuring, betrayals and denials and broken covenants. We cannot change God's nature or character. He cried through
the Pentateuch and the prophets (Deut. 16:19-20;24:17; 2h. 9:8; Amos 2:
6-7; 4:1; 5:7 and 11;6:12; 8:4 and 6). This is mentioned in the poetical
book like the psalms (14 :4; 53:4; 44:12; 72:1-7, 12-13). The book of
Isaiah which was written by several people over a long period of time
espouses the cause of Justice for the poor and needy (Is. 1:17-27; 5:7 and
16;9:7;10:2:16:3 and 5;28:6 and 17;30 :18; 32:1 and 16;33:5;40:14;42:1-
4; 51:4; 56:1;59:8-9 and 11-15; 61:1 and 8). This is the refrain of Jeremiah
and other prophets. It comes out clearly and categorically in Amos "But
let justice roll down like waters, and righteousness like an everflowing
stream" (5:24); in Micah, "He has showed you, O man, what is good; and
what does the Lord require of you but to do justice, and to love kindness,
and to walk humbly with your God" (6:8) and in Hosea, "So you, by the
help of your God, return, hold fast to love and justice, and wait continually
for your God" (12:6; also 2:19). It is important to note that human justice

---

[2]   Hans-Reudi Weber, *Power*, P. 126.

was understood in terms of God's righteousness-in relationship and continuity and discontinuity. Thus it is imperative to maintain the distance and the dialectic between the two and not reduce them or separate them absolutely. That would be to falsify the Biblical witness and diminish the great God. Indeed the cry of God is a cry for justice for the people because basically God is God of justice and righteousness.

b) Apostolic Traditions:

This mutuality or reciprocity of the divine-human existence is reaffirmed and reinforced in the writings of Peter (I pe. 2:4-10), Paul (II Cor. 6:16), and John (Rev. 21.3). Thus there is unity and unanimity about this thinking in the total Biblical corpus. There is an explicit emphasis of the fact the they were no people in the sense that they were a scattered, nomadic tribes. But God in his infinite grace and mercy makes them a people, holy to the Lord. He gives them a purpose and direction. They become a community of people. This is not an exclusive privilege of the people of Israel. Their representative and paradigmatic character is accentuated. They are made a mighty instrument in the hands of God for the liberation of the whole world.

The ancient, apostolic church was conceived in terms of people. St. Paul quotes approvingly from Hosea and asserts the character of the church (Romans 9:24-26). This is the fundamental way in which the church understood herself (Hebrews 4:9). Hellenization of Christianity and institutionalisation of the church after Constantine shifted focus from the people to the organisational, static character of the church. Since then the church became hierarchical, elitist in character, promoting domination of the few and the dependence of the majority people. In such a context easy submission and an uncritical obedience became the way of life for the people. They are not able to exercise their critical faculties and God-given responsibilities with freedom. As a result of this long history of the domestication of the people in the church, she suffers from an ecclesial schizophrenia-it actively advocates democratic forms of government in the political life but permits or even promotes a kind of dictatorship in the church life. The policy and structure of the churches need to be seriously questioned from this perspective. The voice of the people have been stifled and the understanding of the church made very narrow and limited. The early church as illustrated in the Acts of the Apostles and even in ancient Israel, believed in and practised delegation of responsibilities and devolution of power to the people. Moses was asked by his father-in-law, Jethro, to choose able people from all the people, "such as fear God, ones who are trustworthy and hate bribe". And such people were to be appointed as rulers of thousands, of hundreds, of fifties, and of tens. This was an attempt to build confidence and capacities in the people (Exodus 18:11-15). That is the meaning of mutuality growing into maturity.

Peter is able to summarise this way of thinking when he utters,

> But you are a chosen race, a royal priesthood, a holy nation, God's own people, that you may declare the wonderful deeds of him who called you out of darkness into his marvellous light. Once you were no people but now you are God's people; once you had not received mercy but now you have received mercy (I Peter 2:9-10).

The apostolic traditions promote the *exodus* and *anawim* traditions of the Old Testament, Jesus is referred to as the Rock (1 Cor, 10:1-5) and Paschal lamb (1 cor. 5:7) that is sacrificed as a response to the cry of the people. Paul refers to the story of deliverance from Egypt and to the role of Moses. In some ancient mss Jude seems to refer to Jesus as the one "who saved people out of the land of Egypt, (Jude 5). James concretises the demand of the gospel and of the *anawim* tradition by asserting that authentic religion constitutes visiting the orphans, and widows in their afflictions, being impartial, "For as the body apart from the spirit is dead, so faith apart from works is dead" (James 1:27; 2:2-6, 14-17) In his proclamation he warns the rich for exploiting the poor labourers "and the cries of the harvesters have reached the ears of the Lord of hosts" (5:4-6). John goes on to expound the gospel tradition in terms of loving the poor neighbour and asserting,

> if any one says, "I love God", and hates his brother he is a liar; for he who does not love his brother (sister) who, he has seen, cannot love God whom he has not seen (I Jn. 4:20).

We find this thrust and emphasis even in the apocalyptic literature in the Bible. John sees the vision of a "new heaven and new earth". He particularises this in terms of wiping tears from the eyes, putting an end to mourning, crying and pain "for the former things have passed away" and God says, "Behold, I make all things new" (Rev. 21). Indeed the cry of the people have been heard by God and they are liberated. Such is the promise and hope of the people. This has a ring of fulfillment, already in anticipation-in expectation. Thus the language of the apostles sound peculiar and unreal as the language of the law and the prophets in the Old Testament. But it has a basis in the past. It generates hope for the future. We joyfully share in this *kerygma*. The God whom they proclaimed is an acutely sensitive, responsive in essence.

In the apostolic church there were specific structural problems like the relationship between Jews and Gentiles, circumcision and uncircumcision, slavery and freedom. Surely, "Let my people go", came to mean liberation from these problems. The stalwarts like Peter, Paul and Barnabas together made a powerful plea for breaking down the barrier between Jews and Gentiles and being decisively against circumcision of the Gentiles before they became Christians. This was considered unnecessary and irreligious. Peter challenged the audience in Jerusalem by asking them, "Now therefore why do you make trial of God by putting yoke upon the neck of the disciples which neither our fathers nor we have been able to bear" (Acts 15:10). Finally James stood up and clearly proposed, "Therefore my judgement is what we should not trouble those of the Gentiles who turn to God" (15:19), This was passed as a resolution unanimously by the apostles and the elders at that council of Jerusalem. This was considered first of its kind. This resolution is an actualisation of what Paul had written to the Corinthians, "you were bought with a price; do not become slaves of men" (I Cor. 7:23). He went on to assert, "Where the spirit of the Lord is, there is liberty" (II Cor. 3:17). But Paul did not accept unconditional, absolute freedom (See I Cor. 6: 12-20; 10: 23:24). Paul realised that our battle is not against flesh and blood but against "principalities and powers." Therefore it is important that the early church was not prepared to tinker and tamper, do window-dressing and bring about cosmetic changes, which is no change at all. Even if they are changes, they are rather superficial or artificial which do not last. LET MY PEOPLE GO came to mean for the apostles nothing less than justice, From that perspective, we can understand and appreciate the writings of James and also of John (I Jn. 3: 17-18). The Christian faith must be made active in loving and just deeds (Gal 5:6). We cannot miss this loud testimony of the apostles. They were committed people who had been touched and transformed by the power of the resurrection. They were different people realising the reversal of values that had occurred in Jesus. They wanted to extend that ministry in their life and work. They understood, individual acts of charity very often becomes "a screen for injustice and a substitute for justice."

c) Gospel Traditions

Obviously the apostolic tradition grew out of the life and work of Jesus. The gospel is the good news of God becoming one of the people, born in Bethlehem, the son of an ordinary carpenter. God's people becomes people's God in Jesus the Christ. This reversal is the revelation of a God who does not assert, My People, from outside the historical, human milieu. On the contrary, God actualises his words, "my people", by becoming one of them. Thus he is not only for but *from* the people. That is the meaning of the incarnation-total identification. The Book of Hebrews talks about Jesus as the high priest who is able to sympathize because he was tempted like we are but without sinning (4:15); he shared in the human nature and "therefore he had to be made like his brethren in every respect" (2:14 and 17). It is not surprising to hear before and after the resurrection Jesus utter, "These who are well have no need of a physician, but those who are sick; I came not to call the righteous, but sinners" (Mk. 2:17). He asserted the priority of the people over human conventions and traditions like the sabbath (Mk. 2:23-28). That is the stuff of his humanity and that is what he meant by my PEOPLE.

Jesus shares and participates in the prophetic, exodus and the *anawim* traditions of the old Testament. Several times he is compared to or contrasted with Moses, old and new exodus-with the wilderness experience. The Last Supper which Jesus himself instituted recalls, reviews and resolves to appropriate the new covenant made possible through the blood of Jesus. The new convenant is viewed in contrast to the old covenant. Jesus himself makes a promise in response to the cry of God's people.

The *anawim* tradition is very well carried over from the song of Hannah, the mother of Samuel (I Sam 2:1-10) to the Magnificat of Mary, the mother of Jesus (Lu. 1:46-55). Here Mary is not portrayed as a meek, obedient and submissive lady but a politically awakened woman. God's mighty action is understood as scattering the proud, bringing down the mighty from their thrones, filling the hungry with good things and the rich are sent away empty (Lu. 1:46-55). Thus Mary is able to vividly anticipate the mission and ministry of Jesus. It is a powerful declaration of God's intervention in history and vindication of the poor. God establishes his sovereignty in this way. Jesus in in turn picks up the prophetic tradition and commences his ministry with the words of Isaiah 61:1-2 (Lu.4:1618). Consequently Jesus is proclaimed as the prophet (Jn.4:19; 6:14; 7:40). And like the prophets of old, Jesus is radically and relevantly sensitive to the cries of the poor, hungry, the lame, the blind and even the dead. Therefore even when he is in the midst of the thick crowd he discerns the touch of the one who is crying for help.

The Mathean passages (12:18-20; 23:23-28; 25:31-45) raise the issue of justice clearly and categorically. Jesus and justice are intrinsically related. It is not necessary to wait for Karl Marx, Mao Tse Tung, and Che Guevara to hear about justice. It is quite clear that long before such stalwarts of the eighteenth and twentieth century, this becomes evident in his understanding of power, the Pharisees, the Sabbath, the temple system, the legal system and the condition of women. Obviously he questioned the power of Herod and his likes. He wanted his disciples to be servant, not lording over other people, but serving and saving them from bondage and slavery. Obviously he perceived of righteousness as doing the just and the right and not pretending, which is self-righteousness. Obviously he was against idolatry of the Sabbath and willing to engage in liberational actions on that day.[3] He was against the temple system as it operated in Jerusalem in his time (Jn. 2: 13-16). In the story about the woman caught in adultery, he rebuked the people for their self-righteousness, questioned indirectly the legal system that made the woman more vulnerable and on the whole confronted the people with the downright discrimination and deprivation of women in general. It is a powerful indictment of the society of his time (Jn.8:1-11). Thus there is enough indications in the gospel traditions to demonstrate that Jesus was radical and revolutionary considering the attitudes and actions of his time in Israel (nearly 2,000 years ago). He raised questions and counter-questions, spoke about values and reversal of values which expressed and exposed the shallowness or hollowness of the people. He could not stand the false piety and religiosity of the Pharisees. Therefore he demanded a righteousness that would exceed the righteousness of the scribes and Pharisees, which obviously meant leading towards justice.

Jesus was not a timeless religious teacher, philosophizing vaguely and generally on the verities of life. He did not indulge in vague generalisations and sterile abstractions. We know from his ministry that the cry of God had not ceased and the imperative "Let my people go" in various difficult situations, as difficult as the exodus, remained and persisted. He was equally concerned about the whole of life (body, mind and spirit) and the all of life (political, economic,ecological and social). He was against

---

[3]   Read about the "Spirituality of Liberation" in Virginia Fabella et al. *Asian Christian Spirituality: Reclaiming Traditions* (New York: Orbis Books, Maryknoll, 1992).

fragmentation and reductionism. Indeed justice was understood in a radical, redemptive or liberative and creative way, not in a retributive or proportional way (Jn. 3: 16-17; see also Matt. 9: 27-29; 11:2-6; 15:30; Mk. 10:46-51; Lu. 14 : 13-14). In the parable of the Good Samaritan, Jesus showed the structural problem between the Jews and Gentiles and the problem of 'charity'. He went on to assert "I have come that they may have life and have it abundantly" which means in its richness, in its fulness. It is for this reason it is important to make a significant and systematic shift from diakonal service to *dikaiosune* which is justice as understood by Jesus.

The Bible clearly and categorically witnesses to a God who dies, not suffer from *ataraxia* (indifference) and *apatheia* (insensitivity). He is a suffering, crucified God. He asserts his power by going to the periphery, outside the gate. He becomes a servant of the people. Such is the depth and dimension of God's identification with his people.

Seventh CCA Assembly had mentioned.

> The wealth of Asia is in its people. Over half the world's population is in Asia. The people in Asia have a long history and rich culture which spans thousands of years. Many of the finest expressions of the creative human spirit are in Asia. We seldom realise that it is the work of the people that has made it possible for rulers to do the things they claim. A new mood is emerging in Asia—an awakening of the people themselves. Now the deep movements of the human spirit and the growing solidarity of the people are the reference points for a perception of history. Empires rise and fall, kingdoms come and go, but the people remain as the permanent reality of history. Jesus lived with the people and administered to them.

A Theology of the People

Increasingly, Christian theologians both in the North and the South are focussing on people without romanticising or idolising them. Ian Fraser talks of reinventing theology as the people's work—to discern what God has done and is doing for the people and from the people. The paradigm of the exodus and the life and work of Jesus makes this possible. In South Korea there is the advent of *minjung* theology, meaning theology of alienated, marginalised people. According to the Biblical testimony

Yahweh became directly involved with the powerless people and saved them from the powerful Pharaoh. God discloses himself through such saving activity and makes them a people

Park Sang Jung[4] has made a significant distinction between *ochlos* and *laos* as found in the New Testament. According to him *ochlos* (minjung) was introduced into the Gospel tradition by the author of the Gospel of Mark with some specific intention. In the Gospel, *ochlos* appears 36 times while *laos* appears only in two places. We find Jesus constantly with people serving and saving them from problems and difficulties. The common people *ochlos* are placed over against the dominant people of Jerusalem. While the people of Galilee were gathering around Jesus and following him, the ruling class were afraid of Jesus and the people. Jesus associated himself with tax-collectors and sinners (Mk. 2:15-16, Mathew refers to tax-collectors and prostitutes). Galilee was never a part of the mainstream of the history of the powerful people of Israel. Jerusalem was the centre of power for the Jewish people. It is to the people of Galilee Jesus comes preaching good news of liberation (Lk. 4:18-19). The resurrected Jesus left Jerusalem and went ahead of his disciples to Galilee where he had started his ministry of sharing the good news of liberation among the poor, weak and the vulnerable. Indeed Jesus came from the hinterland of history.[5] A similar study and conclusions have been drawn by Ahn Byung-mu, a professor of New Testament in South Korea.[6] The marginalised and the abandoned is the locus of divine activity. We can apprehend what God is by what he has done and is doing for such people.

[4]   Minjung Theology: *People as the Subjects of History* Edited by the Commission on Theological Concerns of the Christian Conference of Asia (New York: Orbis Book, Maryknoll, 1981), pp. 123-137. See also Ian Fraser, *Reinventing Theology as the People's Work* (Madurai: The Unemployed Young People's Association 1985), pp. 20-28; Samuel Amirtham and John S. Pobee, ed., *Theology by the people: Reflections on Doing Theology in Community* (Geneva: WCC, 1986); See also R.S. Anbarasan, ed., *People's Movements: Towards a Perspective* (Madras: Association for the Rural Poor, 1982); Walter Fernandes, ed., *People's Participation in Development: Approaches to Non-Formal Education* (Delhi : Indian Social Institute, 1981); Mathai Zachariah, ed., *The Church: A people's Movement* (Nagpur: NCCI, 1975).
[5]   *Living in Christ with People: A call to Vulnerable Discipleship.* (CCA Seventh Assembly Report, 1981), pp. 67-72
[6]   *Minjung Theology*, pp. 138-151. W.C.C. perspective has been suggested in a book by Ulrich Duchrow, *Global Economy: A Confessional issue for the Churches* (Geneva, World Council of Churches, 1987).

According to C.S. Song, Christian theology has to be conceived in the womb of people's experience. Therefore, their songs and stories, their tears and struggles become the raw ingredients of theologising. According to him tears bring together people in suffering. Tears are signs of life. Jesus is a man of tears, a man of sorrows (Jn. 11:35; Matt. 23:37; Lk. 13:34). God in Jesus the Christ is able to identify and express solidarity with those through a Chinese folktale about the ancient wall of China, how the agony and tears of one Lady Meng could conquer the arrogance and authority of the emperor, Chin Shih Huang-ti (3rd century B.C.). Song affirms that powerlessness can turn to powerfulness through the power of tears because that is the kind of God we affirm in Jesus the Christ.[7] More recently he has reaffirmed:

> The God is not an abstraction of thinkers, but a living reality in the midst of the people. God is not a theological proposition but the moving force of history. God is not to be located in the Holy of Holies but in the company of men, women, and children toiling and struggling for the right to live as human beings. God of the people, God in the people, and God with the people.[8]

A theology of the people has also been advocated by Gustavo Guitierrez who has said that we have to rediscover the Lord alive in the poor and oppressed, living subversively the gladness of Easter right at the heart of a people's movement crushed and repressed. Hither to the ones who have been "absent from history," are beginning to be present and becoming the makers of history. Preference is written into the gospel message itself and Gutierrez states,

> Precisely what so many find insupportable in the preferential for the poor is its claim to announce the gospel within the dialectic of a universality that moves from and through the particular, from and through a preference ... gospel is addressed to every human being: only it has a predilection for the poor.[9]

---

[7]   C.S. Song, *The Tears of Lady Meng: A Parable of People's Political Theology* (Geneva: WCC, 1981).

[8]   C.S. Song, *Tell us our Names: Story Theology from an Asian Perspective* (Indore: Satprakashan Sanchar Kendra, 1985), p. 195.

[9]   G. Gutierrez, *The Power of the Poor in History* (NY: Orbis, 1983) pp. 128-129. See also pp. 199-212.

Indeed for him this sense of particularity and preference becomes the basis of our universal affirmation of the love of God without becoming exclusive or individualistic. Segundo calls this 'partiality' and opines. "A hermeneutic circle in theology always presupposes a profound human Commitment, a partiality that is consciously accepted."[10] It may be good to recall that fifty-one years ago, in 1942 Dietrich Bonhoeffer said:

> We have for once learnt to see the great events of world history from below, from the perspective of the outcast, the suspects, the maltreated, the powerless the oppressed, the reviled—in short, from the perspective of those who suffer.[11]

In this chapter I have attempted to indicate the priority of the people from a Biblical-Theological perspective. By 'people' I have meant primarily the poor people. Theologically, I have endeavoured to demonstrate that we have to affirm the preferential option for the poor people because they hold the key to the understanding of God in Jesus the Christ. Jesus came to give life to people in all its richness and abundance (Jn. 10:10), particularly the marginalised and the abandoned.

People are dear to God particularly, the poor people. He relates to them as subjects and not objects of pity. He becomes one of them. His presence and power is known and acknowledged by the people in various ways. They mourn and groan, murmur and rebel but God remains faithful. God does not give up the people because of their repeated failures and sinfulness. He renews the convenant several times. Such is the nature of God's long-suffering, persevering love. Therefore we have good reasons to believe and hope in such a God who inspires and instigates. Once they were far off, he has brought them close, once they were no people but God has made them a community of people, once they were no body, he has made them some-body a people with a purpose and direction. Such is the nature of God.

God of the Bible is a God of Justice who wants to liberate all people from unjust structures and oppressive systems. Therefore in the Bible,

10   Juan Luis Segundo, *The Liberation of Theology* (New York: Orbis Books, 1982), pp. 33 and 29. See also his *Liberation of Dogma Faith, Revelation and Dogmatic Teaching Authority* (New York: Maryknoll, Orbis Books, 1992) Ch. 12, pp. 234-263.
11   D. Bonhoeffer, *Letters and Papers from Prison* ed. E. Bethge (New York: MacMillan, 1973), p. 17.

"love is the fulfillment of justice, never a substitute for the latter; justice is a necessary instrument of love; and love is for Christians the ultimate norm of justice."[12] I may further crystallise the issue that the fundamental conviction of the law and the prophets including Jesus, was that God demands righteousness in the name of religion; that righteousness has to be viewed in terms of justice which is radically relational and structural in character, this-worldly and corporate. Therefore Christianity is not a privatised, psychological experience but a dynamic theological-ethical experience in terms of justice. Nothing less than this can be our vision and goal. We cannot subvert or sabotage the gospel of justice. We will end this chapter with a story from Rabindranath Tagore,

"Sire", announced the servant to the King, "The saint Narottam has never deigned to enter your royal temple. He is singing God's praise under the trees by the open road. The temple is empty of worshippers. They flock round him like bees round the white lotus, leaving the golden jar of honey unheeded." The King vexed at heart, went to the spot where Narottam sat on the grass. He asked him, "Father, why leave my temple of the golden dome and sit on the dust outside to preach God's love?" "Because God is not there in your temple," said Narottam. The King frowned and said, "Do you know twenty millions of gold went to the making of that great marvel of art, and it was consecrated to God with costly rites?" "Yes, I know it," said Narottam, "It was in that year when thousands of your people whose houses had been burned stood vainly asking for help at your door. And God said, 'the poor creature who can give no shelter to his brothers would build my house.! And he took his place with the shelterless under the trees by the road. And that golden bubble is empty of all but hot vapour of pride." The King cried in anger,"Leave my land." Calmly said the saint, "Yes, banish me where you have banished my God."[13]

[12] Clinton Gardner, *Biblical Faith and Social Ethics* (New York: Harper, Row Publishers, 1960), pp. 262-270.
[13] Rabindranath Tagore, *Fruit Gathering*. Read also "Toward the Liberation of Theology" by Tissa Belasuriya in Curt Caorette *Liberation Theology: An Introductory Reader* (New York: Maryknoll, Orbis books, 1992), Ch. 2, pp. 31-41.

XIV

A Theology of the Future:
A Perspective for Christian Ethics

Introduction

After exploring and analyzing various social, economic and political issues in India using ethical tools, it is important now to provide a theological perspective. To do this firstly, I would like to evaluate and make a selection from among the numerous theologies of the future which have been formulated in various ways beginning from the nineteenth century. Secondly, I would like to relate the chosen theology of the future to our ethical being and doing. In chapters one and ten, I have referred to it.

It is in search for the locus of the good, that I write this chapter. I have become increasingly interested in and aware of the possibilities and dangers of the teleological methodology. For this reason I am venturing into this unknown territory of the future. We are aware of the kind of attitude prevalent towards it in India. Some conceive of the future as something pre-determined and therefore predestined. Life in India seems to be fated and the future foreclosed. The law of *karma*, at the empirical level, has engendered among the people an ethos which is basically characterised by defeatism and escapism. Some feel the weight and burden of the past so much that they cannot move forward. The iron chain of the past seems to hold them back. The future, in this context, is definitively and decisively determined by the past. Such a fatalistic attitude is very well crystallised among scholars in India in the debate between astronomy and astrology. Very often the two are either identified or confused with each other. This kind of an attitude cannot entertain the possibilities of the new. There is a sense of fear and cynicism in the face of this dark future. In such a situation, poverty increases because some people still think it is God-given and human-made. As a result of this, the poor have been muted and defuturised. I am in quest of a theology that would liberate the people from this deterministic mould and save them from conservatism and conformism. Writers like Alvin Toffler in *Future Shock* and earlier George Orwell in his books, *Animal Farm* and *Nineteen Eighty Four* and Aldous Huxley in *Brave New World* have projected a kind of future in the light of the events of their time. Such a future is foreboding and forbidding. This is not the kind of future that we aspire for.

In the following section, I will briefly look at some of the earlier understandings of the future in terms of the Kingdom of God.

Earlier Understandings of the Future

In the Christian affirmation, the future is conceived in terms of the synoptic symbol of the Kingdom of God. That was the "pulsating reality of Jesus' existence". But this concept has been understood and interpreted in various ways. We will briefly refer to some of them which have occurred from the last century.

One group of thinkers have viewed the idea of the Kingdom explicitly in an ethical way. They talked about "building the Kingdom." Albert Ritschl was one of the pioneers in understanding theology in an ethical mode. Therefore his theology had an elliptical character. He represented the Dominion of God (Herrscaft-Gottes) as the spiritual and moral task of those gathered in the Christian community. According to him, the kingdom of God was very much a sociological entity-This-worldly and ethical in nature. Ritschl defined it by saying,

> The Kingdom of God consists of those who believe in Christ, in as much as they treat one another with love without regard to differences of sex, rank or race, thereby bringing about a fellowship of moral attitude and moral properties extending through the whole range of human life in every possible variation.[1]

In an earlier version of this, Ritschl had clearly indicated that the

---

[1]   Quoted in Gosta Lundstrom, *The Kingdom of God in the Teaching of Jesus* (Virginia: John Know Press, 1963), p. 5.

Kingdom is the result and a product of a common human ethical activity. Many critics think that in the process of ethicising the concept, the Kingdom became uneschatological because it completely lost its futuristic dimension. They feel that Ritschl was more influenced by German Idealism of the time and the theology of the Enlightenment rather than the Bible. Later scholars like Johann Christoph Blumbardt and his son, Christoph Blumhardt, gave a social interpretation of the concept. They believed in its organic development. In this light, we can understand the statement, "It is of tremendous importance to labour for this earth, it is not heaven that is to be conquered, but earth."[2] According to them, although it is in one sense a gift of God, it does not come suddenly and unexpectedly through some catastrophe. It is significant to note that in spite of this ethical thrust, the future character of the Kingdom is retained.

This approach to the idea of the Kingdom definitively influenced writers life Washington Cladden, Richard Ely and Walter Rauschenbusch. for Gladden "The Kingdom of god is the whole social organism so far as it is affected by divine influence."[3] The Kingdom would come by the mighty contagion of social injustice and he equated it with Christian social order. Ely had said, "Let it not be forgotten that it is the Kingdom which we are to seek, and a Kingdom is a social state."[4] For Rauschenbusch, the concept of the Kingdom was the unifying force through which he had the social version of a redeemed society. It would overcome the Kingdom of evil in the world with its superpersonal forces. Although the Kingdom is divine in its origin, progress and consummation, it was "humanity organised according to the will of God."[5] On the one hand, he realised its future character, on the other hand, he asserted "The Reformation too brought no renascence of the doctrine of the Kingdom, it had only eschatological value, or was defined in blurred phrases borrowed from the church."[6] Obviously, he does not seem to appreciate the relationship between ethics and eschatology. He saw the Kingdom as a gradual process and so wrote about the maintenance and "upbuilding of God's Kingdom on earth."[7] Evidently these stalwarts of the Social Gospel

[2]   *Ibid.*, p. 18.
[3]   Robert T. Handy, ed., *The Social Gospel in America: 1870-1920* (New York: Oxford University Press, 1966), p. 103.
[4]   Ibid, p. 237
[5]   Walter Rauschenbusch, *A Theology for the Social Gospel* (New York: Abingdon Press, 1977), p. 142.
[6]   *Ibid.*, p. 132-133.
[7]   Walter Rauschenbusch, *The Righteousness of the Kingdom* ed. and int. by Max L. Stackhouse (New York: Abingdon Press, 1968) p. 116.

movement had fallen victims to the nineteenth century cult of inevitable progress, an evolutionary optimism, and even coming perilously close to identifying the Kingdom with a particular social and economic system. But it is important to note that these scholars did not identify the Kingdom with the existing church. Rather they spoke and wrote about Christianising the social order. In such a situation of course the Kingdom became quite a human enterprise and lost completely its futuristic aspect. It came to be identified with geographical region. Richard Niebuhr had made a stringent critique of this way of thinking in his book, *The Kingdom of God in America,*

> It (the Kingdom of God) was secularised by being detached
> from its context of faith in the sovereignty and the experience
> of grace, while it was attached to the idea of human sover-
> eignty and natural freedom. It was nationalised, being used to
> support the feeling of national superiority and of manifest
> destiny. It was confused with the progress of industrialism and
> capitalism.[8]

Such an equation resulted in a sense of triumphalism and false pride. Niebuhr expressed the dilemma of the modern Christian very well when he went on to say, "A God without wrath brought men without sin into a kingdom without judgement through the ministrations of a Christ without a cross."[9] This kind of thinking about the Kingdom made it lose its universality and futuristic character. But it must be said to the credit of the above-mentioned scholars that they used the concept as an "interpretative tool" by which they analysed and evaluated history. But they used it in such a way that they made ethics and eschatology disjunctive and even opposed to each other. For them the futuristic dimension seems to render the symbol of the Kingdom unethical and concomitantly ineffective and irrelevant for the problems of the world. In their usage, the idea became more a descriptive category.

There was another group of thinkers who conceived of the concept in an inward, individualistic and essentially supernatural way. Theologians like Adolf Harnack, Wilhelm Herrman, Johannes Weiss and Ernest

---

[8] Richard Niebuhr, *The Kingdom of God in America* (New York: Harper and Row Publishers, 1937), p. 151. In our own time such a phenomenon has taken place with the idea of secularity. See Harvey Cox, *The Secular City* (New York: Macmillan Co. Ltd., 1965) pp. 110-113.

[9] *Ibid*, p. 193.

Lohmeyer saw the Kingdom as wholly unconditional and anti-ethical. This way of thinking is very well epitomised by Harnack in his statement, "All that remains then is God and soul, the soul and its God."[10] Obviously his idea was of a kind of an individualistic, supernatural religious experience. He argued that the eschatological note in Jesus' teaching was an "alien accretion", or "an incrustation." Therefore he engaged himself to the task of separating the husk from the kernel of the Gospel. He discovered that the eschatological thrust is seen in "co-efficients" of historical forms. Basically he advocated a personal ethic without eschatology. Johannes Weiss challenged his father-in-law, Albrecht Ritchl, and stated that the Kingdom is not the result of an immanent development but the miraculous intervention of God. It is not moral ideal which humanity must bring about, but the highest religious good, which God bestows. Consequently, Weiss did not speak about the righteousness of the Kingdom but righteousness **for** the Kingdom. It is not an ethical entity.[11] So Weiss restores its eschatological dimension but in the process loses its ethical emphasis. Later writers like Gunkel and H.J. Holtzmann tried to establish its ethical and corporate thrust.

With Albert Schweitzer we enter a different phase in the debate regarding the symbol of the Kingdom. He makes the Kingdom exclusively futuristic. This is designated as "consistent eschatology". According to him the ethics advocated by Jesus is not for the Kingdom but it is for the time between the 'already' and the 'not yet', between his (and his disciples) preaching and the coming of the Kingdom of God. He called this "interim ethics", by which he meant,

> that the ethical demands of Jesus all aim at inner preparation for membership of the coming Kingdom and ultimately as justification at the judgement. That is as much as to say that to Jesus an ethic of the Kingdom of God did not exist. This presupposes a supernatural state of the world, in which mankind has lost its earthly mortality, and stands transfigured beyond struggle and sin, good and perfect in every way like the angels.[12]

---

[10]   Adolf Harnack, *What is Christianity?* (New York: Harper and Row Publishers, 1957), p. 56. The Book was first published in 1900.

[11]   G. Lundstrom, *Kingdom of God*, p. 41. Nathan Soderblom agreed with Weiss stating that Kingdom is not a comprehensive term for the moral progress of Christian Humanity. He emphasised its eschatological, transcendental and incommensurable character.

[12]   *Ibid*, p. 74.

He separates the ethical teaching of Jesus from the eschatological *weltanschauung*. According to him, the ethical ideas are not inextricably bound up with the eschatological form-essentially unconditioned by the symbol. It is important to remember that Schweitzer took very seriously the ethical import and implications of the teaching of Jesus. He wrote about Jesus,

> He introduced into the late-Jewish conception of the Kingdom his strong ethical emphasis on love, making this, and the consistent practice of it the indispensable condition of entrance. By doing so he charged the late Jewish idea of the Kingdom of God with ethical forces, which transformed it into the spiritual and ethical reality with which we are familiar.[13]

From this perspective it is important to note that Schweitzer was prompted in his ethical ventures and adventures by this awareness of the future which is called the Kingdom of God.

Rudolf Bultmann agrees with Schweitzer to a great extent by making the Kingdom supernatural and superhistorical. But for Bultmann ethics became eschatology. There is an urgency of decision for God.[14] It is either or crisis: either being controlled by the imminent expectation of the reign of God or being determined by the world. It is a demand for *metanoia*. Ethics becomes for him existential in character, some kind of an inner religious experience. Fundamentally for him, "Jesus was first an existentialist and only afterward an eschatologist"[15] Achievement of the true self became primary for him. The future for him became an existential moment and man stands alone in "empty space". The Kingdom is de-mythologised and in the process it is de-eschatologised. Therefore it is rightly noted, "... Kingdom of God is never represented as really present in Jesus, and that the truly future character of the Kingdom is not established."[16]

Evidently Bultmann is cut off from eschatology and the result is that

[13]   Quoted in Richard H. Hiers, *Jesus and Ethics: Four Interpretations* (Philadelphia: The Westminster Press, 1968). p. 64.
[14]   See Thomas C. Oden, *Radical Obedience: The Ethics of Rudolf Bultmann* (Philadelphia: The Westminster Press, 1974). By radical obedience, Bultmann did not mean following rigidly rules and regulations which are authoritative but where a person understands the demand and affirms it from within himself.
[15]   Heirs, *Jesus and Ethics*, p. 94 and 99.
[16]   Lundstrom, *Kingdom of God*, p. 155.

his ethics turns out to be some sort of a situation ethics. He affirms:

> Jesus teaches no ethics at all in the sense of an intelligible
> theory valid for all men concerning what should be done, and
> left undone...(Jesus) can only leave the decision to the man in
> his concrete situation. If a man really loves, he knows already
> what he has to do.[17]

We have come to realise more than before that love needs to be structured to do justice in our political, social and economic life. Love is used here as a great simplifier of life.

With scholars like T.W. Manson and particularly C.M. Dodd, the Kingdom of God loses completely its futuristic character. It becomes a present reality but with a 'residue'. This is called "Realised Eschatology" or "Presentative Eschatology." Dodd thought of the futuristic apocalyptic imagery of the Gospels as an "accommodation of language." According to him, people should live knowing fully well that they are already in the presence of the Kingdom. He advocated an absolute ethic, a life lived directly and immediately under the reign of God. He refers to the various texts of the Gospels, and shows, "that the eschaton has moved from the future to the present, from the sphere of expectation into that of realised experience."[18]

Finally, it is important to note that writers like Nils Alstrup Dahl, G. Bornkamm and Roman Catholic scholars like, Rudolf Schnackenburg have maintained the dialectical character of the Kingdom, its propleptic character.[19] Later we will indicate why it is vitally important to maintain this dual dimension of the Kingdom for the sake of ethical decisions and actions.

Some Modern Discussions about the Future and Ethics

In this section, I would like to discuss some theologians like Pannenberg, Moltmann and Braaten with regard to the future and Christian ethics. For Pannenberg, futurity is fundamental for Jesus' message. And this becomes the ontological priority on the basis of which he understands the

---

17 Quoted in Hiers, *Jesus and Ethics*, p. 109. John A.T. Robinson and Tillich have used similar language.
18 Quoted in Lundstrom, *Kingdom of God*, p. 116.
19 G. Lundstrom, *Kingdom of God*, p. 259-278.

structure of reality. Jesus proclaimed the rule of God as a reality belonging to the future. Therefore the future becomes the mode of God's being. His being and existence cannot be conceived apart from his rule or power. God's claim on the world is to be understood exclusively in terms of this rule which Jesus called the Kingdom of God. By establishing the "ontological priority" of the future, Pannenberg reverses the time sequence and frees himself from the causal nexus. Past and present do not determine the future but the former have been eventuated from the latter. So in this sense, the future is not the prolongation or completion of the present but is the creative origin of reality. Futurity of the reign of God becomes the power determining the present. The appearance of Jesus makes this future possible. Consequently we have a foretaste or foreknowledge of this future which is in God. The future is anticipated in our time.

This proleptic character of the Kingdom means that it is not external, "out there", isolated and cut off but is constantly releasing its generic power in the creation of the present moment. Therefore while Pannenberg always uses the terms, 'coming' or 'imminent' to describe the Kingdom, Carl Braaten uses the term, 'oncoming' to capture the sense of movement and dynamism. The future is not a static entity somewhere ahead of us, lurking in the dark. It is dynamic and relational. Moltmann asserts that the German word *zukunft*, which is the translation of the Latin word, *adventus*, has this sense of approaching or arriving. Some scholars prefer to use the word *adventology* rather than eschatology. It is therefore good to remember that Braaten has made a significant distinction between "future in history" and "future of history", the former being some kind of an utopia (teleology) or a future that is projected as another time within history and the latter being eschatological future which deals with the final fulfillment or end of history.[20] It is this latter future which is determinative of the structure of reality. Pannenberg also makes this distinction and states,

> Yet in the perspectives that are dominant for secular futurologists the future is anticipated by extrapolating from present tendencies, or models are developed that are intended to represent trends of that sort. Theology, on the other hand, deals with a future that confronts the present world and all its development tendencies and even stands in opposition to it.[21]

[20] Evert H. Cousins, ed., *Hope and the Future of Man* (Philadelphia: Fortress, 1972), p. 43f.

[21] W. Pannenberg, *Ethics* (Philadelphia: The Westminister Press, 1981), p. 176

Reinhold Neibuhr stated,

> Against utopianism Christian faith insists that the final con-
> summation of history lies beyond the conditions of the tempo-
> ral process. Against the other-worldliness it asserts that the
> consummation fulfills, rather than negates the historical pro-
> cess.[22]

Therefore while maintaining the otherness of the future in God, we
cannot negate the historical process which is part of the purpose of God
himself. From this perspective, we can agree with Eller only condition-
ally, when he writes:

> Being God's future, it is to be expected that it lies beyond
> man's control, beyond man's manipulations (however well
> intended), beyond man's utopian constructs, beyond what
> man can envision even as possibility.[23]

We would rather state that being confronted with the contradictions
and ambiguities of life, we will affirm the world with discernment and
discrimination. But we take seriously Eller's desire to maintain the
tension between the future of God and the present which he categorises
as reality and actuality respectively. On the one hand, we affirm the
discontinuous character of this future, thus keeping alive the sense of the
novuum, while on the other hand we must acknowledge its continuity with
the past and the present. The latter have originated from the future of God.
From this point-of-view, we have to take seriously the law of *karma*. This
concept is helpful in the sense that the past is reckoned with. It is not to
be conceived in a fatalistic or deterministic mode but making people
aware of the past and to realise "that the possibilities of the future are in
some sense limited by the past."[24] We cannot completely escape or be
saved from the causal nexus. It is a reminder that there is a moral order
or *dharma* in the universe with its cause and effect. Some of the evil

---

[22] Reinhold Niebuhr, *The Nature and Destiny of Ma*n, Vol. II (New York:
      Charles Scribner's and Sons, 1943), p. 291.
[23] Vernard Eller, *The Promise: Ethics in the Kingdom of God*, (New York:
      Doubleday and Co., Inc., 1970), p. 217.
[24] Eric J. Lott, "The Dilemma of *Karma* and the Dynamics of Hope in Hindu and
      (continued on next page)

consequences of the actions of individuals or groups may be absorbed or transcended by some redemptive actions but all of them cannot be obliterated. There is some sort of a residue of actions. Past, present and future need to be inextricably bound together because they belong to the same continuum.

The proleptic character of the future also makes for discontinuity, for openness and freedom. For both Moltmann and Pannenberg this future is marked by contingency and unity. In the present time, there is diversity and pluralism but it is the future of God that makes things cohere and find their meaning. For Pannenberg, contingency indicates future ambiguity which is essentially indeterminate but not vague. It has a direction and purpose. It is possible to deal with this contingency because the future is personal and to speak of God is to speak of a personal power. In this context of contingency, we affirm the unifying power of the future which can be understood in terms of love. According to Pannenberg:

> Love grants existence and grants it contingently. This means that love grants new existence, in spite of the self-asserting arrogance of that which already is. In love we recognise the intrinsic dynamic at work in the eventuating of contingent events from the future and releasing them in the process of time.[25]

By contingency he means freedom, unboundedness, and discontinuity thus grasping the spirit of the new and the sudden. By unity Pannenberg means love, coherence, fulfillment and continuity in the proleptical sense. On the basis of this contingent character of the future, Moltmann is able to assert the resurrection of Jesus. he says, "Only when the world can be understood as contingent creation out of the freedom of God and *ex nihilo*... the rising of Christ become intelligible."[26]

In concluding this section, we may state with Pannenberg and Moltmann that ultimate future is the new paradigm of transcendence whose power transforms and brings about alteration in the conditions of

---

[24] *(continued from last page)*
   Christian Thought," in *Influence of Hinduism on Christianity* Ed., Gnana Robinson (Madurai: Tamilnadu Theological Seminary, 1980), p. 40.

[25] Pannenberg, *Theology and the Kingdom of God*, p. 65.

[26] Jurgen Moltmann, *Theology of Hope: On the Ground and Implications of a Christian Eschatology* (London: SCM Press, Ltd., 1967), p. 179.

history itself. According to Moltmann it is transcendence in the sense that this future promises something qualitatively new which stimulates the fundamental transformation of the 'systems' of the present. It is the occasion for the possibility of a revolutionary consciousness.[27] From this we realise the ethical and structural aspects of this future. We must also remember that this future for which we hope is based on a promise. Jesus himself shared in this hopeful orientation of the Hebrew people towards the future. According to John Baillie this hope for the future, based on a promise, becomes an emphatic imperative and not just a possibility. He asserts, "It becomes a sin not to hope."[28] It is this future, the oncoming Kingdom of God, which we celebrate and anticipate in our work and worship.

Ethical Implications of this kind of Future

Such a theology of the future can provide the necessary dynamics, perspective and methodology which is distinct from teleological, deontological, and situation (contextual) modes of ethical decision-making. This future becomes the ontological basis of Christian ethics or the key to Christian ethics as Braaten states. This means that ethics is constitutive of this future.

We are aware that in history people have seen visions of millennial hope or utopia which could be characterised as teleology.[29] It is essentially a human construct which may not take seriously the tragic dimensions of human history. This has been the bane of many utopias, while this future which we have discussed has a finality and decisiveness and consequently it can become normative and determinative of human conduct.

It helps to balance vision with discipline which Keeling calls *ascesis*, originally meaning training required to learn a craft Christian *ascesis* is to bring together spirit and body, will and desire towards the goal of the Kingdom of God.

---

[27]   Jurgen Moltmann, *Religion, Revolution and the Future* (New York: Charles Scribner's and Sons, 1969), p. 196.

[28]   John Baillie, *The Belief in Progress* (New York: Charles Scribner's and Sons, 1950), p. 65.

[29]   See Dennis P. McCann, *Christian Realism and Liberation Theology: Practical Theologies in Creative Conflict* (New York: Orbis Book, 1981), pp. 50-51. The terms, "Millennial Hope", "Apocalyptic", "Eschatology" and "Utopia" are clarified and differentiated in this book.

The most important aspect of this future is its integral relation to the present. The promise of the new that we have in Jesus becomes the basis for hope and freedom. Therefore it is not surprising that the World Council of Churches has focused on this theme for sometime trying to deal with the problems of our time. It has become quite clear that this hope is not other-worldly and individualistic but this-worldly and corporate in character. It is being realised through the various meetings of the W.C.C. that this hope for the future has to reckon both with the reign of God and the *realm* of God. So it is not only an orientation but a mode of life. There were constant affirmations of this future at these conferences in the midst of negations of life in Asia, Africa and South America.[30] This hope prevents people from accepting the word, "Nothing new happens under the sun. Hence all is vanity" (Eccl. 1:9). Rather they reaffirms, "Behold, I make all things new" (Rev. 21:5). Out of this affirmation of the new comes the desire to engage in responsible and meaningful actions so that we may grasp this future. In this sense such a future is both a gift (gabe) and a task (augabe).

From this perspective, we must remember that we are not talking about some complacent, naive hope which believes that everything will be alright somehow at the end. Nor are we talking about some kind of a cynical hope which believes that nothing can be worse. This is not some kind of a shallow optimism, romanticising the future. Basically this kind of a future demands responsibility. In this sense, hope and planning are related. Moltmann rightly says:

> Hope and planning are both related to the future but they are
> not identical with one another. Hope and planning represent
> the future in different ways. Yet they are not separated from
> one another, but live with each other and for each other. Unless
> hope has been aroused and is alive there can be no stimulation
> for planning. Without specific goals towards which hope is
> directed, there can be no decision about the possibilities of
> planning: but without planning, there can be no realistic
> hope.[31]

[30] *Faith and Order* Paper No. 86 (Geneva: WCC, 1978). pp. 125-135. See also *Sharing in One Hope: Report and Documents from the Meeting of the Faith and Order Commission* (Geneva: WCC, 1978). They categorically affirmed, "The Christian hope is a resistance movement against fatalism" (p. 8).

[31] Jurgen Moltmann, *Hope and Planning* (London: SCM Press Ltd., 1971), p. 178, See also Sebastian Kappen, *Jesus and Freedom* (New York: Orbis Books, 1977), pp. 61-63.

Such is the hope which demands rational, systematic and purposive actions with definite direction about which we know something from this future. This future gives us freedom and courage to act, risk and struggle knowing fully well that there are disabling or death-forces at work. This future is the enabling power moving us to confront, challenge and change unjust structures and oppressive systems. It is indeed ahead of us. Alves rightly says, "He is liberated from the prison of what he is and made free to think and behave according to possibilities not immanent in this world."[32] By announcing this future of God one is able to denounce all that falls short of the vision. Thus Pannenberg maintained,

> In relation to the God of the future, man is free, free for a truly personal life, free to accept the provisionality of everything, free with regard to nature and society, free for that creative love that changes the world without destroying it, This creative love proceeds from freedom and is directed towards affirming and creating freedom in the world.[33]

Both Pannenberg and Moltmann understand actions, in the light of this future, as political actions which will bring about justice, Pannenberg maintains,

> But the Kingdom of God speaks in a radical way also to those established social forms. Justice and love are relevant not only to the individual but primarily to the structures of human interaction. Obviously, then, the Kingdom of God is pointedly *political.*[34]

In the similar vein, McKeating has said,

> If we hope for the future it must include a **political hope**. If you don't like the word 'political', let me put it in another way; if we have a hope for the future it must include some sort of a

---

32   Rubem Alves, *A Theology of Human Hope* (Indiana: Abbey Press, 1975), p. 57.
33   Pannenberg, *Theology and the Kingdom of God*, p. 69.
34   Pannenberg, *Theology and the Kingdom of God*, p. 80.

vision of what the world ought to be like and how society ought
to be run. But that's politics.[35]

Such is the impact and import of the power of the future driving us to
the political arena to fight for the oppressed and the exploited. Moltmann
believes that this political involvement is imperative to bring about
justice for the hopeless and those consigned to the shadows of the cross.[36]
Pannenberg maintains that a Christian political ethic must be permeated
by the expectation of the Kingdom of god, God's future Lordship over the
world. When Jesus said "My Kingdom is not of this world" (John 18:36),
He did not mean that the Christian faith is in opposition to society and
state. He meant that his Kingdom does not derive its standards and norms
from the world. We work for political changes in the light of the future
because it involves the future of the essence of humanity.[37] It has become
quite clear that belief in the absolute future of God does not make one
indifferent to the present reality, but such an eschatological perspective
enables and empowers one to work in the world with seriousness and
particularity.

It is the tension of the Kingdom which motivates one to act in the world
politically but also with discernment. We have a prophetic and a critical
role to play in our involvements. Pannenberg says that we must not be
reckless with history. He indeed sounds a word of caution. We must not
lose our sense of history and community in our urge to change. We cannot
always start *de novo*. The experience and wisdom of the past cannot be
treated lightly. So Pannenberg rightly affirms, "This positive relationship
to both present and past reality in spite of all criticism of it was established
once and for all by the incarnation of God in Jesus Christ. Belief in the
incarnation means that the future will not simply destroy the past and the
present."[38]

---

[35] Henry McKeating, *God and the Future* (London:SCM Press Ltd., 1974), p.
62

[36] Jurgen Moltmann, *The Experiment Hope* (London: SCM Press Ltd., 1975), p.
118. See also *Hope and Planning*, p. 122 and his *Future of Creation* (London:
SCM Press Ltd., 1979), p. 147. He says, "The ethical consequence is,
because, and in so far as, the coming God already antedates his future, giving
it in advance in history, men and women can and should anticipate this future
in knowledge and deed."

[37] Pannenberg, *Ethics*, pp. 133 and 191

[38] *Ibid.*, p. 177

In eschatological ethics one takes seriously the wider context and not just the immediate situation. It gives us a sense of transcendence and objectivity and a wider frame of reference.

From this perspective, we need to realise the distance and distinction between all our sincere efforts and the coming Kingdom of righteousness or justice. We must be aware of the provisional and partial character of all human achievements. They are preliminary compared to the future that is in God. But this fact does not make our decisions and actions secondary or peripheral. Pannenberg correctly states,

> To love the preliminary is no little thing. Christians are surely right to call for devotion to Jesus. He who despises the preliminary because he waits for the ultimate will not be able to recognise the ultimate in its coming... Hope for the coming Kingdom knows that the ultimate fulfillment is beyond human powers to effect. Yet, far from being condemned to inactivity, we are inspired to prepare this present for the future.[39]

So we must be clear that the Kingdom will not be established by humans. It is most emphatically the Kingdom *of God*. Keeling has noted, "The most basic social creativity of Christianity has been the recognition that there is only one Kingdom, stretching from the creation to the eschaton, encompassing every created existence."[40] In that context, it is our urgent task to demythologise political myths in the midst of our involvement. For this reason Braaten has said,

> Christian ethics is not to be understood as the means of producing the future Kingdom of God, but only as annuncia-tion, anticipation, and approximation, let us say as "signs of the coming Kingdom"...The Coming of the Kingdom in its

---

[39] Pannenberg, *Theology and the Kingdom of God*, p. 126. In another book he asserts, "An awareness of this distance, however, does not, when rightly understood, weaken our readiness to act. On the contrary, the very relation of the distance between the promised future of the divine Kingdom of Peace and the present state of the world can stimulate us to change the present... to eradicate the most obvious faults of our world." *In Faith and Reality* (Philadelphia: The Westminster Press, 1977), p. 119.

[40] M. Keeling, *Foundation of Christian Ethics*, p. 238.

priority and power is the possibility of doing God's will on Earth.[41]

In the light of this, we must learn to relativise and be humble before this future. We cannot depend on our conscience or on some arbitrary and authoritarian imperative for our ethical thinking and doing. But we must depend on the power of the Kingdom which is proleptically present and providing us with criteria and norms.

Finally, we come to a problem related to eschatological ethics. Gustafson noted the problem when he said,

> The current celebration of the openness towards the future is proper in so far as it recognises that the God whose will one seeks to discern for the future is the God who has willed in the past. Much of this celebration refers primarily to human attitude in any case, and as such is insufficient to determine what men ought to be doing in a particular instant. Attitude alone does not determine an act. To be open to the future is not to discern what one ought to do in it.[42]

Even recently he has reiterated his criticism and said:

> It is a theological interpretation of the world from which a basic orientation toward life can be derived but which provides no significant bases theologically, historically, or naturally for the guidance of human action.[43]

We have to take seriously this criticism of specificity and concreteness. It is true that such an eschatological perspective does not provide us with proximate norms and principles. But both Moltmann and

---

[41] Carl Braaten, *Eschatology and Ethics: Essays on the Theology and Ethics of the Kingdom of God* (Minnesota: Augsburg Publishing House, 1974), pp. 110-111. The same concern was expressed by the advocate of Liberation Theology, Gustavo Gutierrez. See his *A Theology of Liberation: History, Politics and Salvation* (New York: Orbis Books, 1973), p. 236.

[42] James M. Gustafson, *Theology and Christian Ethics* (Philadelphia: The Pilgrim Press, 1974), p. 118.

[43] James M. Gustafson, *Ethics from a Theocentric Perspective: Theology and* *(Continued on Next Page)*

Pannenberg again and again refer to ultimate Christian norms of love and justice and shape their ethics accordingly. I suppose Gustafson is looking for some kind of "Middle axioms", which are neither too general nor too particular. This they cannot give because of its *openendedness*. But we need to appreciate what they have given for our ethical thinking and doing. Gustafson himself acknowledges this in terms of attitude and orientation. This we cannot under-estimate for Christian ethics. Gustafson himself says, it must be said to the credit of both Pannenberg and Moltmann that they have addressed themselves to larger macro-ethical problems in the fields of politics and economics. Therefore both of them go beyond attitudinal concerns to the arenas of action. They have given us a viable and valid perspective and a mode of thinking and doing which we feel is of immense value particularly in today's world. It does not lead to passivity and fear but to activity and freedom through which we sight and support those signs of the absolute future in the present. We need to grasp this future and be grasped by it. We are emboldened by the knowledge that the God of the future is actively present and available, forwarding his kingly rule and bringing it to consummation.

43   *(Continued from last page)*
      Ethics Vol. I (Chicago: The Chicago Univ. Press, 1981), p. 35. It is interesting to note that Reinhold Niebuhr in one of his early writings noted that moral activity in end-oriented, that its dynamic is to move towards a transcendent and divine unity of essential reality which is the future of God. See his *Interpretation of Christian Ethics* (New York: Harper and Brothers Publisher. 1935) p. 59 and see also pp. 100-135 of the same book.